Breaking and Entering

Breaking and Entering

Unexpected Sermons for an Unfinished World

Elizabeth Goodman

Foreword by Hannah Fries

WIPF & STOCK · Eugene, Oregon

Wipf & Stock
An Imprint of Wipf and Stock Publishers
199 W. 8th Ave., Suite 3
Eugene, OR 97401

www.wipfandstock.com

PAPERBACK ISBN: 978-1-4982-3434-4
HARDCOVER ISBN: 978-1-4982-3436-8

Manufactured in the U.S.A.

Dedicated to my own personal trinity,
Jesse on whom it all depends,
Tobias who let loose my love,
and Jack who routinely blows the roof off.

As it turns out, it's fun sleeping beneath the stars.

Contents

Foreword

AT THE CRACK OF dawn the women go to the tomb, bringing spices to anoint the body. They are surprised, when they arrive, to find the stone rolled away: instead of death, an empty space. The sun comes up over the horizon, breaks through the opening, illuminates that space, filling the emptiness.

God breaks in.

Present tense: God breaks in, then and now. *Is* breaking: present progressive, ongoing. In the midst of terror and grief, in the midst of the banal everyday, God breaks in. It is sudden and slow, powerful and peaceful, awesome and simple.

Clearly, we aren't talking about petty crime here, though you'd be excused for thinking of "breaking and entering" as an act of violence and a disregard for law or boundaries. When it comes to God, however, Reverend Liz Goodman will likely dissuade you of the former . . . but perhaps not the latter. "This is a god who upsets social convention, preferring instead the freedom of eternal life," Goodman writes. "This is a god who breaks down human culture, preferring instead the Kingdom of Heaven." Think of Jesus, breaking religious law and healing on the Sabbath, breaking bread with all manner of unsavory people, making the authorities uncomfortable.

Break is a word that surfaces a lot in these sermons. In it is the possibility for a grand, divine shakeup that startles us out of complacency and moves us always toward renewal and redemption. Jesus's message of peace is a "radical break" from what's come before; God's grace does not come at some final end time, but is "breaking even now, breaking in even here."

And that is a good thing—a very good thing, according to Goodman. Because it means another world is within our grasp, within the sight of our imagination. We can reach beyond intolerance, violence, injustice, and greed; we can see the Kingdom of God among us.

Yet this kingdom is not defined by power as we know it. It is quite a different kind of power, rising from within and spilling out in the form of "self-emptying love." The reign of God comes "not as an imposition from on high, but as the leaven slowly causing the dough to rise" or as a weed "breaking out" in our midst, "undermining, choking out the good fruits of civilized culture"—that is, the "civilized" culture that still runs on the sweat of exploited workers, that still harbors racism, that still makes outcasts of the poor and sick.

Goodman sees a flawed and wounded world, yes, but one that is still being formed. In this ongoing act of creation, each of us is called to participate, to be co-creators. While visioning and re-visioning this world-in-progress, Goodman returns again and again to the cross as the model of radical self-giving love by which we may know the god we are to follow. Her sermons thirst, palpably, for justice and brim with compassion for the world we have been given; her vision is one of wholeness.

You will not find in these sermons easy answers, quick judgments, or comfortable platitudes. Such things would be impossible with the intellect and curiosity at work (and play) here—Goodman is too comfortable with discomfort. Underneath the expected interpretation is often another perspective, a surprising twist. Behind language and words themselves lurk layers of meaning and opportunities for reinvention.

What you will find in this book is a conviction that God's love is both unsettling and transformative—and larger and more inclusive than we can comprehend. It is here among us, always already breaking among us, and it is reason for joy.

Hannah Fries

Author, *Little Terrarium,* a collection of poems
Member, Monterey United Church of Christ
Monterey, Massachusetts

Shows What a Preacher Can't Do

When it was evening on that day, the first day of the week, and the doors of the house where the disciples had met were locked for fear of the Jews, Jesus came and stood among them and said, "Peace be with you." After he said this, he showed them his hands and his side. Then the disciples rejoiced when they saw the Lord. Jesus said to them again, "Peace be with you. As the Father has sent me, so I send you." When he had said this, he breathed on them and said to them, "Receive the Holy Spirit. If you forgive the sins of any, they are forgiven them; if you retain the sins of any, they are retained."

But Thomas (who was called the Twin), one of the twelve, was not with them when Jesus came. So the other disciples told him, "We have seen the Lord." But he said to them, "Unless I see the mark of the nails in his hands, and put my finger in the mark of the nails and my hand in his side, I will not believe."

A week later his disciples were again in the house, and Thomas was with them. Although the doors were shut, Jesus came and stood among them and said, "Peace be with you." Then he said to Thomas, "Put your finger here and see my hands. Reach out your hand and put it in my side. Do not doubt but believe." Thomas answered him, "My Lord and my God!" Jesus said to him, "Have you believed because you have seen me? Blessed are those who have not seen and yet have come to believe."

Now Jesus did many other signs in the presence of his disciples, which are not written in this book. But these are written so that you may come to believe that Jesus is the Messiah, the Son of God, and that through believing you may have life in his name. (John 20:19–31)[1]

WE'RE ABOUT TO ACCEPT into membership of this congregation several new people, eight, maybe nine. Given that we currently have twelve formal members, this is a seismic jump—and we're making headlines for it. The Massachusetts Conference of the United Church of Christ is featuring us in its email weekly blast called "Spotlight" and in its slightly longer-form blog.

But think about it for a moment. What does this mean, to be a member? What does this mean especially here? Because, as I understand it, people very quickly feel a part of things among us, or they don't. Without

---

1. All Bible citations are from the *New Revised Standard Version* unless otherwise noted.

any formalism, beyond any formal mechanism for joining, free of any fetters that might come with institutionalism and its attendant committee structure and resultant Robert's Rules of Order, this congregation has a mysterious way of enfolding into involvement and active participation new "members" all the time, really on any given Sunday. If some congregations thrive on planning and budgeting, or on envisioning, implementation, and evaluation, we thrive on seeing how it goes and taking it from here.

Not surprisingly, this fits my leadership style, which I explained for the forthcoming blog post. Leadership is often something done from out front. A leader has a vision and then comes up with a plan and then guides a process so to realize the vision. Bigger organizations need such leadership, I imagine. Gould Farm, for example, (I imagine) needs someone out front charting the course and deciding on how to stay it.[2] But another sort of leadership is more responsive, done more from beside and beneath. I've found this is how I lead, and it seems to me this is the sort of leadership that small congregations tend to need.

Incidentally, this also fits with my experience of God. For some, God is felt to have a plan—and this makes sense. After all, one of the persistent claims of the faith is eschatological, that which concerns the end. God has in mind an end of all things, a glorious end in which all is praise, a consummation of the creation and creator. So it must be that God guides all things to that end, and this could be felt as God's plan. But for me, I experience God less as "having a plan" and more as acting in response—responding to what unfolds, responding even to me in forgiveness and grace. I act: God responds. We act: God responds.

Did you know *-spond* is the Latin root meaning promise? So to respond is to renew an already-established promise. There's theological truth in this, then, that God, the one of ancient promises, is also fundamentally responsive, ever renewing those ancient promises. There's also, then, an imperative in this, a claim on us if we mean to be God's people: we're to be responsive. We're to respond to changing circumstances and new developments in hope. We're to respond to needs as they arise in faith. We're to respond with love.

But it strikes me that this microdynamic way of being together doesn't rely so much on "membership." Really, membership, in the context of a

2. Gould Farm is a working farm as well as a residential facility for adults with major mental illness. Situated in Monterey, the farm is a wellspring for the church I serve. On any given Sunday, as much as half the worshipping congregation might come from Gould Farm, be they staff, patients (called here "guests"), or yearlong volunteers.

responsive community, might feel like an "un-necessity" or even a stumbling block.

This is why, currently, many congregations are struggling mightily to give up their old membership model and mindset in favor of something more current—a discipleship model or stakeholder model. The church shouldn't be about making members but about forming disciples. The church shouldn't be about joining, as if it were a club; it should be about sending out, as if it had a mission or were itself a mission.

As it happens, I've read those books and I've attended those conferences; and I always do so as one who's already made that shift, as one serving a congregation that's already come out from under the heavy burden of membership and committees and Robert's Rules of Order, and is now burdened but lightly with freedom in Christ by the power of the Holy Spirit who doesn't stay still for long.

So why, then, would I celebrate as we take in new members today? Why should any of us seek to join, or rejoice that so many are joining, if we mean not to be a club of conformity but to be a mission on the move?

If you're comfortable with those questions, then you're likely uncomfortable with what appears to be John's aim with his gospel narrative. We've heard from John a lot in recent weeks, so we've heard a lot John's insistence that his hearers and readers believe in Jesus. And yet we've fallen far short of hearing many instances of his insistence. In fact, over fifty times in the twenty chapters of this gospel comes in several forms the refrain "so that all might believe through him": "Do you not believe?" "Do you now believe?" "Tell me that I may believe," "We have come to believe," "Lord, I believe," and, as we heard earlier, "Blessed are those who have not seen and yet have come to believe." Really, by this insistence John justifies having written his whole gospel: "But these are written so that you may come to believe that Jesus is the Messiah, the Son of God, and that through believing you may have life in his name."

Maybe you didn't notice all the insistence on believing, though, because so much else is going on here as well.

First, there's this—the disciples locked away in fear of the Jews.

This, though, is more usefully heard as their being locked away simply for fear. The disciples were, after all, Jews themselves; and there was nothing, and is nothing, inherently frightening about Jews (or about any other brand of human group). What *is* frightening, however, is violence let loose, violence now without proper framing or structure or reason or aim.

I mean, violence with those attendant fetters is frightening enough. The violence of the electric chair or the firing squad is frightening enough, but at least it's controlled, somewhat predictable and reasonable. The violence of war is fearsome enough, but at least there's such a thing as "war crimes" that give structure to war and a sense of fair play, if a perverse one. (One of the many things that's so disturbing about the recent police shootings, racially charged and caught on tape, is that it's violence approaching the out of bounds. And once we can't trust the police to use violence "correctly," then we're in a new and very deep sort of danger.)

After all, violence let loose is another matter. And violence, this week, this "Holy Week," had (perhaps?) been let loose. The state working with the priesthood had killed an innocent man, and now his followers were scattered and doing God knows what, proclaiming and planning God knows what. So the fears were real, and likely all around. Among the authorities, would the followers of this Jesus retaliate for all this? Among the followers of Jesus, would the authorities seek to kill off still more of their movement, come after each of them, one by one? And so would any among the disciples break out of their discipline of peaceful resistance and strike back?

Second, there's this: Jesus' coming and standing among them and breathing on them the breath that is the Holy Spirit, the Paraclete as it's called in this gospel. Strictly speaking, Paraclete means "called to one's side," and so is often translated into English as "comforter" or "advocate." Think of a public defender or a health care proxy. Think of someone trained and skilled in a field where you're stuck in mire and unable to fend for yourself. But then consider this, which this Holy Spirit enables the disciples to do: if now they forgive the sins of any, those sins are forgiven; but if they retain the sins of any, those sins are retained.

This has been heard as the founding Scripture for the Christian priesthood, which came to be felt as having the power to forgive and redeem, or not, as the case may be. But what if this passage weren't saying anything so general as all that? What if this detail were most relevant in the context of what's going on here in the story on that very scary night?

Violence was let loose and on the move, and it was either going to keep lashing out and keep claiming more victims or someone was going to have to stop it—by deciding that, though this one had the "right" to retaliate, he or she would not retaliate. In this way, either the sin of the other would be retained and so the acts of retaliation would continue—until everyone everywhere was engulfed in violence; or the sin of the other would be forgiven and so the whole downwardly spiraling dynamic of violence-begetting-violence would be put to rest. This is to say that Jesus, resurrected and returned now in peace, could simply be saying to his friends on this terrifying night, "The choice is yours: forgive and have forgiveness reign, or retain and continue in the path of resentment and violence. The choice is yours."

Third, there's this: Thomas, poor Thomas, whom we condemn as "doubting," but who I think was simply deeply unfortunate. I mean, he was out when all the other disciples received visitation from the risen Christ. And who knows why he was out? Maybe he was out gathering supplies for their lengthening stay behind those locked doors. Maybe he was out getting a sense of things, "doing recon," as it were, to gauge how much longer they'd need to stay locked away, to determine whether it was safe at last to come out. Whatever. The point is that he was out. And then he came back, and everyone told him, "We have seen the Lord! (Oh, but you were out.)"

And we blame him for doubting. Traditionally, the church has condemned him as doubting. Jesus, however, didn't. He simply granted Thomas his request. "Unless I see the mark of the nails in his hands," Thomas said, "and put my finger in the mark of the nails and my hand in his side, I will not believe." So, the following week, Jesus returned and said to Thomas, "Put your finger here and see my hands. Reach out your hand and put it in my side. Do not doubt but believe."

Of course, the reason we might condemn Thomas for doubting is because that separates him from us, and furthermore puts us in company with the "blessed." Yes, to do so puts us in the company of those whom Jesus considers blessed, praises as blessed: "Blessed are those who have not seen and yet have come to believe."

So, now we've come to it—for by this word of blessing from Jesus, our writer John wraps into his story those who come after, his hearers and readers, we who have not seen and yet might believe.

Now we've come to it—John's need for us to believe.

You know what word isn't in our litany for joining the church?

"Believe."

We've got "desire," "seek," and "hope." We've got "promise," "welcome," and "affirm." But we have no "believe."

This is by design. People didn't, and don't, want to have to claim to believe something, especially if they don't believe in it—not this time with these particular new members, nor any prior time in my memory. We're a serious bunch, it seems. We take our words and confessions seriously enough not to want to say something we can't stand with.

And we're not alone, here in Monterey. The whole United Church of Christ is a non-creedal denomination. We have no common creed that we've established as the thing that makes the difference between those who are members and those who aren't.

What's more, this is usually felt as one of its selling points. No creeds! After all, the Christian faith, as perceived and as practiced, has been largely reduced to a set of assertions that you either believe in (and so are Christian) or don't believe in (and so aren't). (Six days to create the world? Yes? You're a Christian! Bible written by God's own hand? Yes? You're a Christian!) I don't suppose any here would celebrate this as a wonderful development in the lived faith.

But remember, "creed" comes from *credo*, as in "I believe," as in the Apostles' Creed: "I believe in God the Father Almighty, Maker of Heaven and Earth; and of Jesus Christ, His Only Son, our Lord . . ." And, though few here, it seems, want to say, "I believe . . . ," it's worthy to recognize what exactly John is committed to having us believe.

That Jesus is the Son of God, that Jesus is the abiding presence of God and the full revelation of God in the world—this is what John needs us to believe. And why? Because people will say all sorts of things are true about God that aren't true: that God hates fags (untrue, if "fag" is taken to mean gays and lesbians); that God blesses slavery (untrue); that God rewards with blessing the especially deserving (untrue); that God punishes with suffering those who deserve it (untrue). This sure knowledge that people will say all sorts of things about God that aren't true is what justified the priesthood and established the church in the first place. We *needed* an authority to resort to when people attempted to assert as true things about God that are not true. But that presupposed the "un-corruption" of the church and the priesthood, which is unfortunately a presupposition that came no longer to hold.

And so came the Protestants, who widened the circle of those with authority, widened it so wide that now everyone has a say—those with advanced degrees, those without advanced degrees, those with no education whatsoever; those with the authorization of an ordaining body, those without such backing, those who'd spit on any such formal authorization; those with congregations, those with a viewership, those with a charismatic personality, a microphone, and an agenda. And so God is said to work in all sorts of ways that may or may not comport with what's true. God gave Tim Tebow victory because he prayed in public. God gave Joel Osteen wealth because he prayed for wealth in just the right way. God gave America the biggest military because we're an exceptional nation in God's sight, but God condemned America with defeat in Iraq because we've legalized abortion.

No.

No.

And how do I know this? Because of the cross.

Because of the cross, this I know: God is cruciform. God is self-giving, self-emptying. God is wounded and killed that we might have peace. The cross is the standard by which we measure assertions about what God is and what God is not, about what God has done and what God has not done.

A standard is an objective and agreed upon measurement that is true and checked for being true by an established disinterested authority. When you go to the gas station, you don't have to wonder whether the gallon you're buying is actually a gallon. It says right there on the pump that it's been checked and authorized by the Department of Weights and Measures.

John means for his gospel assertion about Jesus, and him crucified, to be such a department of theological weights and measures; and John understands the cross as the true measure of God, the true revelation of God's nature, way, and end. God is cruciform. God is self-giving, self-emptying. God is wounded and killed that we might have peace. This is what John is so desperate to have us believe. This is what Thomas had confirmed when he wanted to see not only Jesus but his wounds, his *mortal* wounds.

And why? Why the urgency around this theological claim? Why the persistence in regard to a claim that really seems quite abstract? Because by this the world will be saved—saved, that is, from itself. By self-giving, by *forgiving*, by self-emptying and giving way to the other, by striving not for survival and self-preservation but for eternal and abundant life for all starting now—by these things peace will be won and salvation will be ours, all of ours, for "salvation" means wholeness, perfection. Anything less than salvation for all isn't salvation at all.

This is what we are meant to believe.

Do we believe it?

Do you believe it?

If you do, then we need you—we of this little church with twelve members.

The fact is that church membership is about the less lofty matters of life together. Concerning itself with the facts-of-the-matter—the allocation of resources, the financial assets and the budget, the physical plant and the pastor's time—church membership doesn't have "its privileges." It has its responsibilities.

And they're sometimes quite dull, these responsibilities—cleaning up after communion, picking up the mail, stopping in to turn down the heat when I've forgotten to but realize the fact only after I've arrived back home in Lenox. And they're sometimes quite crucial responsibilities—seeing after the upkeep of the building, or tracking down the rent from the tenant of the parsonage, or approving my annual report and how I prioritize my duties. And they're sometimes quite spirited responsibilities—deciding on whether to refurbish the organ, or to give to Construct, Inc. or to the Crocus Fund (or both), or to invest in more Godly Play stories or hymnals or a piano. Most of all, though, they're responsibilities to be entrusted with those who share in the belief that Jesus is key to what God wants us to know about himself, who have no agenda other than to live by the law of love, and who will stand together as one risen body witnessing to what abides, that is, faith and hope and love.

You know, response isn't the only way by which ancient promises are reaffirmed. It also happens in responsibility—in taking it and entrusting it. So not only are we to be a people who respond, we're also to be a people who take responsibility and who entrust responsibility. It's leadership that's less "beside" and more "beneath" (undergirding, establishing). Membership is one way this is done.

And so we do celebrate new members among us—not as contradictory to our mission but as a needful part of it.

A little over five years ago, on Easter Sunday, as I remember it, I wished that this little church would just die. It's tough to be so small. It's draining to be so tiny. I even said I planned to see if I couldn't kill us.

I see now what I can't do.

Thanks be to God.

Being Suggestive

The Lord God took the man and put him in the garden of Eden to till it and keep it. And the Lord God commanded the man, "You may freely eat of every tree of the garden; but of the tree of the knowledge of good and evil you shall not eat, for in the day that you eat of it you shall die." . . .

Now the serpent was more crafty than any other wild animal that the Lord God had made. He said to the woman, "Did God say, 'You shall not eat from any tree in the garden'?" The woman said to the serpent, "We may eat of the fruit of the trees in the garden"; but God said, 'You shall not eat of the fruit of the tree that is in the middle of the garden, nor shall you touch it, or you shall die.'" But the serpent said to the woman, "You will not die; for God knows that when you eat of it your eyes will be opened, and you will be like God, knowing good and evil." So when the woman saw that the tree was good for food, and that it was a delight to the eyes, and that the tree was to be desired to make one wise, she took of its fruit and ate; and she also gave some to her husband, who was with her, and he ate. Then the eyes of both were opened, and they knew that they were naked; and they sewed fig leaves together and made loincloths for themselves. (Genesis 2:15–17, 3:1–7)

Then Jesus was led up by the Spirit into the wilderness to be tempted by the devil. He fasted for forty days and forty nights, and afterwards he was famished. The tempter came and said to him, "If you are the Son of God, command these stones to become loaves of bread." But he answered, "It is written, 'One does not live by bread alone, but by every word that comes from the mouth of God.'"

Then the devil took him to the holy city and placed him on the pinnacle of the temple, saying to him, "If you are the Son of God, throw yourself down; for it is written, 'He will command his angels concerning you,' and 'On their hands they will bear you up, so that you will not dash your foot against a stone.'" Jesus said to him, "Again it is written, 'Do not put the Lord your God to the test.'"

Again, the devil took him to a very high mountain and showed him all the kingdoms of the world and their splendor; and he said to him, "All these I will give you, if you will fall down and worship me." Jesus said to him, "Away with you, Satan! for it is written, 'Worship the Lord your God, and serve only him.'"

Then the devil left him, and suddenly angels came and waited on him. (Matthew 4:1–11)

SCRIPTURE'S EARLIEST PREACHER IS the serpent. If preaching is interpreting the word of God, then the first one to do this according to the Bible is the serpent.

Just saying.

But that actually gets me thinking. The serpent in the garden and the devil in the wilderness don't share a name, and they don't share a form; many a scholar would caution us against making too direct an equivalence here. But, look, they do share a same technique—suggestion—and that counts for something.

The serpent asks the woman, "Did God say, 'You shall not eat of any tree in the garden'?" It's an ambiguous question; I imagine it's so by design. Consider, does the serpent mean to ask, "Did God say that, of all the trees here in this garden, there are any from which you may not eat?" If so, then this would allow for God to be felt as gracious, having offered the man and woman a great abundance—everything here but one. Or does the serpent mean to ask, "Did God say don't eat from any tree in this garden?" in which case God would be felt as withholding, even cruel, a tempter himself—laying out an abundance before the man and the woman, and then saying, "Don't touch."

We should recognize, of course, that what God actually says according to the story is neither of these. We should recognize that the serpent frames in negative terms what God just prior framed positively: "You may eat freely of every tree of the garden; but of the tree of the knowledge of good and evil you shall not eat, for in the day that you eat of it you shall die." Really, we should recognize that the question as asked cannot be answered. But I imagine that's also by design. As any student of politics knows, the one who frames the debate wins the debate—and the serpent means to win this debate, so indeed to frame the woman and the man.

These two naïfs are no match for the serpent, but their innocence serves them well for a moment. The woman doesn't answer the question as asked; instead, she repeats what God did say. "We may eat of the fruit of the trees in the garden, but not of the fruit of the tree that is in the middle of the garden." And in so saying, she seems to hold on to the hope that God is not withholding, that God is gracious.

But the suggestion otherwise is a potent one, isn't it?

Here's another potent suggestion: "If you are the Son of God . . ." The devil is said to have said it to Jesus twice in the wilderness, the whole temptation essentially energized by this word: *if.* It's a brilliant approach because, though Jesus never claimed such status for himself, it's a pretty powerful one to be pinned with, one that he might want now to prove true.

Ironically, he would prove it by steadfastly resisting the proving of it.

If you feel you've heard this story before, then rest assured you have. This scene appears in all three synoptic Gospels, and so we hear it every year and always on the first Sunday of Lent. It sets up so well the forty days of Lent that are before us, forty days until Easter not counting Sundays. These are to echo the forty days that Jesus is remembered to have spent in the wilderness, away from all the comforts of his culture, away even from the law and ritual that safeguard living and give shape to time. To be in the wilderness is to be on your own, really on your own.

Mark, the earliest written gospel, doesn't recount any details of Jesus' time on his own, really on his own. According to that rendering, Jesus' experience in the wilderness really was empty—a formless void, even, as before when God began to create. Pre-created: we might call it postapocalyptic these days—this entering into chaos, this giving over to nihilism. It all makes Mark's version, to my mind, the most terrifying version, a temptation not about anything but about nothing, about annihilation, about non-being. The driving question to this understanding of the temptation, then, was whether Jesus could withstand self-giving, self-emptying. Could Jesus withstand kenosis, which as the Christ he would have to suffer on the cross?

But none of this is to make light of Matthew's understanding of what Jesus withstood, which was also Luke's understanding—for here, though Jesus didn't face the threat of annihilation, he did face the threat of conscription to serving some master other than God. That he doesn't succumb is perhaps the obvious point.

"[T]he essence of Jesus' sinlessness," writer Gil Bailie claims, "was his immunity to the contagion of desire."[1] This is typical of Mr. Bailie, he for whom a central question in the life of faith is this: Whom are you going to imitate? Who is your model for living? And so, to his mind, and to mine, Jesus' success in the wilderness is about desiring the right thing, desiring to be like the right one. "His triumph over the demonic snares in the wilderness was a triumph over the glamour of mimetic suggestion; but it was an achievement made possible, not by Jesus' strength of will, but by the superior strength of *another* mimetic desire: Jesus' desire 'to do the Father's will,'"[2] that is, Jesus' desire instead to imitate the Father.

1. Bailie, *Violence Unveiled*, 209.
2. Ibid., 209.

So, to sum up, Jesus' triumph in the wilderness was in resisting the suggestions of the devil, which would have made him like the devil; and in continuing to model himself after the One in whose image and likeness he knew himself to have been made. Jesus might have become like the devil, following the devil; but instead he became evermore like the Father, following the Father.

Got it.

But wait. Wasn't it this that God didn't want in the beginning? Wasn't it this that God meant to avoid—that any should be like God? Didn't God mean to be inimitable? Or was that just in reference to regular old people?

"You will not die," the serpent assured the woman and, by mimetic extension, the man. "You will not die; for God knows that when you eat of it [the fruit of the tree of knowledge of good and evil] your eyes will be opened and you will be like God, knowing good and evil." But we're not supposed to seem to be like God, are we?

Certainly, this is what most preaching about Adam and Eve has focused on, at least as far as I know. Certainly, this has made for many a fine preaching point. We should be content in our humanity. We should rejoice in our humanity. We're not in control; God is. None of us is sovereign (not Pharaoh, not Caesar, not the king or the president, certainly not the dictator); God is. When this message is rubbed up against Jesus in the wilderness, the harmony is striking. As Jesus is pushed to act out his divinity but chooses instead to inhabit his humanity, the irony resounds.

Barbara Brown Taylor, writing in *The Christian Century,* claimed (and is often quoted for having done so), "[W]hereas Adam stepped over the line and found humanity a curse, Jesus stayed behind the line and made humanity a blessing. One man trespassed; one man stayed put. One tried to be God; one was content to remain a human being. And the irony is that the one who tried to be God did not do too well as a human being, while the one who was content to be human became known as the Son of God."[3]

And this is lovely, right? The symmetry, the irony—it's lovely. As a preacher, I'd be so tempted to preach it! The problem is that it's based on a lie, or on the suggestion of a liar—the serpent suggesting that God doesn't want us to be like God, that God would have a real problem if we were to become too much like God.

But if God doesn't want us to be like God, then why would God have sent us Jesus? If God doesn't want us to live fully into our resemblance to

3. Taylor, "Remaining Human."

God, then why would God have sent us God's Son who so perfectly imitated God and said also to us, "Follow me," who so completely embodied God's self-giving love and also invited us, "Come and see," assuring us, "I am the Way"? If God doesn't want us to be like God, then why would God have sent us God's Holy Spirit by which we might come together as the church to be formed, informed, reformed, transformed into the mystical body of Christ? If God doesn't want us to have our eyes opened that we might see, then what was with all those encounters between Jesus and blind people that left those once-blind-people now to see? Truly, if God didn't want us to be like God, and yet sent God's Son to stimulate in us such a desire and also sent God's Spirit that this desire might be fulfilled, then God is more tempter than the serpent, more tempter than the devil.

Come to think of it, God would only have a problem with our becoming like God if God were certain things that we know, through Christ, God not to be. (Jesus is said to be Godlike, so it also must be that God is Jesus-like.) So, consider: God wouldn't want to us to be like God if God were all about control—for there can be only one force in control. But God isn't about control. God is about freedom and responsibility, call and response. God wouldn't want us to be like God if God were powerful as the world understands power—for such power secures itself against all who want in on that action. But God isn't about the power that seeks domination. God is about power as expressed in service and self-giving. God, *this* God who is love, who sent his Son to be our shepherd and his Holy Spirit to empower the church: of course God wants us to be like God!

And yet.

There is this prohibition: "[Of the fruit] of the tree of the knowledge of good and evil you shall not eat . . ." What of that, you might rightly ask? Well, perhaps what God didn't want was for us to suffer—to know not only good but evil as well. Or perhaps what God didn't want was for us to attempt to distinguish between these two, good and evil, a process of judgment we so often get woefully wrong. Or perhaps God didn't want us to dwell in the world as if duality were a given condition rather than but one way to conceive of and relate to reality. Or perhaps, according to the storyteller's understanding, this fruit really did introduce death into the dynamic of life, really did mean to explain the mystery of mortality; and God didn't, doesn't, want us to die. Really, this prohibition could be about any number of things. I just don't think it's about what the serpent suggested it was about. After all, though a preacher, he's not necessarily right—crafty, yes, but not always correct.

You might think that what I'm suggesting is that there's something essentially corrupt, crooked about the rhetorical device of suggestion. But that's not what I'm suggesting because, the truth is, this device is one of my favorites. As a way to insight, a way to surprise, a way to sudden laughter, a means for art, suggestion is a powerful mode. What's more, as it happens, I am a member of a most earnest group of people: the clergy. This group, especially Protestant clergy, can be chokingly earnest—and there's seldom much fun in that, much delight or surprise. Most crucially of all, though, is that I most often encounter God's living truth when I find it suggested to me in the many layers of Scripture, tradition, translation, and experience. My faith practice is preparing worship for you, writing sermons for you; and for me the writing of a sermon is a process of unearthing some suggestion and following up on it. For this reason, the question that nearly always spurs a sermon's conclusion is this, a question that I quite literally and often out loud ask myself, an indicting question as it were: Just what am I suggesting? Just what am I suggesting to you about this passage from Scripture, which means to suggest something to us of God?

When suggestion didn't work for the devil, he had to make it plain. "Fall down and worship me," he said, thus stripping away any pretense—at friendliness, at alliance, at well-meaning advice-giver—and making his agenda now known. The previous two statements of temptation were indeed suggestions: "*If* you are the Son of God, command these stones to become loaves of bread. . . . *If* you are the Son of God, throw yourself down from this high place . . . " But at last it's as if someone even asked him, "Just what are you suggesting?"

It's the same voice that asks me every week, as I stand before you yet again: "Just what am I suggesting?" As I speak of things that I couldn't possibly know, testifying to things too grand for any words actually to contain, just what am I suggesting?

Today this is what I'm suggesting: Christ has come to show us what God who is life is like. He has done this that we ourselves might come to be like God, for by this the world will be saved—from its own violence, its own lust for vengeance, its own ravenous short-sightedness. He has done this though the world will do its worst to him, and he has done this for us though we ourselves will participate in this world's worst-doing. But all that will come to nothing, for he yet comes to us with these words even while his wounds are still open: "Peace be with you."

I am suggesting that by this we are all saved and reconciled to God as if we'd never been so cut off as we might have suspected.

That's what I'm suggesting. It's good to say it clear and plain. But it's delightful also to approach slow and slant, a flirtation with the truth that will at last come in consummation.

I pray for a long courtship. I'm enjoying myself quite a lot and would love to work for a world in which all might say so, too.

Thanks be to God.

Casting Spells—Old Testament
An Aside

MY SON, TOBIAS, ONCE asked me, "What's the most powerful word?"

"I don't know," I said, distracted. I was in the middle of something. I'm always in the middle of something.

"Liz," he said.

"Yeah?" I turned my head reflexively, my distraction dissipated.

"That's the most powerful word," he said, "your own name."

I don't believe in magic. Maybe that goes without saying. I mean, who does anymore?

And yet.

For most of us, our first word is *mama*. That's true the world over. *Mama* is, for most of us, the first word we ever speak. The motion—lips, mouth, tongue, breath—it takes to make *mama* mimics suckling. *Mama*, then, means food, nurturance, and so (on the aggregate) means mother.

The moment when a baby can at last murmur *mama* with intent is a watershed moment. It's when the baby can hold mama in mind, can conjure up mama in image and promise, can maybe even make her come, respond! Now the existence of the one who sustains life is no longer snuffed out when simply out of the range of smell or sight. Now the ongoing presence and participation of mama is no longer coupled with her immediate proximity. To be able to say "mama," then, is a power akin to magic.

"Whoshall I tell them sent me?" Moses asked the bush that burned though unconsumed. A voice had spoken to Moses through the bush, had told him that the Lord had observed the misery of the people enslaved, had heard their groans on account of the taskmasters. And so the Lord was sending Moses to Pharaoh, sending him to bring the people enslaved out of Egypt.

Of course, at this Moses wondered, likely incredulous, "Who am I that I should go to Pharaoh?" But moreover, who are you? "If I come to the Israelites and say to them, 'The God of your ancestors has sent me to you,' and they ask me, 'What is his name?' what shall I say to them?"

The stakes were high here. Moses was asking an impertinent thing. It had long been known that to know the name of a god was to have power over that god. Before anyone knew about the Living God (though a few had their suspicions); back when every nation and every people had their own god or pantheon of gods; back when even households had gods, kept them there on the shelf with their pots and kettles—everyone knew that to know the name of the god was to have power over the god.

And so this god, the God of Abraham and Isaac and Jacob, had demurred about his name. He had lots of nicknames. Even according to Scripture, he had lots of referents: El Shaddai; Elohim or Eloyin; Adonai, and simply El, that is, "God." But not until this moment had any person dared to ask God, "What is your name?"

That God answered is an astonishing act of submission. But the answer itself calls that then into question. "YHWH," an utterance that can't really be uttered, a puff of air that signifies being. "I am that I am," or "I am who is," and from then on in Scripture, simply "the LORD."

It's a strange name, imprecise and as mystifying as it is clarifying. But the fact that God told Moses suggests a few things. That God wanted us to know God's name, that God *wants* us to know God's name, that God submits himself to relationship with us—these are all suggestions of the story.

But so are these: that God meant for us to know that knowing God's name is not so straightforward a thing, that God *wants* us to know that to know God's name is to know that God's name cannot be known. We can invoke God, as in a prayer of invocation. But here our power over God ends. Here it becomes instead power with.

We should remember this whenever we mean for God to do our bidding, and we'd be wise to remember this whenever others speak of God as doing their bidding. Like a good mother, God responds. God even provides. But God doesn't obey. And whenever we mean to cast a spell on God, we're opening the possibility that God might cast a spell on us—to do justice, to love kindness, and to walk humbly with God.

Making Bill Maher Laugh

> When the people saw that Moses delayed to come down from the mountain, the people gathered around Aaron and said to him, "Come, make gods for us, who shall go before us; as for this Moses, the man who brought us up out of the land of Egypt, we do not know what has become of him." Aaron said to them, "Take off the gold rings that are on the ears of your wives, your sons, and your daughters, and bring them to me."
>
> So all the people took off the gold rings from their ears, and brought them to Aaron. He took the gold from them, formed it in a mold, and cast an image of a calf; and they said, "These are your gods, O Israel, who brought you up out of the land of Egypt!" When Aaron saw this, he built an altar before it; and Aaron made proclamation and said, "Tomorrow shall be a festival to the Lord." They rose early the next day, and offered burnt-offerings and brought sacrifices of well-being; and the people sat down to eat and drink, and rose up to revel.
>
> The Lord said to Moses, "Go down at once! Your people, whom you brought up out of the land of Egypt, have acted perversely; they have been quick to turn aside from the way that I commanded them; they have cast for themselves an image of a calf, and have worshipped it and sacrificed to it, and said, 'These are your gods, O Israel, who brought you up out of the land of Egypt!'" (Exodus 32:1–8)

THERE'S A MAN WHO had a statue made of the Ten Commandments that weighs about five thousand pounds, two and a half tons. He needs a crane to move it, and sometimes the crane buckles under the weight.

That's a joke.

You're not laughing—which means either the joke isn't funny or you don't get it. But I know it's a funny joke. So let me explain it. (And don't get too down on yourselves. I didn't get it at first either.)

I noticed something last week during worship that I'd never noticed before. The last line of the reading, which was the Exodus version of the Ten Commandments—there are two versions, one in Exodus and one in Deuteronomy—told of the people's response to Moses' encounter with God. They had been watching while Mount Sinai was engulfed in smoke and fire, and while Moses disappeared into the pyrotechnics; they saw Moses then emerge and come down, and they listened as he read what he'd been given—Ten Commandments that are actually better rendered as ten utterances, brief as they are, and even more so in Hebrew.

Here's what the story said about this response: "When all the people witnessed the thunder and lightning, the sound of the trumpet, and the mountain smoking, they were afraid and trembled and stood at a distance, and said to Moses, 'You speak to us, and we will listen; but do not let God speak to us, or we will die.' Moses said to the people, 'Do not be afraid; for God has come only to test you and to put the fear of him upon you so that you do not sin.'"

Here's what's striking about this: Moses' admission that the reason for all the spectacle, the shock and awe, has nothing to do with God's presence, God's essence. There's nothing about God that is fire and smoke, trumpets blasting, thunder thundering. This isn't how God *necessarily* comes to manifest among humans; this isn't how God's essence substantiates. No, this has to do with some *human* need, a human expectation of God.

Not unrelatedly, there's been another shot fired in the culture war about religion. Bill Maher—comedian, and provocateur who's got his own talk show, and mind behind the film *Religulous* by which he meant to strip naked the ridiculous nature of religion itself—made comments about Islam that then had movie star Ben Affleck coming to Islam's defense.

Now, already you can likely guess that the discussion wasn't an intellectually rigorous one. Not that I think these two are incapable of intellectual rigor—I have no idea about that—but I do know the context for the conversation isn't conducive of such a thing: a talk show that is often more of a shout-down. Plus, what little I know of each of these two indicates that neither has any actual experience with Islam or any other "religious" practice for that matter.

So, what superficiality got played out between these two—attacker on the one side and defender on the other—is the idea that there are two kinds of people in the world: there are religious people and their gods, and there are irreligious people and their common sense; there are people who will defend religion (or at least their religion) against any and all attack or critique, and there are people who see religion as, well, "religulous."

Amidst all this straw-man knocking-down is this depth that goes uncovered and unexplored and indeed probably entirely unknown: the idea that Lord himself, the Living One whom we meet in the Bible and with whom many people of the book throughout history and the world over pilgrimage through life to life, is as critical of religion as Bill Maher could ever be.

The Bible is a deeply ironic text. God, whom the Jews first recognized and then, across centuries, witnessed into the world; God, whom Jesus knew intimately as Father, *Abba*, Daddy; God, whom Peter and Paul and the other apostles spread abroad through preaching and baptizing and community-building—this God is a God who is deeply ambivalent about religion.

First, to define our terms: "religion" is famously difficult to define, and "you know it when you see it" doesn't cut it. Knowing this, scholar William Cavanaugh surveyed university religion department catalogs and found courses on the following: "totems, witchcraft, the rights of man, Marxism, liberalism, Japanese tea ceremonies, nationalism, sports, [and] free market ideology."[1] In fact, the whole concept of religion is one that arrived late to the game. Though the practices that fall into this category are as old and persistent as humanity itself, the critical concept of religion is a modern concept, one introduced to study the strange peoples and practices that exploration and colonization had European people encountering the world over.

I always find it helpful, then, to go back to the word's root. *Re-ligio* is a term meaning to re-bind, *ligio* meaning bind, as in *ligature* and *ligament*. So, perhaps religion is any phenomenon that binds people back together— one with another and one with their god, which is the transcendent made imminent. Re-ligio is, then also, that phenomenon which establishes who's in and who's out.

And now we're in some tricky territory. Now we must proceed with caution. It's what God would have us do.

Consider the story of Abraham and Isaac and Mount Moriah—when Abraham bound Isaac at God's command so to sacrifice him, and then un-bound him, at the Lord's command so to let him go. There are those who call this story "The Binding of Isaac," the *Aquedah* in Hebrew; and there are those who call this story "The Unbinding of Isaac." Which is it to you?

And consider this—the scene revealed to the prophet Ezekiel of a valley that was full of dried bones, a mass grave, really, filled with the re-mains of a people slaughtered. But then the bones began to come together, a clattering, bone to its bone. And then there were sinews on these bones, ligaments, so to hold them together; and then flesh. It was a re-binding, this

1. Cavanaugh, "Does Religion Cause Violence?"

scene. It was a re-ligious coming together. The moment of true life for these resurrected bones comes when the breath of God enters each body, but the breath wouldn't have had any place to fill had not the bones been rebound, bone to its bone.

But then consider this—when the king of Aram, Israel's enemy, Naaman, was suffering terrible leprosy and sent for the Jewish prophet Elisha for help, for a cure. And, though he received one, it wasn't what he was expecting, and he was dismayed, outraged actually, by the irreligious nature of the cure—so common a thing, so unspectacular a thing. "Go wash in the river Jordan seven times." He said, in a rage, "I thought that for me he would surely come out, and stand and call on the name of the Lord his God, and would wave his hand over the spot, and cure the leprosy!" But then his servants approached and said to him, "Father, if the prophet had commanded you to do something difficult, would you not have done it? How much more, when all he said to you was, 'Wash, and be clean'?" So he went down and immersed himself seven times in the Jordan, and his flesh was restored "like the flesh of a young boy, and he was clean."

Now consider Jesus and his many arguments with the religious authorities, noticing first of all that his objection was not because they merely abused their authority but because they abused their *religious* authority. Sloppy thinking has had those in the church often hear this as Jesus taking issue with them because they were Jewish. Sloppy thinking has had us sometimes assume Jesus objected to their religious practice because it was the wrong religion, the religious authorities of his day being Jewish while he was the first Christian. But Jesus wasn't a Christian. He was a Jew. He was a Jew living in Jewish territory with other Jews, worshiping by Jewish Scripture and abiding faithfully with the Jewish God. So, no, he didn't object to them because they were Jewish. He objected to them because they were religious, were religious before they were anything else. They led with religious rectitude and never departed from this.

And consider him saying this, as his ministry was becoming more and more focused on the cross: "Come to me, you who are weary; and I will give you rest—for my yoke is easy and my burden is light." The great twentieth-century theologian Paul Tillich claims, "[T]he burden He means to take from us is the burden of religion."[2] And he goes on to say that, when it comes to knowing and abiding with God, "Nearly nothing is demanded of you—no idea of God, and no goodness in yourselves, not your being

2. Tillich, *Shaking*, 102.

religious, not your being Christian, not your being wise, and not your being moral. What is demanded is only your being open and willing to accept what is given to you, the New Being, the being of love and justice and truth, as it is manifest in Him whose yoke is easy and whose burden is light."[3]

Finally, consider Jesus in the last week of his life, according to the Gospel of John, when he went to the grave of his friend Lazarus who had recently (though really) died. To no one in particular or to the grave or to the power of death, Jesus said this of the bands of cloth used to wrap a dead body, and more specifically to have wrapped Lazarus's dead body: "Unbind him, and let him go."

But then be mindful that on the night of his arrest, Jesus said to his disciples in reference to bread, said to all of them together (the "you" of this plural): "Take, eat; do so in remembrance of me;" And of the cup, he said, "This is the cup of the New Covenant; whenever you drink of it, do so in re-membrance of me." And consider this, that if to remember is to re-member or to reattach what has been dismembered or cut off, then this could well be understood as a sacrament of re-binding, of re-ligion.

And yet once dead, Jesus' passion is said to have had this effect: the temple curtain torn in two, that is, the curtain that separated the inner sanctuary from the Holy of Holies, that innermost sanctuary into which no one could enter but the High Priest on the High Holy Day—this very seat of religious observance and cultic practice—yeah, that curtain. It was torn in two, as if to say there is no separation between the holy and the mundane, between the divine and the created order or even among those within the created order; there is no such dismemberment, or at least not anymore; and so there is no formal need for reattachment, for re-ligion.

This is what the Bible has to say regarding religion: it's good, it's bad; it's a blessing, it's a dreadful trap; you don't need it, here it is as a fulfillment of your need; take and enjoy, take care and be very cautious.

Ambivalence, anyone?

Walter Brueggemann has something interesting to say about the golden calf. This is often thought to be an idol. This is often taken as the first transgression against the recently given Ten Commandments, one of which is, "You shall not make for yourself an idol, whether in the form of anything that is in heaven above, or that is on the earth beneath, or that is in the water under the earth. You shall not bow down to them or worship them; for I the Lord your God am a jealous God." The golden calf is often

3. Ibid., 102.

taken as just such an idol, which means it took the people all of ten chapters to break their covenant with the Lord. But Old Testament scholar and quite fiery preacher (from what I'm told) and member of the United Church of Christ (go, team!) Mr. Brueggemann suspects it's not so simple. He suspects that the golden calf "is an alternative representation for God . . . not idolatrous but simply a competitor to the ark of the covenant as a proper sign of divine presence."[4]

This makes some sense to me. What's more, as far as competitions go, this one seems epic. The golden calf is an appropriated fertility symbol—appropriated from Egypt, perhaps, and their bull god Apis; or from Canaan, perhaps, and their god Baal, imaged as a bull. This is to say the golden calf is a religious artifact plain and simple. Endowed with a power based on the people's belief that it has power, and perhaps on the fact that the materials of which it was made are materials considered of great value, and so perhaps worth fighting over—peoples' gold jewelry which they surrendered, though by what force or coercion we can only imagine—the golden calf carries no critique of itself, no warning of the power it purports to possess and exercise.

The Ark of the Covenant, on the other hand, is but a box (a gold-plated box, yes, but still just a box) in which the people could carry around the law, those two tablets of commandments by which a people might live together in peace. No magic, no spectacle, these were simple guidelines as to how love is lived out, how love behaves, so to enable life together and life abundant. The binding these guidelines offered the people—the religion contained and offered therein, so to speak—is a voluntary binding one to another. And it comes with the critique written right into it: "I am the Lord your God, have no other gods before me, and make no idols for worship. Rather, to be my people, honor your elders, remember the sanctity of time, and restrain from violating one another out of misplaced desire."

Of course, this box was eventually imagined as having power of the more spectacular sort. When the Philistines had it in their possession after making war with the Israelites, all sorts of bad fortune that befell them was credited to their having this box. And then there's the portrayal of the powers of this box in the movie *Raiders of the Lost Ark*—it burning the skin off any Nazi who tried to steal it. Yes, it's true that this box came to be imagined as having great and terrible power—but I wonder if that, as Moses said, was

---

4. Brueggemann, *An Introduction*, 64.

all just God putting on a show to put the fear of God into the people so we would not sin.

The cost of sin, after all, is quite high. When a people, a nation, falls out of the bounds of a commonly held law and sense of authority, a common acknowledgement of who's in charge and to be listened to and respected, it's not an overstatement to say that all hell breaks loose.

Have you seen the news lately?

Here's how another scholar sees it. Gene Tucker characterizes what Aaron was up to in authorizing the making of the calf: "Aaron, as a religious leader, responds to a religious need with a religious solution."[5] And that such a solution was an abomination to the Living God is but one more hint that God's not necessarily a fan of religion.

And yet God does have mercy for our need for it, and so does apparently try to fulfill it—though in ways that actually give life rather than take it, and in a way that actually widens the circle of who's in and who's out so that it's indeed a circle that has a center but no outer edge. God has mercy for our religious needs, and through time has met those needs with religious rites increasingly simple, increasingly light. And what we do here on any given Sunday is the most responsible thing we can as regards our need for religion—we hold it in the light of consciousness and good intention.

Light, indeed!

But, hey, did you hear the one about this guy who made a statue of the Ten Commandments, those utterances, those ineffable puffs of air by which God meant for the people simply to abide together in peace? The statue weighs five thousands pounds, two and a half tons! He needs a crane to move it around, and move it he does. He goes around the country with it so people can see it. Sometimes the crane buckles under its weight.

Now do you get the joke? It might even make Bill Maher laugh—and I don't mean scoff but really laugh. I know it does me, but then I'm always up for a laugh.

Thanks be to God.

5. Tucker, "Proper 19 [24]." 406.

Obey.

After these things God tested Abraham. He said to him, "Abraham!" And he said, "Here I am." He said, "Take your son, your only son Isaac, whom you love, and go to the land of Moriah, and offer him there as a burnt-offering on one of the mountains that I shall show you."

So Abraham rose early in the morning, saddled his donkey, and took two of his young men with him, and his son Isaac; he cut the wood for the burnt-offering, and set out and went to the place in the distance that God had shown him. On the third day Abraham looked up and saw the place far away. Then Abraham said to his young men, "Stay here with the donkey; the boy and I will go over there; we will worship, and then we will come back to you."

Abraham took the wood of the burnt-offering and laid it on his son Isaac, and he himself carried the fire and the knife. So the two of them walked on together. Isaac said to his father Abraham, "Father!" And he said, "Here I am, my son." He said, 'The fire and the wood are here, but where is the lamb for a burnt-offering?' Abraham said, 'God himself will provide the lamb for a burnt-offering, my son.' So the two of them walked on together.

When they came to the place that God had shown him, Abraham built an altar there and laid the wood in order. He bound his son Isaac, and laid him on the altar, on top of the wood. Then Abraham reached out his hand and took the knife to kill his son. But the angel of the Lord called to him from heaven, and said, "Abraham, Abraham!" And he said, "Here I am." He said, "Do not lay your hand on the boy or do anything to him; for now I know that you fear God, since you have not withheld your son, your only son, from me." And Abraham looked up and saw a ram, caught in a thicket by its horns. Abraham went and took the ram and offered it up as a burnt-offering instead of his son. So Abraham called that place "The Lord will provide"; as it is said to this day, "On the mount of the Lord it shall be provided." (Genesis 22:1–18)

MUCH HAS BEEN MADE of Abraham's obedience to God's command: "Take your son, your only son, Isaac, whom you love . . . and offer him there as a burnt-offering." Much is made of his obedience to God. A model of faithfulness, people have said, a role model in the life of faith.

And why not? After all, not only was it a terrible command that he was ready to obey—"ready" being perhaps a better translation of the Hebrew word *hinneni* than the more common rendering, "Here I am." Not only was it a violent command that he was ready to obey—violent, yes, toward Isaac but also toward the promise God had been making to Abraham all along, that he and Sarah, in spite of barrenness and old age, would become the parents of a great people, a promise whose fulfillment had been dubious and delayed and laughable even. No, not only was it a terrible and violent command, it was also cruel, worded in such a way as if not merely to test Abraham but to terrorize him. Why else belabor the identity of the one whom Abraham was to take to a mountain that God would show him: "your son, your only son Isaac, whom you love"? Why else but to bring it closer and closer to home, closer and closer to Abraham's heart: "your son, your only son Isaac, whom you love"?

This overemphasis comes in contrast to the otherwise spare story, which spares no detail. Plodding and suspenseful, it notes that Abraham rose early in the morning and saddled his donkey. He took two of his young men with him and, of course, his son, his only son, Isaac, whom he loved. He cut wood for the burnt offering, which Isaac would soon enough carry—bound to him before he was bound to it. Methodical if mean, the story notes every fine act on Abraham's part, every movement he makes toward Moriah and then, now alone with his son (his only son, Isaac, whom he loved), farther into the place that God had showed him.

Unswerving obedience, we might hear in it all—Abraham's building an altar and binding Isaac to it, Abraham's taking out his knife to kill his son. (And what of Isaac, he who was strong enough to carry his own wood and to hike for three days so was certainly strong enough to fight his old father off? What of him?) Faithful obedience: we marvel at it and we wonder of ourselves, Would we? Could we? I have, anyway. I wrote my senior thesis at divinity school in large part about this very question.

Would we? Could we?

Do we have to?

You know, I'm beginning to suspect that all this time I've been marveling at the wrong act of obedience. Really, I'm growing convinced that all this time *we've* been marveling at the wrong thing.

It is impossible to say how common a practice child sacrifice was in the ancient Near East. We have nearly no archeological evidence that it was prevalent. But, of course, a lack of evidence proves nothing. We have lots of narrative mention of it, but often that's in reference to something other peoples do—and that's always hard to interpret. Was it written as propaganda, in order to justify enmity of one people for another? Or was it written as fact, or perhaps even warning, in order to caution the members of one people away from another? It's hard enough to know why people say what they say when they're among the living and you can still ask them follow-up questions. It's hard enough to know what motivates even the people closest to us. How much harder it is, then, to know the motivations of people long dead, of an utterly different time and place.

All that said, there is reason enough to believe, at least for our purpose today, that child sacrifice was a familiar practice if not a common one— something the Moabites did, something the Ammonites did, something that might well have been done in Ur, the land out of which God called Abraham in the first place. (And maybe this was one reason why.) Perhaps even the earliest Israelites did it.

Consider: the place called *gehenna* that Jesus spoke of, a word rendered in English as "hell," was an ever-burning garbage dump that's believed to have been a once-sacred site used for child sacrifice.

Consider: the lovely assurance the prophet Micah issues, that all the Lord requires of the people is for them "to do justice, to love kindness, and to walk humbly with your God." Indeed, consider that this comes in direct response to this question posed: "Shall I give my firstborn for my transgression, the fruit of my body for the sin of my soul?" which indicates that such a thing was a possibility, a possible requirement for getting right with God.

Consider: Abraham, though loving of Isaac, yet perhaps doubted that God's promise to him would be fulfilled through Isaac because, of course, the call would come for Abraham to give Isaac back. The call would come, that common call to slaughter your own child for righteousness' sake. And Abraham would do it, the common, culturally dictated thing to do. And Isaac would comply, having perhaps lived his whole short life under the shadow of this dark question: Will I be allowed to live or will I be chosen to die?

Consider (if you can) all the things you do because it's what we do in this culture. Militarism. Consumerism. Racism—the unshakeable idea that there are different races within the human race and that these reveal essential value and capability and character. The eating of animals that have been brutalized and enslaved. The burning of fossil fuels over which wars are waged and by which whole ecosystems are devastated while the many climates of the whole world wobble and warm.

Consider (if such a thing is even possible) all the things you don't even question doing because our cultural framing of reality doesn't allow for such questioning. (The tricky thing about assumptions is that you don't know what your assumptions are, you don't even know you *have* them, until something radical—radically strange, radically other—comes along and reveals them to you, sometimes to your dismay, sometimes to our shame.)

Of course, Abraham would walk with Isaac to the land Moriah. Of course he would! The wondrous thing is that together they walked home.

Yes, of course! The marvelous act of obedience on Abraham's part wasn't when he obeyed the call of God to offer his beloved son, but was when he obeyed the call of the angel of the Lord not to lay a hand on him.

There's a funny thing in this story that I can't ever get past—the name of the deity changes midway through the narrative. See: that while it's *God* who tested Abraham and it's *God* who told him to take his son, his only son, Isaac, whom he loves, to the land Moriah; while it's *God* who showed him the mountain that these two would climb together and it's *God* whom Abraham believed would provide the lamb for the burnt offering (a confession so ominous it's chilling, said to Isaac, "God will provide the lamb for a burnt-offering, my son"); yes, while it's *God* whom Abraham was praised for fearing, and rightly so, for it's *God* whose word is terrible and violent and cruel; it is yet the *Lord* whose angel calls from heaven to say, "Abraham, do not lay your hand on the boy or do anything to him"; and it is yet the LORD in whom Abraham does at last confess faith, upon seeing the ram caught in the thicket, upon offering it up instead of his son, calling the place where this all happened, "The LORD will provide," as if to say, "The LORD, and not merely God, will provide." At the peak of the story, at the watershed moment when Isaac's life is spared and the LORD's promise to Abraham moves evermore toward fulfillment, the deity's referent changes from "God" to "the LORD."

Why?

There are two ways in the Hebrew Bible by which the deity is named. *El* and its many variants (*El Shaddai, Elohim, El Olam*, etc.) is the more generic term, most often translated "God" and used in reference both to the God of the Israelites and the gods of other peoples. The other is an unpronounceable name referred to as the tetragrammaton, meaning a word having four letters, these being YHWH. This is the name that Moses heard uttered from the burning bush when he asked it, "Whom shall I say sent me?" It's rendered in English, "I Am," or alternatively, "I Am that I Am," or, "I Am that I Shall Be," or "I Am that Is." It's been turned into a name that can be pronounced, *Yahweh*, or this earlier version, *Jehovah*, or this most common among English Bibles, printed in capital letters, "the LORD." But here's the crucial point about "the LORD"—that the only god ever called the LORD is Israel's God, which is to say Jesus' God, which is to say our God. The only God ever called the LORD is the God known to us in the life, death, and resurrection of Christ.

This is a god who upsets social convention, preferring instead the freedom of eternal life.

This is a god who breaks down human culture, preferring instead the Kingdom of Heaven.

Standing in contrast to all those countless gods of human assuming and arranging—the primitive gods of human sacrifice and sacred violence, the political gods of imperialism and authoritarianism, the contemporary gods of capitalism and militarism and consumerism—the LORD is a God sovereign over all, casting in full relief the falseness of these functional gods and promising that, though what is will fall away, what abides is absolute blessing for all.

Calling to us from beyond the boundaries of the world as we know it—boundaries of what's expected and appropriate, what's customary and conventional, what's a given and taken for granted and accepted as just the way things are—the LORD is a God who goes ever before us, leading us out of what we think we know is true and into the realm we know only in our hope and our imagination, where the rule is love, the dynamic is redemption that nothing is lost, the aim is reconciliation that all might be one, and the end is life free of death, life that has no end.

Much has been made of Abraham's obedience—or rather much is made of it in certain circles. In other circles, though, obedience would be the last posture in life worthy of amazement and admiration. In some circles, obedience is considered worthy only of derision. Originality: this is what's worthy of praise. Self-determined originality: this has value these days; this is a primary objective. Self-made men. Self-actualized women. Expressive teenagers. Children who've found their "passion."

I was a teacher of high school English students for a short while. I remember writing assignments in which students struggled after originality. It was either the content of the papers, or their form. How to be original? Writing backwards, capitalizing only the improper nouns, appropriating punctuation (but hadn't e. e. cummings already done that?). How to be original? It caused no small amount of angst. In fact, in a couple cases it caused a great deal of angst, troubling these two teenagers whom I have in mind, troubling these who were already quite troubled. Evidence of the struggle was indeed the last paper one girl handed in before committing suicide that weekend. And, though I doubt it was a straight line, though I doubt that her recognizing herself as at least somewhat derivative is what suddenly made life too difficult to take, I *do* think there's something here to explore. I *do* think the pressure to be original is real.

Poet Mary Oliver is known in a most beloved poem, "Wild Geese," for assuring people of our need not to be good, merely to be. She likely meant to comfort with this. If comforting, though, it would mostly be so to people raised on a steady diet of obedience. My offering for these latter days, for those brought up to find their passion, is this: "You don't have to be original." Indeed, I don't think you can be. I think none of us can be wholly original (though each of us is certainly unique). And it's this: it's this that made me so very sad in the wake of the girl's death. This is what had me so stricken—my own conviction that everyone obeys someone, everyone obeys something, that this isn't some failure to be self-determined but is simply the way things are, the way we are. The questions, then, for us are: What do we obey? Whom do we obey?

This story of Abraham and Isaac in the land of Moriah seems difficult because of that first dreaded command ("Take your son, your only son Isaac, whom you love"). But what actually makes it difficult, challenging, urgently challenging, is the fact of the second command—for this would have us search ourselves as to whether we're listening to the right voice in life and obeying the right commands.

There's an irony here. The voice we're to listen to, the commands we're to obey, would have us question so many of our conventions, defy so many of our habits and ways of life. The voice we're to listen to, the commands we're to obey, would have us recognize our assumptions for what they are, and would have us bring them into the light so we can discern and decide whether they're true and therefore worthy of our obedience, or not.

Obedience as defiance, obedience as pushing forward and outward, finding some new way—who knew church could invite such adventure? Why, even the kids might want to get with this.

Thanks be to the Lord.

Religious but Not Spiritual

Who is wise and understanding among you? Show by your good life that your works are done with gentleness born of wisdom. But if you have bitter envy and selfish ambition in your hearts, do not be boastful and false to the truth. Such wisdom does not come down from above, but is earthly, unspiritual, devilish. For where there is envy and selfish ambition, there will also be disorder and wickedness of every kind. But the wisdom from above is first pure, then peaceable, gentle, willing to yield, full of mercy and good fruits, without a trace of partiality or hypocrisy. And a harvest of righteousness is sown in peace for those who make peace. Those conflicts and disputes among you, where do they come from? Do they not come from your cravings that are at war within you? You want something and do not have it; so you commit murder. And you covet something and cannot obtain it; so you engage in disputes and conflicts. You do not have, because you do not ask. You ask and do not receive, because you ask wrongly, in order to spend what you get on your pleasures. (James 3:13–4:3)

They went on from there and passed through Galilee. He did not want anyone to know it; for he was teaching his disciples, saying to them, "The Son of Man is to be betrayed into human hands, and they will kill him, and three days after being killed, he will rise again." But they did not understand what he was saying and were afraid to ask him.

Then they came to Capernaum; and when he was in the house he asked them, "What were you arguing about on the way?" But they were silent, for on the way they had argued with one another about who was the greatest. (Mark 9:30–34)

I *LIKE THE LETTER* of James. It was Martin Luther who had a problem with it. He called it an "epistle of straw"—which I suppose is true enough. He claimed there was too little of Christ crucified in it—which I suppose is true enough. Words of wisdom, words of common sense: okay, it's not profound, but it is useful. Placed more in the Old Testament tradition of Proverbs and Ecclesiastes, the Letter of James meant to make clear the sort of attitudes and behavior entailed in living a Christian life, which it does quite well, beautifully, in fact. Preacher Will Willimon has said that reading the book of Proverbs is like taking a long road trip with your mother.[1] If

---

1. McThenia, "A Missionary Vocation."

so, then the letter of James is as if your mother were a Waldorf method preschool teacher.

Actually, it sort of reminds me of a new book, *Religion for Atheists*.[2] Alain de Botton wrote it, a Swiss-born now Englishman and self-proclaimed atheist. I'll admit I haven't read the book, but I did read the opinion piece he wrote for the *Wall Street Journal*[3] and the book review Aengus Woods wrote for NPR.[4]

De Botton's central thesis is that secular modernism has resulted in a loss of a sense of community, which he believes is something the great religions of the world managed to create very well. So he means, by his own admission and in his own words, to "steal" from religions the practices that create community. While leaving behind the belief systems that he finds absurd and that he assumes most people guided by common sense would also find absurd, de Botton would like to see a flowering of *agape* restaurants, for example, wherein people who are strangers might eat together so to become friends.[5] Rich and poor, young and old, smart and simple, senator and janitor—all would be welcome, would sit shoulder to shoulder, and would feast.

Incidentally, this is quite a switch from what I'm used to hearing, that people want spirituality without all that religion. Here's someone who wants all that religion but without the silly spirituality. I have to say it's refreshing. I'll admit it's also irritating. De Botton is going to let common sense be the guide for building a commonly held sense of community.

But the problem, which the NPR book review points out very well, is that common sense isn't so common. Everyone thinks they've got it, and that some other people might have it as well. "[Y]et most of us can usually identify large chunks of the population who conspicuously lack it," writes Woods. "To make matters worse, in any projected breakdown of global common-sense distribution, we can't even agree on which folk constitute the haves and [which] the have-nots. However, one thing is always certain: I myself possess it. Definitely. Absolutely. No question."[6]

---

2. de Botton, *Religion for Atheists.*

3. de Botton, "Religion for Everyone."

4. Woods, "'Religion for Atheists.'"

5. The agape meal, sometimes also called a love feast, comes to us from early Christianity. The first "followers of the Way" would gather for meals that were distinct from the Eucharist yet were free and open to all.

6. Woods, "'Religion for Atheists.'"

Woods continues, "This conundrum of common sense is what makes a writer such as Alain de Botton so attractive and so infuriating. He is a master of the well-heeled, chatty and above all reasonable tone. . . . But scratch the veneer, and one quickly finds myriad competing common senses screaming to break free."

Here is one of the competing common senses that scream in my mind to break free: when I gather with strangers at an agape meal: whose voice is authoritative? Whose sense and sensibility will we adopt in common? Alain de Botton's—so reasonable, so calmly assertive? Well, then I'm not interested. I've met educated white guys with a calmly overdeveloped sense of reason. They make me want to run screaming to my nearest women's studies class.

But about one thing he might be right, though not as sweepingly so as his sweeping statement suggests. He writes, "Insofar as modern society ever promises us access to a community, it is one centered on the worship of professional success. We sense that we are brushing up against its gates when the first question we are asked at a party is 'What do you do?,' our answer to which will determine whether we are warmly welcomed or conclusively abandoned."[7] And this reminds me of what the disciples were arguing about as they walked along the way.

It's surprising that they fall into this argument, isn't it? An argument over greatness, over what is greatness and who among them will be deemed greatest—that this is where their conversation goes is surprising given that what comes before is Jesus teaching them about his own suffering and death. "The Son of Man is to be betrayed into human hands," or more accurately translated, "is to be handed over, and the humans will kill him, and three days after being killed, he will rise again."

This is one of three times that Jesus mentions his fate on the cross. Sometimes it's said that he foretells it—his own crucifixion. This time it's said that he teaches it. It's a distinction that I'll now perhaps make too much of. To foretell it is to tell me about something that's to happen; to teach it is to tell me about something that I should try to do as well. As a follower of Christ, as a disciple to be disciplined in the way of Christ, I should live a cruciform life; I should form my living in the shape of the cross—self-giving, self-emptying.

And it *is* a discipline. It *is* something that needs to be taught to me, that I need reminding of and practice in—because it isn't the human's natural

7. de Botton, "Religion for Everyone."

predisposition, or at least not the human's *only* natural predisposition. We like power, and the power to be found in vulnerability is a little counter-intuitive. We like glory, and the glory to be found in giving love is not as self-evident as the glory to be found in wearing pretty clothes, or living in a fancy home where you can throw parties that everyone wants an invitation to, or holding a job that pays you millions of dollars and where you get to employ lots of people and fire a few too.

The bitter envy, the selfish ambition that James mentions in this open letter—these are so common! It might not be so, as James writes, that we want something and do not have it, so we commit murder. It might not even be so that we desire something and cannot attain it and so we engage in disputes and conflicts. No, the reactions to such feelings might not be ours in such extreme. But certainly these feelings, so familiar to me, are familiar to each of us; and certainly they do pose a threat to our relating, to our participating in community. Otherwise, why write an open letter? If envy, if ambition, if competition, weren't so commonly at work within us, if these are evils that afflict only a couple of people, then why not just write that one guy who has this thing called envy that seems to spoil his relationships; otherwise, why not just write that one girl who is out of the norm because of her ambition?

The disciples didn't understand the teaching. They didn't understand what Jesus was saying, and I can relate. Every time I'm to preach on one of these occasions when Jesus has spoken of what awaits him—something I'm to do a lot, since three times in the three synoptic Gospels he speaks of his own coming suffering, which means that three times a year outside of Holy Week the cross is there for us to wrestle with again—my initial thought is, "Oh, I've done this before; I'll whip this sermon out." But then I sit with the text, and with the formula to which it testifies—that the cross is God's revelation of good news for us, that the Crucifixion is made a means of God's grace, God's amazing grace—and I realize that once again I don't get it, that I need to start from scratch and figure it out anew. Why is the Crucifixion good news? Why does the cross save? How and why and from what does it save us?

The cross is good news because it means humans even at our worst are little match for God's goodness—God's love, God's forgiveness, God's peace. The cross is good news because it reveals that God's glory is in weakness, God's strength is in vulnerability, God's might is in self-giving, God's victory is in self-emptying, and God's Christ is that guy—not some superstar but just some guy, some gentle, forceful, regular, exceptional guy for whom there is no place in this world of powers and principalities and death-dealing dynamics and might-makes-right, and so who must be expelled from it, yet only to return and to say for starters not this, "I'm back, and I'm pissed, and you're gonna get yours," but this, "Peace be with you." And the Crucifixion saves because it reveals to us humans the power dynamics to which we are enthralled, a revelation that in turn gives us some measure of self-understanding and therefore hope for stepping out of such a downward spiraling. The Crucifixion saves because it lays bare the lie by which we largely live, that violence can and will save us from violence, which in turn gives us some measure of unblindness and unforgetting and therefore hope of ending cycles of violence. Finally, the Crucifixion saves because in it and through it and in spite of it, God has done something—something wonderful, something new (behold!), something miraculous—that plants in the earth a seed of peace, a seed of hope, a seed by which God's Kingdom will grow even here.

Liz Garrigan-Byerly—our once member and then seminarian and now associate pastor of Wellesley Village United Church of Christ—Liz Garrigan-Byerly and I used to play with this question: The salvation that comes through the cross, does it come because of what we do in response to what we've learned in witnessing the cross and resurrection; or is it something God did, has done, continues to do, in the mystery of the cross? And at her ecclesiastical council, when those gathered, having read her ordination paper, might now question her on certain aspects of it, I asked the inevitable atonement question. There's always one, in every council, someone who asks the dreaded atonement question. "How does the cross save us? It's not that the blood of Christ is what God required in order to slake God's wrath. That was our answer once—for about a thousand years; but now we know better. So, does the salvation come of what we do in response to what we've seen and heard? Or is it something God has accomplished in Christ and the church?" I asked it, and she smiled back at me knowingly: this was coming. Her answer: "Yes."

Imagine: an either/or question whose answer is yes.

Okay, so the disciples didn't understand. Clearly, the more things change the more they stay the same. But they at least had the chance to ask follow-up questions; they at least could have asked Christ, "Could you say that again, and this time slower?" That they didn't out of fear softens my judgment in their regard. That they didn't ask because they were afraid to ask has me feeling some compassion for them. I've been there. A math teacher stands at the chalkboard and says, "$A^2 + B^2 = C^2$," and I sit at my desk and nod my head because, you know, whatever. Fear comes because I know I have no hope of understanding, and the test is coming up, and this is probably going to be on it.

Jesus, for his part, seeing that the disciples haven't learned from his teaching, arguing as they were moments later about greatness, decides to give it another go. "Show, don't tell" is some common wisdom, and so he does, taking a little child and putting it among them—this powerless, voiceless, vulnerable scrap, probably dirty, perhaps disowned. Here is the guest of honor.

It makes a huge difference to me, at least, in whose name I join a group—in whose name and by what spirit. It matters, probably more than it should, in whose name and by what spirit I join in. Alain de Botton has invited us to a meal; so has Jesus. I've been to meals of the sort de Botton has in mind. They do nothing to address the cravings that are always at war within me, and (I sort of hope) are always at war within and among us all. (I don't want to be alone in my insecurities.) They, in fact, tend further to stoke such internal conflict: to tell the funniest story or to listen graciously while awaiting your turn, to amuse and sparkle in conversation or to try to blend in with the wallpaper, to impress or to come across as someone who really couldn't care less. I've also been to the meal Jesus had in mind—been to it in sanctuaries of stone and stained glass, been to it kneeling at an altar and sitting in a pew and standing at the table myself breaking the bread, been to it in conference rooms at annual meetings and in this plain sanctuary of restrained beauty. It always addresses that which is at war within me and us—the things James's letter means to address and Jesus' self-giving and servanthood do clearly address. It addresses it by spelling out and laying bare just exactly who I am (frail, foolish, in need of confession) and having me at the table anyway. It addresses it by saying implicitly if not outright, "Come as you are; serve as you can; eat as you need; taste and see that the Lord is good."

If you can get that self-emptying spirit into a restaurant dedicated to a secular agape meal, then God bless it. Take it away, Alain. But if you can't, then we're here. Just look for the sign of the cross and you'll find us.

Thanks be to God.

What Awe Serves

Six days later, Jesus took with him Peter and James and John, and led them up a high mountain apart, by themselves. And he was transfigured before them, and his clothes became dazzling white, such as no one on earth could bleach them. And there appeared to them Elijah with Moses, who were talking with Jesus. Then Peter said to Jesus, "Rabbi, it is good for us to be here; let us make three dwellings, one for you, one for Moses, and one for Elijah." He did not know what to say, for they were terrified. Then a cloud overshadowed them, and from the cloud there came a voice, "This is my Son, the Beloved; listen to him!" Suddenly when they looked around, they saw no one with them any more, but only Jesus. (Mark 9:2–9)

PHIL ZUCKERMAN IS A sociologist aiming to give awe its due.

I don't imagine we here would have it any other way. I don't imagine any here would prefer that awe be ignored or discounted. "It's just a chemical blip in the brain." "It's a dopamine burst." No, I imagine we're all fans of awe, appreciators of its reality and hold on us.

As fundamental to the human experience, to human creativity and curiosity; as perhaps one of the qualities and capabilities that makes us human: awe. Who wouldn't uphold this as an experience worthy of further exploration and appreciation?

Come to think of it, one of my favorite characters in one of my favorite pieces of contemporary literature or theater or performance art, or whatever it is, is Trudy, a homeless woman in Lily Tomlin's one-woman show *The Search for Signs of Intelligent Life in the Universe*, written by Tomlin's now-wife Jane Wagner. Trudy wanders New York, speaking to what she calls her "space chums," showing them around while they visit from another planet or another plane.

One night, under the dim stars of the city sky, she suddenly finds herself in awe.

But it doesn't stop there. It goes on: "Then I became even more awestruck at the thought that I was, in some small way, a part of that which I was in awe about. And this feeling went on and on and on. . . . My space chums got a word for it: awe-infinitum. Because at the point you can comprehend how incomprehensible it all is, you're about as smart as you need to be. . . . And I felt so good inside and my heart so full, I decided I would set aside time each day to do awe-robics. Because at the moment you are most in awe of all there is about life that you don't understand, you are closer to understanding it all than at any other time."[1]

Right? Awe as gateway to insight, to wisdom—what calls us to worship (quite literally this morning, in the Call to Worship). I'm not about to call that into question.

But Zuckerman's intention around his experiences of awe goes astray, to my mind, when he speaks of "awe*ism*." He does so in his recent book *Living the Secular Life: New Answers to Old Questions*, a book I haven't read and (to be honest) don't intend to. I learned of it, and a bit of its contents, from an article on Religious News Service by religion reporter Kimberly Winston. She seems to give it a fair hearing.[2]

According to her, Zuckerman, who counts himself among "secularists"—these being, as he lists them, atheists, humanists, agnostics, and other self-described "nones"—aims to explain how such people "raise their children, decide right from wrong, and build communities without the benefit of religion."[3] I'm not sure to whom he means to explain it. To religious people who perhaps assume the irreligious are without moral orientation? Or to more hardline secularists who reject any talk or thought of transcendence? I don't know who his audience is, and perhaps he doesn't either. This is a sort of scholarly memoir.

Whatever. According to Zuckerman, secularists might live and socialize and decide by this guiding experience, awe, which Winston summarizes, perhaps quoting Zuckerman, as a "nonreligious impulse you can't explain."

Frankly, this is a description I think so vague it's nearly meaningless. A nonreligious impulse you can't explain. But pressing the issue, I wonder what's meant by "can't." Is it that you aren't able to explain it or that you aren't allowed to?

Remember, hardline ideologues come from all camps.

The editor of *Free Inquiry*, Tom Flynn, rejects awe almost altogether, criticizing Zuckerman's project because awe has a referent, a source back to which awe is offered. "To the degree that reverence is understood transitively—as denoting awe, veneration, or respect toward something beyond"— to that same degree it must be rejected. "The domain of everyday experience can't be transcended," he claims. "There is nothing above it,

---

1. Wagner, *Search*, 205–206.
2. Winston, "Welcome."
3. Ibid.

nothing beyond or over it, nothing to revere . . . only reality."[4] Of course, what qualifies in his mind as reality he doesn't say.

And again, I wonder what's meant by "can't" here, because of course everyday experience *can* be transcended. People do it all the time: in prayer and meditation; with music—listening to it, performing it; in relationships—marriages, parenthood, lifelong commitments come what may; in physical activity and challenges. A hiker reaches the top of Mount Washington: I doubt he'd merely explain the experience as a long series of footsteps, though that certainly is the "real" "everyday experience" just embarked upon. So, by saying that "everyday experience *can't* be transcended," our "freely inquiring" Flynn must mean that he won't allow for such a thing.

So much for free inquiry.

I remember once a little boy at a playground took some woodchips and threw them toward other children playing. His mother, meaning to discipline him, told him, "You can't do that." Looking puzzled, he glanced down to the wood chips lining the playground, picked up another handful, threw them, and then looked at her as if to show, "Yes, I can! And you could, too, if you tried."

"You can't explain this impulse, awe."

"Well, maybe you could if you tried."

But back to Zuckerman. As for how he describes this impulse: it's a "profound, overflowing feeling," which he knows best in fleeting moments: "playing on the beach with his young daughter, eating grapes from his grandparents' backyard, sledding in the dark of a January night, dancing with abandon at a favorite concert."[5]

As for aweism, Zuckerman explains that this "is the belief that existence is ultimately a beautiful mystery" and has the capacity to "inspire deep feelings of joy, poignancy and sublime awe." [6]Our friend Trudy, homeless, hearing voices, wandering New York City, might say the same, and, since I go with her, I would agree.

Zuckerman continues, though, and now defensively, as if anticipating the attack from his harder-line secularists: "Aweism . . . though steeped in existential wonder and soulful appreciation, is still very much grounded in this world. It is akin to what philosopher Robert Solomon dubs a

---

4. Ibid.

5. Ibid.

6 Zuckerman, blog. http://atheistnexus.org/profiles/blogs/aweism-1

'naturalized' spirituality: a non-religious, non-theological, non-doctrinal orientation that is right here, in our lives and in our world, not elsewhere."[7]

As to aweism's end, its goal, Zuckerman explains, "An aweist just feels awe from time to time, appreciates it, owns it, relishes it, and then carries on."[8]

And concluding about aweism, Zuckerman assures any who would worry about a religious agenda being set upon them: "My awe stops there."[9] He's not trying to *do* anything with his awe. He's not trying to get anyone to join him in awe. He just feels it, notices it, keeps it to himself, stops there.

Huh.

Trudy might call it "Awe interruptus."

Peter might say, "It is good for us to be here. Let us make three dwellings."

Peter, Jesus' near constant companion; Peter, the disciple who, only verses earlier, confessed that Jesus isn't merely a reiteration of the ancient prophet Elijah or John the Baptizer redux, but is the Christ, something unique and one-time in the world, the anointed one of God; Peter, the rock on whom Jesus would establish his church, which is to say the foundation upon which would be built up a beloved community and community of belovedness: Peter, right here on this mountaintop, amidst this private, awesome experience, did in effect say, "Let's stay here, build three little temples, and never go anywhere else, never go down the mountain, back to the people, back to work. It's good for us to be here. Let's stay here."

And, why not? He'd been personally invited to this experience, after all. Jesus had taken him and James and John, and led them up a high mountain apart, by themselves; and Jesus was transfigured before them, his clothes becoming dazzling white like no laundress could make them; and there appeared also Elijah and Moses, which is to say representatives of the Prophets and the Law. Jesus had allowed these three disciples in and no others, as if Peter and James and John were special somehow, uniquely qualified to witness this.

What qualifications Peter had, he perhaps demonstrated, or even developed, six days prior to this, when Jesus was walking with his disciples to the villages of Caesarea Philippi. On the way, Jesus asked them, "Who do people say that I am?" and they answered what they must have heard:

7. Ibid.
8. Ibid.
9. Zuckerman, 211.

"Elijah or John the Baptizer or one of the prophets." Jesus then asked, "But who do you say that I am?" and Peter answered, "You are the Messiah."

Of course, what he might have meant by this is an open question. To say someone is the Messiah is to say that one is the anointed one of God. But what is meant by that is hardly more clear. Really, it just begs questions: Anointed for what? Anointed as what? Speaking very concretely, to be anointed is to have one's head smeared with oil, which has the aim or effect of setting one apart from others, setting one to some special status and task. So, clearly, to be anointed is to be special; and so, clearly, to be the anointed one of God is to be super-special. But what does this specialness lead to? What does it mean?

Peter assumed it meant this: getting to stay on the mountaintop, getting to glimmer and glow, getting to pass time with the superstars of their tradition. It's a vaulted position, this being the Messiah of God.

But God had something else in mind, which Jesus also had in mind, these two being of the same mind. This is what God said, following the Transfiguration and following Peter's assertion that they should stay on that mountaintop: in effect, "No."

"This is my Son the Beloved; listen to him."

I have to say, I love this command: "Listen to him." It's something I've said to the children when they're running roughshod over their father, and something he's said when they're running roughshod over me. "Listen to your mother!" "Listen to your father!" It's by way of saying, we stand together. It's by way of affirming someone's authority by lending them yours. God saying of Jesus to Peter, "Listen to him," calls Peter back from running roughshod over Jesus.

But what, we might wonder, was Peter exactly to listen to? What, Peter might have wondered, had Jesus said that he was to listen to?

As it happens, the last thing Jesus is said to have said is that the Son of Man must undergo great suffering, and must be rejected by the elders and the chief priests and the scribes, and must be killed, and three days later will rise again.

Perhaps it's this that Peter was to listen to, to hear.

He didn't at first. He didn't when Jesus first said this, six days earlier, while walking among the villages of Caesarea Philippi. An exchange that came just following Peter's confession that Jesus is the Christ, the anointed one of God; an exchange just following Peter's having got it right—now Peter got it terribly wrong.

Jesus said he must undergo great suffering, he must be rejected by the elders, and must be killed; and three days later he will rise again. And Peter rebuked Jesus, in the other synoptic Gospels remembered even to have said to Jesus, "God forbid it, Lord. This must never happen to you!"

Because, really, why suffering? Why submission to death? Why not resistance of this, refusal, avoidance? Why not fight the powers-that-be so to preserve his life?

Yeah, why *not* self-preservation? Why *not* self-defense? He had so much work yet to do. He had so much good still to do. He could hardly do that while hanging from a cross, right?

And, really, if anyone could self-preserve through the gauntlet of imperial power, and do it justified, it would surely be Jesus, the anointed one of God, the Son of Man, the beloved Son of God.

Right?

But at this, Jesus then rebuked Peter: "Get behind me, Satan [which is to say 'adversary' or 'stumbling block']! For you are setting your mind not on divine things but on human things." And at that he turned then to the crowd, perhaps speaking over the heads of the disciples or perhaps still also addressing the disciples (maybe he hadn't given up on them entirely); and he said, "If any want to become my followers, let them deny themselves, and take up their cross, and follow me." And he explained, "For those who want to save their life will lose it, and those who lose their life for my sake and for the sake of the gospel will save it."

None of this apparently stayed with Peter. Most of this apparently slid right off him, for only days later he was right back to aweism—up the mountain, witness to this private revelation, privileged to be partying with the superstars of his tradition. Just days later, he was right back to proclaiming, "It's good for us to be here. Let's build private temples and stay right here."

Forget that down the mountain are people in need.

Forget that those who've sought Jesus (the sick, the poor, the unclean, the disgusting) are still seeking Jesus (to be recognized, to be healed, to be saved, to be loved).

Let's just stay here.

Dietrich Bonhoeffer—from the cell in which Nazis had imprisoned him, while Germany beyond cannibalized itself and Europe descended into a nihilist frenzy—famously claimed, "Only a suffering God can help."

What he might have meant was, if not for a suffering God, then it's just "Good for God, and to hell with everyone else."

But God isn't in this to make it out alive, everyone else be damned. God is in this to make of this old creation something new, to make of this old world enthralled to the power of death a new realm in which life is the fuel for life.

The cross assures us that death is not the ultimate power it seems.

The cross encourages us that true life is much more than self-preservation, survival.

The cross affirms the simple reality amidst the created order of suffering, the painful fact that suffering simply is and the hopeful assurance that it's not all that is.

And a suffering God goads us past our own private experiences of awe into social self-giving in the hopeful faith that by such self-giving all can be made better, all can be awe, all is praise and glory, all the time—and not only for a privileged few (those who have big backyards in which to eat homegrown grapes, those who have healthy children and long stretches of clean beaches on which to watch them play) but for all, the rich and the poor, the sick and the well, the lonely and the closely held, the faithful and the frightened.

When the topic of aweism popped up on the daily Facebook post out of our denomination's national office a couple months ago, I got worked up and so weighed in: "I get feeling spiritually moved when seeing something beautiful, when experiencing something lovely. But what can 'aweism' say or do in face of all the ugliness and injustice in the world? For that, I think you need a self-giving savior who says, 'Take up your cross and follow me.' The world needs fewer people of privilege enjoying awe and more people of all sorts who, once awestruck, then commit themselves to building up a beloved community that won't quit even after the awesome feelings fade." And maybe I laid it on a little thick, but I have increasing impatience for people keeping private what blessing God intends for all.

I will give Phil Zuckerman this, however. Ever since I became a pastor, which is to say ever since I staked my life on the reliability of God's presence, God's word (still speaking), and God's promises to us, I'll admit to being less and less frequently surprised by the awe that Zuckerman so appreciates. It hardly sneaks up on me anymore. It hardly arrests me anymore—stopped in my tracks for the beauty or mystery of something.

I trust it and rely on it, so it's no longer surprising to find.

There's a loss in this.

There's also a gain.

As many of you know, I've taken up rowing again, and recently attended a rowing camp. This had me in Florida, in the sunshine, while New England suffered under still more freezing temperatures. But that wasn't the best of it. The rowing was. It was, actually, truly awesome. There's just nothing like being in a women's eight.

But on the last morning away, when the rowing was finished and my flight wasn't until later, my plans for one last swim in the ocean and a walk in a nature preserve skidded off course. A woman in the lobby of the hotel—someone I'd noticed on other mornings, strong and beautiful as she seemed—collapsed next to me over her oatmeal. In fact, she'd have fallen on the hard floor if I hadn't caught her.

The lobby, which doubles in the mornings as a breakfast buffet, was empty but for the two of us.

Unknown to me, but apparently all alone, she was my person now, at least for the time being. She was mine for whom to call 911, mine to take a quick inventory (as the 911 operator asked me to do) of what food she'd eaten and what medication she might be on. (The unmarked pill bottles in her bag indicated many and unprescribed.) She was mine to accompany to the hospital with her sister on the phone—who was apparently familiar with this routine, frustrated, frightened, and close to giving up on it all.

We made it to the hospital.

And then, with her coming to consciousness and then refusing care, we made it back to the hotel where she grew more and more pissed at me but no less needful, pushing away while clinging close.

I stood over her as she rummaged madly through her things in the hotel parking lot beside her rented car, and I noticed then, though not for the first time, a cross that loomed over the palm trees to the southeast. There was a Methodist church that wanted to make itself noticed, which might have struck me as aggressive at some other time. That morning, it was a witness.

Coming off the awesome experience of being on the water with all those very talented rowers, I could now serve this stranger who wasn't making it a gratifying experience. What it cost me was one final morning of beachcombing and wave-jumping, one final morning carefree in the sun. But what could I do? All week long, I'd been awestruck, and I wasn't about to let that experience go unrecognized.

Trudy might call it "awe terminus" or "awe perfectus."

Of that stranger, I know very little. I imagine her tragedy continues, but I have hope in her regard—that she'll find recovery. As for me, as for *us*, children as we are of awe, I rejoice that this isn't something meant only for us to hold and to keep, but is meant for us to spread that it might abound.

I can't say exactly how such abundance might happen, but not because I'm not allowed to. On the contrary, I am meant to, we are *meant* to. To speak of the things God has done and God will do, to proclaim the promises of God who is good—we can't fully and truly say such things, and yet we're meant to try to say such things.

Here is my most recent attempt.

Thanks be to God.

That Little Light of Yours

An Aside

JOHN THE BAPTIZER WAS Jesus' cousin. About six months older than Jesus, John was Jesus' herald in life, sent to prepare a way for the Lord. Look for him as you read through the gospels, if you ever do. Look and see that John surfaces in the story of Jesus like a driving undercurrent. John's preaching and gathering disciples cleared a way for Jesus' preaching and gathering disciples, John's imprisonment haunted Jesus, and his execution at Herod's reckless hand unnerved Jesus nearly to the point of him abandoning the path, his own ministry. After all, where goes John, there goes Jesus and (it's important to remember) Jesus didn't *want* to die.

All that said, significant as he was, John understood himself largely in terms of what he was not.

"Are you the Messiah?" some people asked him, according to the Gospel of John.

"I am not he."

"Are you Elijah returned?"

"No, I am not."

"Are you one of the prophets?"

"No."

The questions all drip with import. The people wanted, *needed,* the Messiah. The people would have rejoiced at Elijah coming back. The people would have listened with care to a prophet. But what strikes me about this exchange is John's clearly understanding: "I am not."

John's gospel is the gospel of "I Am" statements. Jesus is remembered throughout this narrative to say, "I am . . ." "I am the good shepherd," "I am the living water," "I am the true vine," "I am the Way, the Truth, and the Life." Recalling the Lord's first self-revelation and self-naming before Moses when the Lord spoke from a burning bush to introduce himself to his first prophet: "I Am that I Am." Jesus comes to us quickened by this same spirit of eternal being.

And, apparently, John does not. Three times he says or implies: "I am not . . ." And, of course, this gospel is very eager for people to understand Jesus, and none other, as the Messiah. So, it's no surprise that this gospel would have John say, in no uncertain terms, "I am not he." All that makes perfect sense.

But where it becomes interesting to me is where I am indicted in it, where I am called to task.

Notice John's so totally glorying in someone else's light. Notice the way in which John can so eagerly recognize all that he's not, and that he admires and anticipates someone else to be.

You know the song, "This little light of mine, I'm gonna let it shine." You learned it as children, or you sang it at summer camp, or you hum in the shower because it's there to be sung.

And it's good to be sung. It's a good thing to sing—because it's true. We are light that we should allow to shine. We are, each and all, light that should shine.

But this also would be good: to sing just as joyfully of the light that we don't shine, that I don't shine, and that someone else does.

John, among many other things, it seems to me, teaches us how to relate with someone who might otherwise be a rival to us, stoking in us petty envy and a thirst for vengeance, however wild or mild. John, among many other things, shows us the way for participating in a salvation that the whole world needs and desires but no one of us could manage on our own. John, it seems to me, shows today what it means to be human, full of aspiration and empowerment, but also humility and grace.

Really, amidst a long list of biblical characters whose relationships were rivalries—Cain and Abel, Jacob and Esau, Joseph and his brothers, Moses and Aaron, Saul and David, Peter and Paul—John the Baptizer breaks the mold. His cousin is the Christ, and this strikes him as good news. He'll go along for that ride. He'll even cut its course, and all because the One the world so needs is not him.

You know, it's also not me—or not me *alone.*

Flowers That Are Looked At

Now when Jesus heard that John had been arrested, he withdrew to Galilee. He left Nazareth and made his home in Capernaum by the lake, in the territory of Zebulun and Naphtali, so that what had been spoken through the prophet Isaiah might be fulfilled: "Land of Zebulun, land of Naphtali, on the road by the sea, across the Jordan, Galilee of the Gentiles—the people who sat in darkness have seen a great light, and for those who sat in the region and shadow of death light has dawned."

From that time Jesus began to proclaim, "Repent, for the kingdom of heaven has come near."

As he walked by the Sea of Galilee, he saw two brothers, Simon, who is called Peter, and Andrew his brother, casting a net into the lake—for they were fishermen. And he said to them, "Follow me, and I will make you fish for people." Immediately they left their nets and followed him. As he went from there, he saw two other brothers, James son of Zebedee and his brother John, in the boat with their father Zebedee, mending their nets, and he called them. Immediately they left the boat and their father, and followed him.

Jesus went throughout Galilee, teaching in their synagogues and proclaiming the good news of the kingdom and curing every disease and every sickness among the people. (Matthew 4:12–23)

YOU ARE BEING WATCHED.

You are being seen.

Which of these is good news to you—or is neither good news to you?

I'm watching you.

I see you.

Which of these is comforting, reassuring—or is neither so?

If they don't strike your hearing as different, then that makes sense. There's no reason why they should. The words, to watch and to see, don't have essentially different implications. And yet they do have different implications to my hearing.

I'd rather be seen than be watched. Over the course of my life so far, the times when I've felt seen are times when I've felt recognized, even appreciated, or at least acknowledged and responded to, whereas the times when I've felt watched are more oppressive. To be watched is to be scrutinized, judged, and perhaps then condemned.

To be seen, for me, has been an experience of *metanoia*. To be watched is an experience of paranoia.

This is the second thing Matthew's gospel remembers Jesus to have said: "Repent, for the kingdom of heaven has come near." An inaugural sermon that, I regret to say, is so very much shorter and more efficient than that one you're about to get.

This is also the very thing John the Baptizer is remembered to have proclaimed, and from the first: "Repent, for the kingdom of heaven has come near." Cousins, these were, Jesus and John; and so similar, they were, their proclamations exactly the same, word for word. But they were also quite different in implication—both the men and their proclamations.

The first thing Jesus is remembered to have said he says just prior to his baptism in the river Jordan by John. John, seeing Jesus ready to submit to a baptism by John, balked at this. "I need to be baptized by you," he said to Jesus, "and do *you* come to *me*?" to which Jesus replied, "Let it be so for now; for it is proper in this way to fulfill all righteousness."

And it seems fitting that these would be the first words of such a ministry: "Let it be so for now." It seems fitting that this would give initial word to the mission of this one whose coming would indeed change the world but not in the sudden, even forceful, way that some might have hoped. Yes, if Jesus' life and ministry are understood as bringing the kingdom of God to this world—of bringing the kingdom of peace and eternity to this world of long and conflicted history, of broad and jangling diversity, of persistent but often perverted hope that all shall be well and all manner of things shall be—then it could truly be said that Jesus' first proclamation is the means by which his mission shall come complete: "Let it be so for now." Jesus would upset history, but by being born into it and therefore powerless over it. God in Christ would bring history at last to a peaceful and redeeming end, yet not by being in control or by manipulating and machinating, but by being among—ever one of humanity's choices in our God-given freedom to choose. If Jesus is the one who brings eternity to time, then here is the means: let it be so—for now.

But we'll rightly remember John as not so patient. We'll rightly remember John as more zealous than this. "You brood of vipers!" he said to the religious authorities who had come to him for baptism. "Unquenchable fire," he promised for those whom the Messiah would surely decide were not wheat but chaff. "Are you the one who is to come," he wondered of Jesus when Jesus was behaving in ways unbecoming John's idea of savior, "or are we to wait for another?" We'll rightly remember John to have been more fiery and fervent in his expectation of what Christ would be.

And this is perhaps the righteousness that was to be fulfilled in Jesus submitting to a baptism by John—this baptism that would reveal to the world, but also, and moreover to John, that it is the likes of Jesus who is the beloved son; that is it the likes of Jesus, persistent yet also patient, hopeful of the *shalom* he would bring about yet also faithful that time would be its medium and all humanity would be its means, restless yet also purposeful in playing life as a long game. This is the beloved Son of God. Yes, this is perhaps what righteousness such a baptism would bring about: that the likes of John, zealous and fiery, would come to see that God conquers the world not by militant force and the fear of death but by life force, the power of love.

Okay, they were different, actually very different. And so it might come as a surprise that immediately following John's arrest, Jesus picked up John's proclamation just as John had left it: "Repent, for the kingdom of God has come near." Surprisingly, despite all their differences, Jesus would fill the void made by John's arrest, fill it word for word.

He did this, though, after some time in withdrawal; and it's significant that Jesus is said to have withdrawn. Not merely to have moved from Nazareth to Capernaum, he is said to have withdrawn, which is also strange since Nazareth was quite a bit smaller than Capernaum, smaller and more remote. Generally, when we think of withdrawing, we think of going from somewhere busy to somewhere quiet. But withdrawing from Nazareth to Capernaum is to do the opposite, like withdrawing from Monterey to Pittsfield.[1]

From what, then, was Jesus withdrawing, and why?

Nazareth was perhaps so small as to squeeze, suppress; was perhaps for Jesus a place where there was no privacy, no place to withdraw. And John's arrest was a disturbance to Jesus. His cousin, his way-maker, John was someone whom Jesus loved and followed. He would follow him in life and ministry; he would follow him in terrible death. And so every trauma to occur to John would send Jesus into withdrawal. Was this still the path Jesus would walk?

---

1. Monterey is one of the hill towns of Berkshire County. It has a year-round population of about 1,000. Pittsfield is the county's biggest city, of which there are two. It has a population of 44,000.

The time of withdrawal in Capernaum apparently led Jesus to "yes." Like John, Jesus would now proclaim, "Repent!" and like John, Jesus would now gather disciples: "Follow me."

Immediately, they did. That's what the story says. *Immediately* they did.

It's worth saying here that this call to discipleship likely didn't come out of the blue. As we consider the way by which we might be called, and the way to which we might be called, it's worth knowing that this original call of Jesus to his disciples likely didn't come out of thin air. Though Capernaum was bigger than Nazareth, it wasn't so big that Simon and Andrew, James and John, wouldn't perhaps already have known Jesus, wouldn't already have crossed paths with him. There was, after all, a synagogue in town, and so a place where they would likely have been in the same place at the same time. Really, they probably all knew each other, though how well is impossible to say. So, this encounter with Jesus as he walked by the Sea of Galilee was likely more familiar than extraordinary—a known acquaintance approaching and saying, "Hey, follow me. Come here!"

It's also worth saying and knowing that these newly called disciples likely, after a time, and from time to time, returned to their nets and their boats and their relationships at home. Their following Jesus away from these things that decisive afternoon shouldn't close off to us the likelihood that they would return—even perhaps later that afternoon.

This is all worth bearing in mind as we consider what sort of call we might listen for in our lives, because the church, I think, has tended to think of this original call of the disciples as radical, even magical. The voice of Jesus, "Follow me," is as the voice of the angels over the shepherds rather than the voice of a man speaking to men, all of whom might well have been friends. Likewise, the call to follow in a new way is heard as a breaking off from that which has come before rather than a building on, an adding to. And all of this would have us latter-day would-be disciples listening for a voice from on high call us to a lifestyle all together other from how we are already living. And *this* could well have us dismissive of anything that seems just too mundane. And yet most often, in my life at least, the call that proves itself later to have mattered most comes to me in the guise of the ordinary, the familiar—just made deeper and more purposeful.

Of course, what Jesus said as he began his ministry, what he said in gathering steam to call the disciples, what both he and John said, itself sounds like a grand, even spooky thing: "Repent, for the kingdom of God has come near." But I think we've gotten this wrong, too.

"Repent" is a word that doesn't rightly capture the concept it's meant to name. We might hear it as a word heavy with judgment, the sort of thing painted on sandwich boards worn by street preachers whose hollering and hectoring would have us run in the other direction. We might hear it as conjoined to condemnation: "You'd better repent or else . . ." In an effort to wrest it back from such brimstone implications, cooler-headed scholar-types have insisted that the word "merely" means a turning—a turning away from or a turning toward. To repent, then, the thinking goes, is to turn away from that which is not of God and to turn toward that which is.

But this doesn't quite do it either, at least not for me. As sound an idea as this is, and as worthy a thing to aim for and pray for as this is, it's rather bloodless—hardly an invitation that would ignite or excite, which Jesus' invitation seems to have done.

Repent is the dull English rendering for the Greek word *metanoia*—*noia* for "knowledge" and *meta* for both "change," as in metamorphosis or metabolism, as well as to name that which is behind or before or beyond. So *metanoia* is better understood as a change in knowing—a transformation from knowing only that which is self-evident, the superficial, to knowing that which is before and beyond, that which demands not merely cognition but also recognition, that which is not only profession but confession.

Metanoia, I've said before, is submitting our mind to the mind of God that our knowing might be enlarged.

Metanoia, I've also said before, is a concept I hear in contrast to *paranoia*, the sort of thinking that is divided from itself and conflicted within itself, the sort of thinking that is divisive and driving of conflict.

T. S. Eliot, in the first poem of his Four Quartets, "Burnt Norton," writes of some roses: " . . . the roses / Had the look of flowers that are looked at."[2]

Rowan Williams, recently retired Archbishop of Canterbury, considers these roses that had the look of flowers that are looked at in the first chapter of his book *Faith in the Public Square*. The chapter is entitled "Has Secularism Failed?" and in it he defines "secularism" as "rest[ing] upon the assumption that our attitudes to one another [and toward the world around us] in the public realm have to be determined by factors that do not include

2. Eliot, "Four Quartets," 118.

reference to agencies or presences beyond the tangible [and provable]."[3] In such a world, of course, to recognize some roses as bearing the look of flowers that are looked at is absurd. I mean, just exactly who would be the subjective "looker" at roses that bear the look of flowers that are looked at?

But secularism hasn't done away with the notion of being looked at all together. No, indeed! On the contrary, the modern secular world in which we all live has fashioned all sorts of ways that we're looked at—watched if not truly seen. The stuff of totalitarian regimes and dystopic literature, the stuff of feminist critique regarding the "male gaze" and of privacy advocates regarding targeted Internet marketing, the stuff of the recent NSA revelations—now to be looked at has a menacing, policing, controlling sense to it. A most material manifestation of this secular phenomenon is the Panopticon, a circular prison developed in the eighteenth century whose cells are arranged around a central well from which prisoners could be observed at all times yet could not themselves observe the observer. It was developed to make prisons safer, less violent, as prisoners would become their own wardens, internalizing the policing presence that would make them better citizens. The man who developed it, Jeremy Bentham, described it as "a new mode of obtaining power of mind over mind" and as "a mill for grinding rogues honest."[4]

But in case this isn't all disturbing enough, we must consider the way in which this modern milieu has imagined God to have adopted this same agenda in looking upon us—that is when such an unprovable idea as the existence of God is considered at all. And when it is, it's often considered in this same confined spirit—the eye in the sky always watching you. The secular would have us live in such a closed, managed universe, and "God" would become one more tool for social manipulation and control.

Worst of all, the secularized church, that is the church of the modern world, which expresses itself as either liberal or fundamentalist, offers itself as one more option in the marketplace of ideas, enticing with either feeble pep talks for "make the world a better place" or with fierce threats that amount to a paranoid religion inspiring a paranoid response. "Repent, or else . . ."

---

3. Williams, *Faith*, 12.

4. "Panopticon," *Wikipedia*, http://en.wikipedia.org/wiki/Panopticon. The article featured these two quotes, pulling them from Jeremy Bentham's own writings, the first from *The Works of Jeremy Bentham*, vol. 4 (1843) 39; and the second from *The Works of Jeremy Bentham*, vol. 10: *Memoirs Part I and Correspondence* (1843).

A comic strip going around the Internet pictured Jesus knocking on someone's door. "Let me in," he said, and the voice on the other side asked, "Why?" "So I can save you," was Jesus' response. "Save me from what?" came the question. "From what I'm gonna do to you if you don't let me in."

Now, Rowan Williams, considering those roses: "[B]ut how are they looked at exactly?"[5] It's a question whose answer he finds in the work of yet another writer, Raimond Gaita. His book, *A Common Humanity*, understands that a vital morality has more to do with seeing "the other" as a special sort of object for a subjectivity not your own rather than with the seeing "the other" as a subject equal in value to yourself. "Often we learn that something is precious only when we see it in the light of someone else's love."[6] And he relays this fact: "One of the quickest ways to make prisoners morally invisible to their guards is to deny them visits from their loved ones, thereby ensuring that the guards never see them through the eyes of those who love them."[7]

We are to be roses that bear the look of flowers that are looked at, and we are to recognize in others the sort of loveliness that bears the look of loveliness that is recognized. Any given rose is just a rose—"A rose is a rose is a rose," the staunchly Modernist writer Gertrude Stein is known to have declared. Likewise, any given person is just a person, one of a type and, odds are, not a particularly fine specimen of that type. All of this is true, as far as it goes, true but for God who looks upon us all with love.

This is repentance. This is the metanoid move that John invited us to make, though I do doubt whether he understood the full implication of what he proclaimed. This is the metanoid move Jesus invites us to make, though I think this elusive phrase takes on such meaning now more than when John first proclaimed it. To repent is to recognize God's loving gaze upon each one of us, God's countenance lifted lovingly upon every part and particle that participates in the creation. To repent is to look past all the secular, societal, security-minded monitors—those calculating, controlling, condemning eyes-in-the-sky—to the God that is above and before and beyond them all, looking upon us in love. Love.

You should see the view from where I stand. All of you, gathered here: you bear the look of flowers that are looked at. Lovely!

Thanks be to God.

---

5. Williams, *Faith*, 17.

6. Gaita, *Common*, 24.

7. Gaita, *Common*, 26.

This Is Not a Pony

> Immediately he made the disciples get into the boat and go on ahead to the other side, while he dismissed the crowds. And after he had dismissed the crowds, he went up the mountain by himself to pray. When evening came, he was there alone, but by this time the boat, battered by the waves, was far from the land, for the wind was against them. And early in the morning he came walking towards them on the lake. But when the disciples saw him walking on the lake, they were terrified, saying, "It is a ghost!" And they cried out in fear. But immediately Jesus spoke to them and said, "Take heart, it is I; do not be afraid." Peter answered him, "Lord, if it is you, command me to come to you on the water." He said, "Come." So Peter got out of the boat, started walking on the water, and came towards Jesus. But when he noticed the strong wind, he became frightened, and beginning to sink, he cried out, "Lord, save me!" Jesus immediately reached out his hand and caught him, saying to him, "You of little faith, why did you doubt?" When they got into the boat, the wind ceased. And those in the boat worshipped him, saying, "Truly you are the Son of God." (Matthew 14:22–33)

YOU HAVE HEARD IT said that, if you but have faith, you can walk on water. But I say unto you, that's not what this story is about. You have heard it said that, if your faith overcomes your fear, you'll never falter like Peter did. But I say unto you, if we're going to shame Peter yet again, let's at least do it for the right reasons.

Immediately, Jesus made the disciples get into the boat and go on ahead of him. And they probably didn't notice this as significant at all. You probably didn't either. I did, but only after a couple days thinking on this story. Then the fact woke me from a late afternoon doze on my sofa—Jesus making the disciples go on ahead of him, while he dismissed the crowds.

And crowds there were—five thousand men, not counting the women and children, which means there may have been as many as ten thousand or even twenty thousand people in that deserted place by the shore of Galilee. They were fed now and satisfied, and from just five loaves of bread and two fish—the wonder of which is less that they were satisfied by such a small amount of food and more that they were satisfied at all. They'd just learned of John's death—John the man who'd perhaps baptized many of them in the river Jordan, who'd later been imprisoned in Herod's household but whom Herod feared to have put to death because the crowd regarded him as a prophet.

Well, now it had happened: John had been killed. Worse, he'd been killed as dinner-party entertainment when Herod told his stepdaughter—she who'd danced so compellingly for all his guests—that whatever she wanted he would grant her.

I imagine it was a boozy promise, Herod all heady from too much wine and too much of his daughter. But since it was one made in front of all his dinner guests, he had to fulfill it.

It's true that he feared the crowd and their having foresworn John as a prophet of the Lord, and so he'd always been careful when it came to John. It's true also, according to the Gospel of Mark, that Herod "protected" John, knowing that he was a righteous and holy man, and that he liked listening to him, though "when he heard him, he was greatly perplexed."

Herodias, for her part though, had long resented John for his condemning her marriage to Herod. The reasons for this are confused by the many ancient records that aren't themselves too clear and, taken together, are downright confounding.

As for Salome, she would get what she asked for, and that very evening. After all, John was nearby, in one of Herod's prisons (where he was protecting him?), perhaps even in the cellar of his palace.

When the girl was given it—John's head on a platter—she passed it along to her mother.

As for the body, the pathetic broken body, John's disciples came and collected it and laid it in a tomb.

Then they went to Nazareth to tell Jesus.

And then Jesus withdrew from there in a boat to a deserted place by himself.

John's story runs through the gospel narrative like a slubbed thread running through otherwise fine tapestry. John is the roughhewn foil to Jesus. A few months older, John was the only son of old parents, while Jesus, a few months younger, was the first son of a woman very young. As such, it's reasonable to imagine Jesus' parents looking to John's for guidance, and Jesus in turn admiring and emulating John. I think of my little nephews' attitude toward their big cousin Toby—asking their mother, my sister, about him; wondering what new wonders this great seven-year-old has mastered.

Of course, as they grew older, they realized their differences. But still the admiration was there. Remember, John said to Jesus when Jesus had come down to the river Jordan, "Do you come to me? I should be baptized by you!" For his part, Jesus praised John for his fiery integrity in face of many who wished he'd tone it down: "What do you look for in John? A reed shaking in the wind? A man dressed in soft robes?" People wanted everything from John. As we want our celebrities to be today—doing their own stunts in action-adventure movies but also dressing up nice for the red carpet at premiers—people wanted John to be a prophet but also polite at a dinner party. In defense of each of these two opposites, Jesus mocked such fickleness: "John came neither eating nor drinking, and people said, 'Look! He has a demon!' [I] come eating and drinking, and people say, 'Look, a glutton and drunkard! A friend of tax collectors and sinners!'"

On Jesus' part, though, there was the added fact that John was the herald of the Messiah, the one to go before him to prepare the way. In sum, as went John, so would go Jesus. And now John had been killed—executed in a most humiliating way.

And so, when Jesus heard this, he withdrew from there in a boat to a deserted place by himself.

But when the crowds heard it, they followed Jesus on foot from the towns. For what reason, we don't know. To comfort Jesus? To be comforted by him? Or for some reason even less reasonable, some compulsion just to seek him out? Whatever it was, Jesus had compassion for them, sitting them down when it was evening to have the disciples give them something to eat.

It would have been easy to do otherwise, you know. It would have been easy to rally them as troops deployed for some sweet revenge. It would have been easy to make of this crowd the very thing Herod had feared and so had kept John alive.

But, of course, he didn't do that. Instead, he calmed them down and sat them down and, when evening had come, he had the disciples serve them supper, until all ate and were filled.

And this is the really amazing thing of it, less that is was a mere five loaves of bread and two fish that so filled them, and more that they were satisfied by anything less than Herod's head on a platter. A tale of two dinner parties, this chapter from Matthew's gospel might be called: two pericopes best understood in the contrast that together they lay plain.

Then Jesus made the disciples get into the boat and go on ahead to the other side, to Galilee, while he dismissed the crowds. And this is a throwaway point, right? Yes, it's strange that Jesus would want to be alone when dismissing the crowd, that Jesus would go to such effort to send the disciples off so he could do something alone that he might have more easily done with help. But otherwise it's unremarkable—unless you consider that Jesus would tell the disciples something similar to this at another time later on, similar but also quite different.

It was the night of his arrest, when Jesus took a loaf of bread and, after blessing it, broke it and gave it to the disciples and said, "Take, eat; this is my body." He then, of course, took a cup and gave thanks for it and gave it to the disciples and said, "Drink from it, all of you; for this is my blood of the covenant, which is poured out for many for the forgiveness of sins." And it was then that he said it: "You will all become deserters because of me this night . . . But after I am raised up, I will go ahead of you to Galilee."

"I will go ahead of you to Galilee."

It's another contrast that begs our notice. Especially since these, as his first words spoken after being put to death and then raised to life, really aren't all that profound. It's by contrast that they might be seen as significant, might have us awaken (for example) from a nap, suddenly hearing them together and wondering why the change and also when the change—from his making the disciples go ahead of him to he himself going ahead of them.

I think it happened during that night of grievous prayer.

We're not supposed to think about Jesus betraying his friends. The night in Gethsemane before his crucifixion when he prayed—"Take this cup from me; yet not my will but yours be done"—this is supposed to be the night, the only night, when Jesus contended with second thoughts. To be the Christ or not to be the Christ: that was the question that one night alone. And even then, his second thoughts didn't cost his friends a thing. Sleeping the night away nearby, they were never at risk as Jesus begged to be spared.

Not so here. Not so on this stormy sea. When Jesus sent his friends ahead, something real was at stake for them, especially as evening fell and the boat was battered by waves and far from land, especially as Jesus stayed on the mountain by himself until morning, apparently able to see the boat at sea but unmoved to help. We're not supposed to conceive of Jesus behaving in this way.

There was a YouTube video that made the rounds a year or so ago. It had a male voice-over inviting the viewer to imagine a church where every member is passionately, whole-heartedly calling the shots. Then there's a clip of a young man saying, "What about a church that starts when I get there?" and the voice-over answers, "Okay, when you arrive, we begin." Then there's a clip of a young woman watering her flower garden. She says, "I'd like a pastor to come to my house to deliver the sermon." The voice-over answers, "No problem. Expect a knock at your door within twenty-four hours." An older woman puts down her book then and lifts her reading glasses. "When I'm in the church service, can my car get a wash and a buff?" "Not just that," says the voice-over, "but an oil change and a tune-up." The final clip is of a boy on a bicycle. "I'd like a pony," he says into the camera. "Look in your backyard," says the voice-over, which has the boy agog and then running away, ditching his bike.

I have no idea if this video was earnest or facetious—an earnest attempt of some church to appeal to everyone (their website was certainly earnest: hip and slick as conservative megachurches can be; but still, fundamentally earnest), or if it was a facetious critique of the consumer mentality so often brought to religious practice. Whatever. It made me laugh when I saw it months ago.[1] Then I forgot about it until the middle of the night a few days ago, when I was again awoken about this story.

Jesus walking across the water to the disciples in their storm-tossed boat is a spectacle so awesome that the rest of the story often gets overlooked. Here's what else we might want to notice.

When the disciples were afraid at the sight of what they took to be a ghost, Jesus answered them, "Take heart. I am." If you didn't hear this when I read the story earlier, it's because the translation doesn't do this justice. *Ego eimi* is how it reads in Greek, and almost everywhere else this is translated as "I am." "I am the resurrection and the life; I am the good shepherd; I am the way, the truth, and the life." Each of these echoes the Lord's naming himself at Moses' request when Moses found himself talking to a burning bush. "Who shall I say sent me? What is your name?" Moses had asked, and the bush said, "Tell them, 'I Am' has sent me." All of this is to say that when Jesus said, "Take heart. I Am," he was proclaiming himself as ready once more, ready once again for his being at one with God.

Here's something else we might notice. When Peter said, "Lord, if it is you, command me to come to you on the water," he was speaking another familiar phrase. But last time we heard it, it came from the tempter's mouth and mind. "*If* you are the Son of God," the tempter said to Jesus when he had gone out to the wilderness for those trying forty days, "then command these stones to be turned to bread. *If* you are the Son of God," the tempter

---

1. It is now nowhere on the web to be found.

said to Jesus, "then throw yourself down from this great height." But unlike when Jesus heard this from the tempter –that time long ago when he'd been strengthened by John's just prior presence, John having just baptized him in the River Jordan—here Jesus was perhaps still shaken, shaken perhaps by John's sudden and violent absence. For here he granted a tempter's appeal. (*Et tu*, Peter?) Here Jesus granted Peter's wrongful request: "*If* it is you . . .," Jesus did indeed grant Peter his dubious request, and Peter ended up sinking and more frightened than before.

(Incidentally, this is a mistake Jesus wouldn't make again. Sending the disciples ahead of him, responding to requests that come of the wrong impulse, these are mistakes Jesus wouldn't make again. I know this in considering when Peter listened as Jesus foretold for the first time his death and then had this to say: "God forbid it! This must never happen to you!" This time, Jesus got it right: "Get *behind* me, Satan. For you're a stumbling block to me.")

I have to say I like the idea of Jesus going ahead of me. I know Camus's sweet turn of phrase, "Don't walk in front of me; I may not follow. Don't walk behind me; I may not lead. Walk beside me and be my friend." I like that, too. In regard to many relationships, I really do. But I also like the idea of Jesus going on ahead of me, going on ahead of us. I imagine him—a sower of seeds far ahead in my path, a sower of seeds that I'll come to enjoy and rejoice in when I arrive where he's been. I imagine him lighting a way into our shared future—a future that is dark with unknowns and yet may be light by him that we can make our way into it with hope and wonder. I imagine this as real in time and in eternity, and it spurs me to continue on even when I fear there's much to fear.

And so it follows that I don't like the idea of Jesus faltering. I don't like the idea of Christ making his friends go on ahead because he's not up to the task of going first, because he's not up to the task of leading. I don't like the idea of Jesus saying, "You first," now that the task seems terrible and terrifying—taking on the powers and principalities, as John did; redeeming the stupid violence of history, as not even John could.

So I went back to the story to find a better preaching point—something I actually wanted to say, something that would actually sound good as it should, something like a pony waiting for you in the backyard.

But this isn't the church of me, as that video encouraged its viewer to imagine. This is the church of Jesus Christ, and I'm not always going to get what I want when I want it. Not every story in Scripture can be bent and shaped for the purpose of our edification, of our fortification. Some stories some days just aren't about us. This one is about Jesus and John, and then Jesus alone, and then Jesus and God to whom he returned, by prayer, to be one and to make all things one.

You know, there *is* some reassurance in this: that though Jesus might have faltered, he then regained his strength; that though he might have slacked, he was then resolved. The reassurance is that the path he traveled from fumbling to faithful is one we can travel, too. For ahead of us he does go. Perhaps our prayers should be with him.

Thanks be to God.

No Redeeming Qualities Whatsoever

Later the following events took place: Naboth the Jezreelite had a vineyard in Jezreel, beside the palace of King Ahab of Samaria. And Ahab said to Naboth, "Give me your vineyard, so that I may have it for a vegetable garden, because it is near my house; I will give you a better vineyard for it; or, if it seems good to you, I will give you its value in money." But Naboth said to Ahab, "The Lord forbid that I should give you my ancestral inheritance." Ahab went home resentful and sullen because of what Naboth the Jezreelite had said to him; for he had said, "I will not give you my ancestral inheritance." He lay down on his bed, turned away his face, and would not eat.

His wife Jezebel came to him and said, "Why are you so depressed that you will not eat?" He said to her, "Because I spoke to Naboth the Jezreelite and said to him, 'Give me your vineyard for money; or else, if you prefer, I will give you another vineyard for it;' but he answered, 'I will not give you my vineyard.'" His wife Jezebel said to him, "Do you now govern Israel? Get up, eat some food, and be cheerful; I will give you the vineyard of Naboth the Jezreelite."

So she wrote letters in Ahab's name and sealed them with his seal; she sent the letters to the elders and the nobles who lived with Naboth in his city. She wrote in the letters, "Proclaim a fast, and seat Naboth at the head of the assembly; seat two scoundrels opposite him, and have them bring a charge against him, saying, 'You have cursed God and the king.' Then take him out, and stone him to death." The men of his city, the elders and the nobles who lived in his city, did as Jezebel had sent word to them. Just as it was written in the letters that she had sent to them, they proclaimed a fast and seated Naboth at the head of the assembly. The two scoundrels came in and sat opposite him; and the scoundrels brought a charge against Naboth, in the presence of the people, saying, "Naboth cursed God and the king." So they took him outside the city, and stoned him to death. Then they sent to Jezebel, saying, "Naboth has been stoned; he is dead." (1 Kings 21:1–21)

One of the Pharisees asked Jesus to eat with him, and he went into the Pharisee's house and took his place at the table. And a woman in the city, who was a sinner, having learned that he was eating in the Pharisee's house, brought an alabaster jar of ointment. She stood behind him at his feet, weeping, and began to bathe his feet with her tears and to dry them with her hair. Then she continued kissing his feet and anointing them with the ointment.

Now when the Pharisee who had invited him saw it, he said to himself, "If this man were a prophet, he would have known who and what kind of woman this is who is touching him—that she is a sinner." Jesus spoke up and said to him, "Simon, I have something to say to you." "Teacher," he replied, "speak."

"A certain creditor had two debtors; one owed five hundred denarii, and the other fifty. When they could not pay, he cancelled the debts for both of them. Now which of them will love him more?" Simon answered, "I suppose the one for whom he cancelled the greater debt." And Jesus said to him, "You have judged rightly."

Then turning towards the woman, he said to Simon, "Do you see this woman? I entered your house; you gave me no water for my feet, but she has bathed my feet with her tears and dried them with her hair. You gave me no kiss, but from the time I came in she has not stopped kissing my feet. You did not anoint my head with oil, but she has anointed my feet with ointment. Therefore, I tell you, her sins, which were many, have been forgiven; hence she has shown great love. But the one to whom little is forgiven, loves little."

Then he said to her, "Your sins are forgiven." But those who were at the table with him began to say among themselves, "Who is this who even forgives sins?" And he said to the woman, "Your faith has saved you; go in peace."(Luke 7:36–8:3)

IF YOU ASK ME, Jezebel deserves to have her name dragged through mud. It certainly has been. According to one dictionary, a "jezebel" is an evil or scheming woman.

It's not a definition inherent in the word; the word literally means something else—"Where is your prince?" And, as it happens, Jezebel's prince was in the foreign land of Israel, his name Ahab, whom she married though remained devoted as a Phoenician to the gods Ba'al and Asherah.

For this devotion, when Jezebel and Ahab rose to power in Israel, she then proceeded to suppress the worship of Yahweh, the God of Israel, the Living God whom we worship this morning. She also disregarded Israelite custom as we heard in the story this morning—of Naboth who had not only the desire but also the duty to keep his ancestral land for his own sons and grandsons.

That it was in conflict with his duty to serve his king is unfortunate, the stuff of tragedy. It's hard to know what would have been most right here, most dutiful. I'd say that the king should have backed off, should never have asked for the land in the first place. But it's within the right of a king to do so—eminent domain. And, really, a king who backs off isn't king for long, and isn't a good king in regard to the safekeeping of his people.

You know, this is exactly the sort of situation Yahweh was seeking to avoid in denying the people Israel a king. They didn't need a king, he meant to imply, because he was their king—their king and their God, according to one of the Psalms. But the people insisted on a more conventional king. Yearning to be like other nations, they wanted their God to be remote and their king to be real.

They got what they wanted.

And they did indeed begin to resemble every other nation on earth—a people consigned to the whimsical rule of royals, and a king made crazy and dangerous with power.

Clever, though, that God did something of an end run around royalty by awakening the prophets to see and to speak, to bear witness to what's true. It's a familiar trajectory—from Moses the slave who spoke truth to power, to priests who formalized the religious cult, to kings who built temples and government, God, it seems, rises in rank. And yet, here God is to be found more immediately among the lowly—moving the likes of Naboth to stand his ground, moving the likes of Elijah to speak what's true. The view from below, Dietrich Bonheoffer called it, as the only perspective we truly can trust, as the perspective of the God of the gospel. A sky-god? No way. This one took on flesh and became a slave, humbling himself—obedient to the point of death, even death on a cross.

This is the God Elijah served as the first great prophet under a king. Yet even he was frightened by Jezebel, this evil schemer. It's worth saying, of course, that Jezebel might have been made all the worse by Ahab, whose courage could be screwed not to a sticking place but only to his own sullen sulking on his bed. This likely made Jezebel all the more ruthless.

Thank goodness the lectionary serves up another woman this morning—and one whose remorse counterbalances Jezebel's ruthlessness. I'd be willing to bet everyone's sympathies lay with this woman weeping over Jesus' feet as we listened to the story told. Mine lay with her most of the week from when I first read it.

After all, she's serving as a point of contrast to the Pharisee, and every churchgoer knows the Pharisees are bad. These are the ones who antagonized Jesus until at last they put him on trial and condemned him to the

Romans for crucifixion. These are the bad guys. And since any enemy of my enemy is my friend, this woman must certainly be a good woman, likely an oppressed woman (as all were), a woman whose (likely many) virtues have been subjugated under male domination just like everything else about her. She's probably a woman driven to desperate measure by desperate circumstances beyond her control. Really, she's probably a hooker with a heart of gold, which is not only a mainstay of American popular culture but perhaps even one of our favorite character types. Who couldn't love Julia Roberts in *Pretty Woman*? I tried not to. Really, I tried. Every time I saw the movie, I tried not to love her again.

But the story doesn't call this weeping woman a prostitute. It says only that she's a sinner—this, a word we're even more apt to dismiss as devoid of actual content. I mean, it's just so like a Pharisee to call some poor sod a sinner. Pious people are always calling someone a sinner. It only means that this one isn't religious in the right way, or the same way, as the one doing the name-calling. But look, it's not the Pharisee who first calls this woman a sinner. It's the narrator; it's "Luke." So maybe this judgment isn't as devoid of content as we might like to think. Maybe she was really bad news: manipulative, abusive, cruel. Some people are, you know.

I say this as much to myself as to you. I really have a hard time coming around to the fact that some people are bad news. I remember the story two years ago of a young woman from Italy, an artist who embarked on a project to promote world peace and to prove the goodness of humanity. Dressed as a bride she would hitchhike from her home to the Middle East, saying she wanted to show she could put her trust in the kindness of local people. And I have to say, fool that I am, this woman could easily have been me at her age but for the fact that I've never liked to leave home. After she was found murdered in Turkey, her sister released this statement: "Her travels were for an artistic performance and to give a message of peace and of trust, but not everyone deserves trust."[1]

This statement sounds absurd because it's so very true, and nearly everyone knows it. Really, some people mean only to ruin things. They mean only to cause pain, and worse they find it empowering or amusing. This might be one of the aspects of my current service in Berkshire County's grand jury duty that is exhausting to me—the realization that some people really are up to no good. Though none that I've heard of so far (and thank God!) are murderers, some people really aren't trying to contribute to the

---

1. BBC News, "'World Peace.'"

commonweal, and they're not sorry about that. They're not worried about how they're affecting you or your community, your children, your neighbors. They really, really couldn't care less. Some people are people you really should just stay away from.

So, what if Simon just meant for Jesus to know this wasn't a woman you wanted to be near? And not because she was ritually impure (which she probably was) or socially inappropriate (which she definitely was)—both reasons we could dismiss as typical pharisaical mean-spiritedness. What if it was that she was downright destructive—someone like Jezebel, though without the power? What if Simon's apprehension about her wasn't piety but street smarts and, moreover, concern for this man, Jesus, whom he might have wanted to have as a friend? Haven't you ever wanted to take under your wing that new person in town—tell her what's what, introduce him to the right people? Maybe the fact that Simon remained unmoved by this woman's weeping was about the fact that he'd seen the act all before.

And this is where the story gets interesting. Because it's one thing if Jesus sees some hidden virtue in this poor sinning woman, some seed of redemption that everyone else has missed. It's one thing if she has some secret deservedness about her or within her, and Jesus has the sort of insight to see value in even the most overlooked and dismissed. But it's another thing if Jesus looks upon someone with no such seed ripe for cultivation, no such secret virtue hidden like a pearl in the grotesquerie of an oyster. It's another thing altogether if he looks upon someone lacking any redeeming quality whatsoever, and yet says, "You are forgiven. Go in peace."

If we're thinking people, this story should not only disturb us but offend us, because it means either that Jesus is a fool—a hitchhiking bride who has no idea the horror that awaits him—or that the God whom he represents is reckless with forgiveness, is lousy with love. It means either that Jesus is something like Little Red Riding Hood, set out into the woods where even wolves will fool him ("The better to see you with, my dear!"), or that the God whom Jesus makes present is amoral (that is, lacking the sort of moral code that makes society possible), unethical (that is, operating in reckless disregard of what's right), impossible.

Suddenly this feels less like a story fit for Sunday school and more like something Flannery O'Connor would put us through—where the redeemed one is the character who shoots an old, churchgoing lady in the face at close range.

This is God?

The translation of the Bible I've been using off and on over the last several weeks provoked one of our beloved members to "violent anger," something she told me with gentle irony. Would that all violent anger was like this! Joking aside, I'm glad she told me—and for many reasons. Hearing from you helps me in my future planning for worship. It calls me to be intentional about things I might otherwise not be. It reminds me of the obvious—that the decisions I make affect each of you, in ways however small. It reassures me that I'm not alone in taking our life together seriously. And it moves me that worship is a time when you're open and even vulnerable, and that my offering you something you don't expect can be, though sometimes a blessing, other times a violation. One thing it doesn't do is make me feel like a slave to your wishes. I don't feel the need to avoid everything everyone dislikes (which would be impossible since everyone doesn't like at least one thing we do) or to do only things everyone likes (which would have us do nothing at all—which itself would be something no one would like). Given this, I'm going to read from it now—Eugene Peterson's translation he calls *The Message*. I offer it because I find it helpful. Though it sacrifices beauty for utility and contemporaneousness (not always a good trade), I find it helpful particularly when the words translated are Paul's.

Paul is a convoluted writer of complex ideas that don't translate easily from one language to another or (moreover) from one century to the next. The reading this morning that we didn't hear comes from Paul's letter to the Galatians—written to Jewish-Christians in defense of the inclusion of Gentiles in the church. "We Jews know," he writes, "that we have no advantage of birth over 'non-Jewish sinners.' We know very well that we are not set right with God by rule-keeping but only through personal faith in Jesus Christ. How do we know? We tried it—and we had the best system of rules the world has ever seen! Convinced that no human being can please God by self-improvement, we believed in Jesus as the Messiah so that we might be set right before God by trusting in the Messiah, not by trying to be good."[2]

Though Paul is writing about religious law, what he has to say pertains to all life under any law. And this is how I hear it—not as a follower of the Jewish law (something I'm not) but as a follower of civil American law (something I excel at). Really, as I sit on the grand jury, I realize how law-abiding I am, and how unappealing a life lived in violation of the law would be to me.

2. Peterson, *The Message*, 292.

We should make no mistake: being a chronic criminal is stressful and chaotic; it's unrewarding and even nihilistic. It makes you vulnerable to people who'll exploit you as honor among thieves seems to me only spottily applied and as turning state's witness brings on a whole new set of risks and vulnerabilities. A life of crime causes you to depend upon people who are undependable and trust people who are untrustworthy. And all of this goes double if you're a woman. In sum, provided that the law is moral (or mostly moral), living beyond its bounds makes you terribly unfree.

But though abiding the law might make me more free, might open the way for a less stressful and chaotic life, it doesn't make me good. On the contrary—and this seems Jesus' point—what the lawbreaker has going for him or her is at least a greater potential for knowing she's not good, for knowing he's downright bad, for realizing that the only hope any of us has is in God who is merciful, just, and forgiving. While I who obey the law hedge my bet on the goodness of God, while I in my obedience to the laws of the land protect myself from my own need of God, the one who's fallen through the net of the law has no hope but to be caught up by God's grace.

It seems to me this might be what brought this party-crashing jezebel to such flowing tears. For while an encounter between a lawbreaker and a law enforcer might just escalate antagonisms and deepen defenses, an encounter between a lawbreaker and someone who forgives and loves might just open a way for grace.

And, of course, it might not. Some people will take advantage of another's forgiveness. Some people will take another's offer of love for an amusing ride. So we should admit that we don't know what this woman will make of her own remorse; we don't know how long lasting her own repentance will be. We don't know if she'll shake off this encounter with Christ as soon as she gets home—back to her ugly life, back to her angry world. We don't know if grace will be a moment that becomes merely a memory, and one that embarrasses; or if it will be a prolonged phase, but one that passes; or if it will serve as foundation for a new life. We don't know. What we do know is that it seems to matter little to God.

Forgiveness is giving before—giving before the gift is known to be desired and desirable, giving before the gift is known to be needed, certainly giving before the gift is deserved (thus making it a gift and not a reward). Forgiveness comes before confession; grace comes before repentance, which makes the one who truly gambles in this to be God. While we do-gooders hedge our bets, God doubles down, and does so for the likes of the jezebels of the world, those people who deserve to have their names dragged through the mud and yet whose names God has written on God's heart.

People, here is your God—not fair, but good.

We might prefer the former, but we can rely on the latter.

Thanks be to God.

Casting Spells—New Testament

An Aside

I DON'T BELIEVE IN magic. I already said as much.

And yet.

Jesus' Sermon on the Mount begins with beatitudes that are untrue, unkind, impossible—or some sort of spell.

"Blessed are the poor in spirit, for theirs is the kingdom of heaven." But that's not true. The poor in spirit are actually suffering a sort of hell—and if it's you who happens to be poor in spirit, and you're moreover unable to discern in such poverty the kingdom of heaven, then, well, you're not very faithful either.

"Blessed are those who mourn, for they shall be comforted." But that's not true. Those who mourn shall be avoided because they bring everyone else down—and if it's you who happens to be the one in mourning and you find no eventual comfort, then you're really in a hole.

"Blessed are the meek, for they shall inherit the earth." Wrong. It's the imperialists who inherit the earth. And if it's you who happens to be meek, then I've got some real estate in Florida for you.

Shall I go on?

If you hear these beatitudes as indicative (indicating, describing how things are), then they're wrong, statements of aggressive denial. And if you hear them as imperative (commanding of how things should be, commanding of how each of us who mean to please Christ are to live), then they're so demanding as to court failure and giving up.

And some would say that's the point. Indeed, some have said as much—that the point of these was to set so high an ideal as to make it clear what good Christian living actually entails, to make it clear that, no matter how hard we strive, we'll never fully achieve, and so to make it clear how very badly we need Jesus, how very much better he was than we are.

Others would say, indeed have said, that this is all meant to speak of an inward disposition. Jesus was describing where our hearts should be, what our attitudes about life should be. What we can't manage to do with our outward living, we should at least manage to do with our intention.

Neither satisfies me.

I don't believe in magic. But I do believe Jesus, in preaching, was casting a spell; I do believe that he, in preaching the Sermon on the Mount, and most specifically these beatitudes, was conjuring a world that he meant to hold forth as an alternative to where we usually live. Imagine a place where a poverty of spirit is met with blessing. Imagine a place where grieving people aren't denied but are made central. Imagine a place where meekness is given access to life-giving power, where those who thirst for righteousness are slaked by truth and witness, where peacemaking isn't compromised when the going gets rough but resists such temptation in favor of faithful discipleship and witness that withstands. Imagine a place where the outcasts of the world are given sanctuary, are embraced to the heart.

"Yes, yes," Christians have said throughout the centuries, "heaven will be a great place!"

Jesus' preaching confronts us: "Why wait? Do it now."

What Jesus conjured up is a people, a visible body. What Jesus conjures up is a politics that stands and withstands, like a tree beside the waters. No private affair this, Jesus is spelling out something that is to be embodied, enacted—a community of blessing. This is so to be witnessed and recognized by those in need of blessing. This is so that the church might be found by those who seek it.

You know, such people may be out there. Let's spell it out for them, then. "You are welcome, desired, needed, beloved here." If we say it, perhaps it will come true.

Don't Believe the Bumper Sticker

> Now he was teaching in one of the synagogues on the Sabbath. And just then there appeared a woman with a spirit that had crippled her for eighteen years. She was bent over and was quite unable to stand up straight. When Jesus saw her, he called her over and said, "Woman, you are set free from your ailment." When he laid his hands on her, immediately she stood up straight and began praising God. But the leader of the synagogue, indignant because Jesus had cured on the Sabbath, kept saying to the crowd, "There are six days on which work ought to be done; come on those days and be cured, and not on the Sabbath day." But the Lord answered him and said, "You hypocrites! Does not each of you on the Sabbath untie his ox or his donkey from the manger, and lead it away to give it water? And ought not this woman, a daughter of Abraham whom Satan bound for eighteen long years, be set free from this bondage on the Sabbath day?" When he said this, all his opponents were put to shame; and the entire crowd was rejoicing at all the wonderful things that he was doing. (Luke 13:10–17)

A BUMPER STICKER I see from time to time proclaims, "Freedom isn't free." My thought every time I see it is, "Yes, it is."

Anyway, this story from Luke is likely familiar—or if not this particular story, then certainly this scenario. Jesus heals someone; the religious leaders balk; the one healed plays the middle but is also poised for decision: Whom to follow, tradition or upstart? Really, these stories probably comprise the first thing we think of when we think of Jesus—we who know him from spending most Sunday mornings with him and we who know him from less frequent encounters or even from overhearing and assuming. He was a healer, a miracle-man. Yes, this story about Jesus from the gospel reading sketches a likely quite familiar scenario. We get it: Jesus was something of a magician. Good for him. Good for everyone who was lucky enough to be healed by him.

Now what?

* * *

There are two times in the Old Testament when the Sabbath day is established and the keeping of it is explained. Both are in the laying out of the Ten Commandments, which are themselves laid out twice—once in the book of Exodus and once in the book of Deuteronomy.

Did you know this—that there are two versions of the Ten Commandments? And they're quite similar but they do differ. Naturally, the differences are as telling as the similarities.

Listen to the Exodus version of the fourth commandment:

> Remember the Sabbath day, to keep it holy. Six days you shall labor, and do all your work, but the seventh day is a Sabbath to the LORD your God. On it you shall not do any work—you, or your son, or your daughter, your male servant, or your female servant, or your livestock, or the sojourner who is within your gates. For in six days the LORD made heaven and earth, the sea, and all that is in them, and rested on the seventh day. Therefore the LORD blessed the Sabbath day and made it holy. (Exodus [ch?]:verse[with en dash if it is a range])

Do you hear that the reason for the Sabbath is to imitate God—God who labored for six days and who rested on the seventh? The founding story for the Sabbath is the Creation story—when the world and all that is within it were made, and when God then rested.

Now listen to the version found in Deuteronomy:

> Observe the Sabbath day, to keep it holy, as the LORD your God commanded you. Six days you shall labor and do all your work, but the seventh day is a Sabbath to the LORD your God. On it you shall not do any work—you or your son or your daughter or your male servant or your female servant, or your ox or your donkey or any of your livestock, or the sojourner who is within your gates, that your male servant and your female servant may rest as well as you. You shall remember that you were a slave in the land of Egypt, and the LORD your God brought you out from there with a mighty hand and an outstretched arm. Therefore the LORD your God commanded you to keep the Sabbath day. [Deuteronomy [ch?]:verse[with en dash if it is a range])

Do you hear that the reason for the Sabbath is so the people might remember when they were enslaved and might be foresworn never to subject themselves to such slavish living again, nor to subject others to such slavish living? The founding story for the Sabbath is the Exodus—slavery and freedom, labor and then rest. This means that the purpose of the Sabbath is freedom, freedom to serve the Lord and only the Lord, one way of which to do so is to rest—like the Lord and with the Lord, to rest.

The religious authorities knew this—or at least I like to think they did. I like to the give the religious authorities the benefit of the doubt, and not just because I am one. Though they often come across as the bad guys, though in our hearing we often cast them as straw men, the religious authorities, I think, are better heard as people with power, yes, and with good intentions. Really, it deepens and enriches the whole story if we see all the players in the story as people we could well know, people we might well be, real people who are caught in complicated circumstances and trying to do their best with what they've got and what they know.

What's more, if the people Christ bested were mere straw men, then this reveals Jesus as not much to write home about. Anyone can knock down a straw man. But if the people Jesus bested were the best people of their time—the wisest; the most thoughtful and considerate; the most broad-minded, well-intended men of their time; and foresworn themselves to safeguard the people from potential lawlessness and chaos—then Christ truly does have something to teach us.

So the religious authorities knew that the Sabbath law was just, and that by it justice was made possible. After all, it was by this commandment of the Law that freedom was ensured—freedom for men and women, freedom for owners and servants, freedom even for livestock, for fields! This was a radically progressive and broad-minded commandment.

Likewise, the religious authorities trusted in the Law—the Torah law code, which was both a religious law and a civil law at work—as the means by which society's ideals of freedom and justice for all were proclaimed and realized, held forth as vision and moreover made real every week, every Sabbath.

It was this Law that Jesus violated. It was the commandment that Jesus was seen to transgress. And, of course, whether good or bad, a law transgressed has people imagining life beyond its bounds. Laws now violated quickly lose their binding force, all too soon lose their power to cohere a people as a people. Break too many laws and where does that leave us?

Syria engulfed in "civil" war comes to mind, as does Egypt. Cormac McCarthy's *The Road* comes to mind, as does Mad Max.

This is what was at stake when Jesus healed the woman stooped over.

Here's the conflict: as the religious authorities (most likely) knew, so did Jesus know that the Sabbath was the rite by which freedom is proclaimed and made real. But he also knew that this woman had for years now not had a Sabbath herself.

Consider her ailment: to be stooped over is to be in a permanent position of servitude. Ever bowing, never to make eye contact, never to see the sky for God's sake—this is slavery manifest in the body, which Jesus apparently recognized. This is why he said after the healing, "Woman, you are *set free* from your ailment." This is why also, when the leader of the assembly then said to the people who had gathered apparently to be healed of ailments themselves, "There are six days on which work ought to be done; come on those days and be cured, and not on the Sabbath day." Jesus emphasized the version of the fourth commandment that establishes the Sabbath as a day for freedom: "Does not each of you on the Sabbath untie his ox or his donkey from the manger, and lead it away to give it water? And ought not this woman . . . whom Satan *bound* for eighteen long years, be *set free* from this *bondage* on the Sabbath day?"

(Incidentally, the woman herself seemed to recognize this too, seemed to recognize that what had just happened to her was an exodus in miniature. Freed from her bondage, she comes immediately to praise God. Like those early Israelites now on the other side of Red Sea who just couldn't help it, just had to thank God, so this woman, freed from bondage, knew indeed what her freedom is for: it is for serving the Lord and only the Lord.)

Both desire freedom for the people. Both the religious leaders and Jesus are convicted in the notion that moreover this is what God desires, freedom for the people. The difference? Jesus will stop at nothing to make every single one free, no one unfree left behind.

But you can't really do this, can you? There must be scapegoats. There must be slaves. Who else will do the dirty work?[1]

* * *

There is only one major monument in the United States to the emancipation of the American slaves. In Lincoln Park of Washington DC, it features a statue of a standing President Lincoln and before him a kneeling, though perhaps rising, black man. Shackles on his wrists and ankles are loosed from their chains. The look on his face is either strong and set in its forward looking and upward looking, or is cowering and worshipful of the white man who stands over him.

The so-called Great Emancipator, meanwhile, has one hand outstretched above the once-slave's head. It could be in blessing, blessing his rise; though if it is this, we should at least acknowledge that this is a very masterful thing to be able to do. It could also be seen as setting the height

1. Please listen to Joni Mitchell's song "Passion Play," which is on her album *Night Ride Home*.

to which the man might rise: "This high and no higher." In the other of his hands is what's taken to be the Emancipation Proclamation.

For those who don't know, as I didn't quite know, the Emancipation Proclamation is an executive order Lincoln made on January 1, 1863, and so is something whose sesquicentennial anniversary we as a nation recently cycled past. What this order did was proclaim the freedom of slaves in the ten states that were still in rebellion—whose number was three to four million people. Some things it didn't do: it didn't compensate the once slave-holders who had now lost their labor force; it didn't itself outlaw slavery; and it didn't make ex-slaves now citizens. Brief as it was, 1754 words, it made as explicit goals of the Civil War the eradication of slavery and the reuniting the Union, and it also ordered that black men who qualified could be enrolled into the paid service of the US armed forces—which many of them did do. This put them in the position potentially to fight against their former asters, which could be supposed as every slave-based society's greatest fear, or greatest wish depending on whether you were master or slave.

The fact of the possibility of black men in the army was a fact memorialized in the first plan for this monument, a plan drawn up by sculptor Harriet Hosmer. She had in mind another image of Lincoln, him prone, having passed away. Surrounding the platform on which his body lay at peace—a platform that was to be about sixty feet high, making it the highest memorial statue in Washington, had it been built—was a circle of black men, a circle that was to tell the narrative of black people in America since their beginning. From a slave in chains to a soldier in uniform, these represented black Americans as agents of their own freedom, standing from the start, rising from there. Honoring the deceased president who had proclaimed them emancipated, this circle of African-Americans represented the long, painful journey that as a people they had made, had risen to that freedom and now stood grateful guard.

I wish this were the monument that got built. I'm not alone. Historian Kirk Savage, author of the book *Standing Soldiers, Kneeling Slaves,* though appreciative of all the reasons why the one got built and the other didn't, nonetheless regrets the fact. He claims that the decision for the kneeling slave, low beneath Lincoln's hand—who is, incidentally, also pleading his case, "Am I not a man and brother?"—"speaks to a much larger cultural failure to rethink our society in the wake of the end of slavery."[2]

2. Savage, http://backstoryradio.org/shows/henceforth-free/.

* * *

One thing distinctive about this story of Jesus healing the woman stooped over is that she didn't ask for healing and she didn't earn her healing. This wasn't a case of someone pleading her cause, begging some favor of Jesus. This wasn't a case of "your faith has made you well." This was simply a case of freedom freely offered and freely received.

I like to imagine the once-stooped-over woman now looking Jesus in the eye, looking for a long time, meeting recognition with recognition before embarking on her Sabbath privilege and duty of praising God.

* * *

I know that the bumper sticker I see from time to time is making a statement about the American military. It isn't attempting some theological claim. No, it's making a claim about American military purpose, presence, and practice. To claim that freedom isn't free is to claim the American military is necessary as it is, and should receive our full support. It's also to bring to awareness the fact that soldiers often pay dearly for what freedom their service might have won.

That's a position needful of serious study and debate, which I'm not attempting to do right now. My objection is simply to it as a statement.

Freedom *is* free—a free gift of God who intends for us freedom. To claim otherwise is blasphemy. To claim that freedom is a gift of the state, a well-defended state, makes us slaves to the state.

Freedom *is* free. It is freely offered that we might of it freely receive. It is ours to take up and to live into, ours never to violate by enslaving others or by submitting ourselves for enslavement. We are to be free to serve the Lord in whose service there *is* no dirty work.

Do I believe this? Yes. Can I imagine this? Yes. Are we there yet? No. Tomorrow then, we rise again and get to the good work of building up the kingdom. As for today, for right now, we rest.

Thanks be to God.

Where to Start[1]

Comfort, O comfort my people, says your God. Speak tenderly to Jerusalem, and cry to her that she has served her term, that her penalty is paid, that she has received from the Lord's hand double for all her sins.

A voice cries out: "In the wilderness prepare the way of the Lord, make straight in the desert a highway for our God. Every valley shall be lifted up, and every mountain and hill be made low; the uneven ground shall become level, and the rough places a plain. Then the glory of the Lord shall be revealed, and all people shall see it together, for the mouth of the Lord has spoken."

A voice says, "Cry out!" And I said, "What shall I cry?" All people are grass, their constancy is like the flower of the field. The grass withers, the flower fades, when the breath of the Lord blows upon it; surely the people are grass. The grass withers, the flower fades; but the word of our God will stand for ever. Get you up to a high mountain, O Zion, herald of good tidings; lift up your voice with strength, O Jerusalem, herald of good tidings, lift it up, do not fear; say to the cities of Judah, "Here is your God!" See, the Lord God comes with might, and his arm rules for him; his reward is with him, and his recompense before him. He will feed his flock like a shepherd; he will gather the lambs in his arms, and carry them in his bosom, and gently lead the mother sheep. (Isaiah 40:1–11)

The beginning of the good news of Jesus Christ, the Son of God. As it is written in the prophet Isaiah, "See, I am sending my messenger ahead of you, who will prepare your way; the voice of one crying out in the wilderness: 'Prepare the way of the Lord, make his paths straight.'"

John the baptizer appeared in the wilderness, proclaiming a baptism of repentance for the forgiveness of sins. And people from the whole Judean countryside and all the people of Jerusalem were going out to him, and were baptized by him in the river Jordan, confessing their sins. Now John was clothed with camel's hair, with a leather belt around his waist, and he ate locusts and wild honey. He proclaimed, "The one who is more powerful than I is coming after me; I am not worthy to stoop down and untie the thong of

---

1. I preached this sermon on Sunday, December 7, 2015, the Sunday after the grand juries considering the cases of the killing of Michael Brown and then Eric Garner came back with no true bill.

his sandals. I have baptized you with water; but he will baptize you with the Holy Spirit." (Mark 1:1–8)

THE BEGINNING OF THE good news of Jesus Christ: this is how Mark begins his gospel. Never one to waste time is Mark. That's one reason why it's my favorite gospel. The urgency of it, the immediacy of it: it's a book fueled by purpose. Sure, the beauty of Luke's writing has great appeal, and the theological depth that John's gospel plumbs is majestic. Sure, even Matthew, in his fury—particularly aimed at the likes of me, the religious authorities—is a crucial voice. But Mark charms me.

This is so, in part I imagine, because he's hardly a writer up to the task set before him, yet he succeeds wildly—and because of his shortcomings. The first person (as far as we know) to write a narrative of Jesus' life, ministry, and passion; perhaps spurred by the fact that the generations of people who'd known Jesus were dying off—Mark answers the call (for it must surely have been a call) to write it all down.

But such a thing is impossible! How do you write down the living word without killing it in the process—without fixing it in place, nailing it to the ground?

With unpolished prose, apparently. Really, it's the raw quality not only of his writing, but also and therefore of his Christ, that speaks to some quality of the gospel that more mannered rhetoric would miss. He's like one of the prophets, each of whom knew he was the last person in the world who should be expected to succeed at the task to which he'd been called—Moses with his speech impediment; and Jeremiah so young, too young; and Samuel not even recognizing God's call, thinking it his teacher, Eli, calling to him. None of the true prophets considered themselves worthy.

And, yes, we don't know Mark's response to the spur to write it all down; we don't even know "Mark's" (which is to say our writer's) real name. We don't get any backstory at all, no context from which this emerges. This is all we get to start: "The beginning of the good news of Jesus Christ."

As we proceed through Advent and approach Christmas, with the nativity narrative front and center, we might be surprised that Mark considers the beginning of the gospel of Jesus Christ not Jesus' conception and birth, as both Matthew and Luke do; and certainly not the birth of the whole cosmos and creation, as John does. No, Mark's understanding of where it all began is Jesus' baptism. For Mark, the beginning of Jesus as the Christ—that is, as the anointed one of God—comes when Jesus was already grown.

It's as if being the Christ was a becoming, something he became, rather than an original condition of his existence.

Incidentally, this is one of those events in Scripture that belies biblical literalism. Read as contradictions, these all three can't be true. And so, read from the framework of modernism—this which insists that there's fact and then there's fiction, there's true and there's false, there's either/or—read from that framework you either have to conclude that the biblical story can't get itself straight and therefore must be simple fabrication, or you conclude that every word is a literal fact on its face, and you memorize the words, not taking too close a look at meaning.

But literalism's worst offense in regard to the gospel isn't superficiality; it's in making the gospel of Jesus Christ smaller than it should be—far smaller. Consider that each assertion about Jesus as the Christ might have truthful implications, and to lose any of those is to lose something essential. Each assertion—Mark's that the anointed one becomes anointed in life, perhaps growing into the role; Luke and Matthew's that the messianic promise is woven into Jesus' conception and birth; John's that the Christ was there in "In the beginning [as] the Word"—these are all revealing of the mystery and truth revealed in Christ.

Okay. But we're with Mark now, which means Jesus was anointed as a man to serve as the Christ—no special birth, no cosmic embodiment, just a man, but one called and quickened and full of the Holy Spirit. What truth, then—of Christ and us and the world—is implicated in such a one? Ruminate on that for a while, and see what you come up with.

You know, we might be just as surprised at Mark's gospel's ending as at its beginning, as unconventionally as it begins. We'll discover it (or perhaps rediscover it) soon enough, on Easter—this ending that remembers Mary and the other women at Jesus' grave; and their finding it empty; and their being told by a man all in white who was sitting in the tomb, told to go back to Galilee for this is where they'd find Jesus just as he'd told them; and their running off in terror.

Yes, according to Mark, the Easter emotion is terror.

More on that later. (Easter is coming, always coming.) For now, it's simply worth recognizing that Mark's gospel ends where it begins: in Galilee where Jesus appears. When the angel or the man in white or the whatever-that-was in the otherwise empty tomb told the women to return to the place where it had all started for there they would see him, there's a "go back and try again" quality to it all.

Go back and try it again.

One of my sons is practicing the piano and he reaches the end of some piece he's to learn; and it was a rough journey, a clunky trip across those keys; and there's time left in the practice session. So I tell him, "Go back and try it again."

I'm on the ergometer, rowing, rowing, sweating, rowing; and I pull back on the chain from the catch to the finish, and the number on the speedometer dips (the stroke wasn't as strong as it might have been—if I'd been thinking about my legs, thinking about breathing). So I go back up the slide and I try it again.

I'm preaching a sermon and I don't get the whole of the gospel into it; all of its implications, all of its manifestations. I can't squeeze it all into the twenty minutes I'm allotted; so much is left out, too much is made too simple. So I look forward to the next Sunday when I might try it again.

Jesus' spiritual emissary telling the disciples to go back to Galilee is like telling them to go back and to try following Jesus through life again. What's more, Mark's telling of Jesus' friends being told to go back and try it again is like Mark telling his readers to do the very same—to go back and try following Jesus in life again. They didn't quite manage it that first time; they didn't quite succeed. (If they had, they wouldn't have bothered coming to this tomb. After all, hadn't Jesus said that he wouldn't stay dead?) We haven't quite managed it; we haven't quite succeeded. So we need to go back and try it again.

And, granted, it's difficult; it's a difficult thing to do, maybe the most difficult thing to do. Following Christ may even be impossible: following Christ right up to the cross (and then *through* it), right up to our cross (and then *through* it), each of us *self*-giving on any number of crosses (those things that threaten death but, by God, give way to new life if only we dare to take them on). Such voluntary self-giving—impossible! We are, after all, like grass, and our consistency is like the flower in the field.

This, by the way, is most likely Second Isaiah's thought as to why he wasn't worthy of serving as a prophet for the Lord. (Yes, there's a Second Isaiah, and a Third. Yes, this one book of the Bible is actually probably three, proclaimed and then transcribed by three different prophets from three different periods in the life of the people Israel. First Isaiah prophesied prior to the fall of Jerusalem, and he was largely a prophet of doom. Second Isaiah prophesied during the exile, and he spoke in hopeful terms of restoration. Third Isaiah goaded the people on, now able to return to their homeland that they might rebuild their society, but this time do it right. ["Go back and do it again."])

Second Isaiah was called to preach: "A voice says, 'Cry out!'" which is better rendered, "Preach!" And Second Isaiah replied, "What shall I preach?" The punctuation, though, in most translations implies then that it's not Isaiah who goes on to say, "All people are grass, their consistency is like the flower in the field." But the formal convention implies that the punctuation is in the wrong place, that the quote continues, that Second Isaiah is in fact the one who goes on to say this of the people and their consistency, goes on to say: "The grass withers, the flower fades, when the breath of the Lord blows upon it. Surely the people are grass." In other words, the reason Second Isaiah hesitates to preach is because it won't make any difference. No, he hasn't got a speech impediment or an age impediment or a hearing impediment. No, it's the people who have the impediment: they are consistent only in their inconsistency. So why bother?

Really. Really. Why bother preaching?

Here's why, according to the Lord: "Yes, the grass withers, the flower fades; but the word of God stands forever. So get you up to a high mountain; lift up your voice with strength and say, 'Here is your God.'" Faithful and true, persistent and patient: here is your God, by whom you can indeed go back and try it again, try walking in this self-giving way again, trying until you get it right.

* * *

In case there's any doubt that white privilege exists in America, consider that I didn't start this sermon today in Ferguson or Staten Island. I started it with Mark our gospel writer, and John the Baptizer, and Jesus still offstage, all in Galilee. And, yes, it's entirely right to start a sermon with Scripture. It's entirely proper and appropriate for Jesus to be the first name we utter as we gather in Christian worship. But consider also that in predominantly black churches this morning, Jesus is likely going by the name "Michael" or "Eric."

We know the story, or we likely do. Michael Brown died at the hand of police officer Darren Wilson. Eric Garner died at the hand of police officer Daniel Pantaleo. Both dead men are black, both police officers are white, and both officers were exonerated for their actions on duty. We all know the stories surrounding these deaths; we all know the two terrible still points around which storms have gained force. We all know that race is playing a dominant role in these two incidents, and in so many others like them—race, and even racism, in all of its twisted and dodging and self-denying complexity.

And the fact that these two, Michael and Eric, aren't first in my mind when I wake in the morning, aren't first in my mind when I think through my day and my parenting, my ministry and my preaching, is because of white privilege. I'm not going to get shot in the street: I'm white. My sons aren't going to get choke-held to death: they are white. I don't have to be guided by morbid caution to get through my day—of this I'm confident. This is a confidence denied black people in this country, and we must change that.

"I can't breathe," chants the movement of protest following Eric's death and Officer Pantaleo's exoneration: "I can't breathe," quoting Eric's final words. Well, I can breathe, and it's a great feeling—so great, in fact, that I wish everyone could claim it as theirs. It's the gospel that has me convicted in the faith that such a thing is possible; it's the gospel that has me charged with the duty of helping to make it so. It's been so long, too long. It's time to go back and try it again.

What, then, should we do?

Charles Blow of the *New York Times* claims we should stop trying to find the "perfect victim" on which to build a case for the fact that our justice system is racist.[2] That Michael Brown wasn't a perfect victim, that Eric Garner wasn't even a perfect victim, that both men were committing crimes: stop trying to do that. (As a Christian, I can't help but notice that we already got our perfect victim, and even that hasn't stopped us from sacrificing others. Jesus was supposed to be that perfect victim, after which we would stop acting as if we really believed violence will save us from violence.) Blow's argument is less christological, is more societal: stop waiting for the perfect, flawless black man to be killed before we decide enough is enough.

Former attorney and now blogger Jenee Woods concurs. In her list of "12 Ways to Be a White Ally to Black People," number two is "Reject the 'He was a good kid' or 'He was a criminal' narrative and lift up the 'Black Lives Matter' narrative."[3] She goes on to explain that Brown's death is a travesty of justice not because he was a "good" person (though he might well have been) but because he was a person.

2. Blow, "Perfect-Victim Pitfall."
3. Woods, 12 Ways.

As you can guess, there are other considerations on her list of twelve. It's good reading, and I recommend it. But I'd add a thirteenth to her list.

Of all the things I've ever read about race and racism in America, and by implication my own whiteness, this has stayed with me most helpfully—the opening two lines of Pat Parker's poem from 1978, "For the White Person Who Wants to Know How to Be My Friend." She wrote, "The first thing you do is to forget that i'm Black. / Second, you must never forget that i'm Black."[4] It's a koan. It's a paradox. It's the sort of thing people of faith should especially be able to cope with. So ruminate on that for a while, and see what you come up with.

And then recognize this, this presumption of a rather basic thing—that a white person would want to be a black person's friend, and that a black person might be open to such a thing as well.

Another recent online article explores the so-called racial empathy gap, the persistent fact that people often struggle to feel empathy for people of other races, and that black people—actually, people with black *skin,* and its degree of darkness matters—receive the least empathy of all in America. Seeing it pierced evokes the least empathy in the observer.[5]

Still another article suggested that one solution to this problem is friendships that bridge racial divides.[6] The more black people that white people know as friends, the less those white people hold racist views. This was proven in a formal study. As for less formal settings, of course, this could be coincidental or it could be causal. It could be that white people who have black friends started out less racist, or it could be that having black friends makes a white person less racist. My thought is that it's dynamic: one feeds the other. But, whatever. It has a beneficial effect. To the deadly disease of racism, there is a most enjoyable course of treatment: make friends.

So I've been trying it out. I've been intentional lately about cultivating friendships with black people, which is an embarrassing thing to say, if not offensive, because, of course, friendship doesn't develop out of an agenda and personal relationships won't easily conform to a quota system. Nor should they.

On the other hand, I can't help but notice how predominantly white my world yet is. Because of where I live, where *we* live; because of what I do, pastor in a denomination whose history and present is overwhelmingly

4. Parker, https://muse.jhu.edu/journals/cal/summary/v023/23.1parker01.html.

5. Forgiarini, et al, "Racism."

6. McGlothlin, et al, "Social Experience."

white: I am a white person among mostly white people, and I want not to be so protected anymore from the fact of my own privilege and entitlement.

Actually, I need not to be so protected anymore.

I say "need" because racism is no longer something we can afford—as if we ever could. Racism is no longer something we can live with—neither the ones who die of it nor anyone else. We're called to higher living. This has ever been true, but is more pressingly true at this moment. And, yes, to say we need to go back and try again is to risk trivializing the severity of the problem. But I'll say it because what underlies such apparently pedestrian encouragement is nothing less than the gospel—this persistent revelation that we're not there yet, this faithful promise that there is somewhere good where we might go.

Of course, this which we can no longer afford will cost us in other ways. For white people to renounce racism that is not only attitudinal but also structural will cost us. It will cost us dominance, privilege, security, control. It will also cost personally, for to feel empathy with those who suffer is to suffer yourself. Yes, it will cost us white people—or better perhaps to say, as Ta-Nehisi Coates does in his book *Between the World and Me,* us people who've been taught to believe we're white.[7] It will cost us, and to say otherwise is to deny what's at stake.

But this is what the gospel of Jesus Christ is all about. This is what the truth that begins yet again today is all about. We give up the life that we think secures us life, we open ourselves to something bigger and riskier and more gracious, and we receive the life that truly is life—justice rolling down like waters and righteousness like an ever-flowing stream; a fullness of joy; a glimmering of that shining peace.

People who believe yourselves to be white, don't you want that?

I want a dynamic peace more than I want dominance and privilege. I want joy more than I want control.

The challenge and the promise that we might have such things is the thing at whose beginning we find ourselves again this morning. We've gone back. We try again. Maybe this year, by grace, we'll do better, we'll get it right.

Thanks be to God.

---

7. This is Ta-Nehisi Coates's way of naming white people, which recalls James Baldwin's phrasing, and which would have us understand whiteness not as an established fact but as a cultivated, not to mention self-serving, notion that then has all too real an effect.

Money

The word that came to Jeremiah from the Lord in the tenth year of King Zedekiah of Judah, which was the eighteenth year of Nebuchadrezzar. At that time the army of the king of Babylon was besieging Jerusalem, and the prophet Jeremiah was confined in the court of the guard that was in the palace of the king of Judah . . . Jeremiah said, "The word of the Lord came to me: Hanamel son of your uncle Shallum is going to come to you and say, 'Buy my field that is at Anathoth, for the right of redemption by purchase is yours.' Then my cousin Hanamel came to me in the court of the guard, in accordance with the word of the Lord, and said to me, 'Buy my field that is at Anathoth in the land of Benjamin, for the right of possession and redemption is yours; buy it for yourself.' Then I knew that this was the word of the Lord.

"And I bought the field at Anathoth from my cousin Hanamel, and weighed out the money to him, seventeen shekels of silver. I signed the deed, sealed it, got witnesses, and weighed the money on scales. Then I took the sealed deed of purchase, containing the terms and conditions, and the open copy; and I gave the deed of purchase to Baruch son of Neriah son of Mahseiah, in the presence of my cousin Hanamel, in the presence of the witnesses who signed the deed of purchase, and in the presence of all the Judeans who were sitting in the court of the guard. In their presence I charged Baruch, saying, Thus says the Lord of hosts, the God of Israel: Take these deeds, both this sealed deed of purchase and this open deed, and put them in an earthenware jar, in order that they may last for a long time. For thus says the Lord of hosts, the God of Israel: Houses and fields and vineyards shall again be bought in this land. (Jeremiah 32:1-3, 6-15)

As he was setting out on a journey, a man ran up and knelt before him, and asked him, "Good Teacher, what must I do to inherit eternal life?" Jesus said to him, "Why do you call me good? No one is good but God alone. You know the commandments: 'You shall not murder; You shall not commit adultery; You shall not steal; You shall not bear false witness; You shall not defraud; Honour your father and mother.'" He said to him, "Teacher, I have kept all these since my youth." Jesus, looking at him, loved him and said, "You lack one thing; go, sell what you own, and give the money to the poor, and you will have treasure in heaven; then come, follow me." When he heard this, he was shocked and went away grieving, for he had many possessions.

Then Jesus looked around and said to his disciples, "How hard it will be for those who have wealth to enter the kingdom of God!" And the disciples were perplexed at these words. But Jesus said to them again, "Children, how hard it is to enter the kingdom of God! It is easier for a camel to go through the eye of a needle than for someone who is rich to enter the kingdom of God." They were greatly astounded and said to one another, "Then who can be saved?" Jesus looked at them and said, "For mortals it is impossible, but not for God; for God all things are possible."

Peter began to say to him, "Look, we have left everything and followed you." Jesus said, "Truly I tell you, there is no one who has left house or brothers or sisters or mother or father or children or fields, for my sake and for the sake of the good news, who will not receive a hundredfold now in this age—houses, brothers and sisters, mothers and children, and fields, with persecutions—and in the age to come eternal life. But many who are first will be last, and the last will be first." (Mark 10: 17–31)

IMAGINE SECURING OFFICE SPACE in the Twin Towers on September 12, 2001—the day after.

Imagine buying several homes in the St. Bernard Parish of New Orleans on August 30, 2005—the day after.

Why would you do that? Why would anyone?

This reading from the prophecy of Jeremiah likely didn't impress you. Unless you're a real estate attorney, this reading probably didn't even interest you—except perhaps as a warning that you were in for a very dull sermon.

This is unusual for Jeremiah. He's usually interesting, which is to damn him with faint praise. Really, he's usually compelling to the point of a little spooky. The challenge he typically presents for the preacher—or at least for this preacher—is in keeping up with his extreme message without sounding extreme yourself, without freaking the congregation out. Jeremiah, not typically so fixed on legal minutiae, is most often weeping or railing or raging or disconsolate with grief. The people to whom he prophesies break his heart. The God for whom he prophesies pushes him to the brink. He warns the people of sacked cities and a desolate countryside. He accuses the Lord of abusing him, perhaps even of raping him: "O Lord, you have enticed me, and I was enticed; you have overpowered me, and you have prevailed." Persecuted by a fellow priest, put in the stocks for what the Lord had told him to say, Jeremiah wants out of this triangulated relationship, but he can't get out. "I have become a laughing-stock all day long; everyone mocks me. For whenever I speak, I must cry out, I must shout, 'Violence and destruction!' For the word of the Lord has become for me a reproach and derision all day long. If I say, 'I will not mention him, or speak any more in his name,' then within me there is something like a burning fire shut up in my bones; I am weary with holding it in, and I cannot. For I hear many whispering: 'Terror is all around! Denounce him! Let us denounce him!' Cursed be the day on which I was born!"

And now comes this rather dull real estate deal. No detail unmentioned, no stipulation overlooked, this isn't prophecy or poetry; this is contract law.

And yet I'm impressed because of what I know, that the kingdom of Judah was teetering. It had been several centuries since David had ruled over it and Israel—and what days of glory they had been! But now Israel had long since fallen—to the Assyrian Empire; and now Judah was pressed between two empires as well, passed as a pawn between Egypt to the south and Chaldaea to the northwest. Judah eventually aligned with Egypt, so when the Chaldaeans overtook Egypt, Judah also fell. The Chaldaean emperor, Nebuchadnezzar, placed a puppet king on the throne in Jerusalem— King Zedekiah. He had a soft spot in his heart for Jeremiah, Jeremiah who urged surrender to Zedekiah's own people, surrender for survival's sake. But Zed took the advice of a more militant element in Jerusalem, those who would realign with Egypt and would eventually stage a rebellion against all imperial power.

Jeremiah was clear that such a rebellion was doomed. It would doom the city, doom the temple. It would be the end of the people in their land. They could not assume the Lord God would enter battle for their sake. They could not assume the Lord was on their side, for it had been a long time since they'd been on the Lord's side. They were a nation called into being for the sake of justice; and they had become terribly unjust. They were a people who had come through the waters and into the Promised Land to be upright and moral, but they had become decadent and lax. God had fashioned them to be a people who served the poor among them, who saw to the well-being of the downtrodden, the orphan, the widow; and they had become divided among themselves, rich and poor, clean and unclean, powerful and powerless.

But they still had their pride, their sense of exceptionalism.

Well, Jeremiah was clear that such pride doesn't make for wars won, and he said as much—first during the siege of 597 BCE, and then, even more so, during the siege of 587 BCE. With the Chaldaeans at the gates of the city, while those in power urged further military action, Jeremiah told Zedekiah to seek terms of surrender. With Nebuchadnezzar prepared to mow down the city (which he later did), to blind and murder his own puppet-king Zed (which he later did), to take the best into exile and to leave behind only the least wanted to fester among the ruins (which he later did), those in power sought heightened military action while Jeremiah urged the people to face reality, to surrender, and to seek peace. And for this, the militants in charge sought Jeremiah's death by throwing him down a well. But Zedekiah rescued him and tucked him away as a prisoner in the court of the guard, kept like a miserable pet.

And still, he spoke; still he prophesied.

And one day he decided to get into real estate.

I wonder what the vineyard looked like. It was between sieges when Hanamel came to Jeremiah and said, "Buy my field that is at Anathoth for the right of redemption is yours." It was sometime in that decade between the first and second siege, which is to say things were bad, but they could get worse: they *would* get worse. The city was sacked but not yet burned down. The temple had been violated but not yet destroyed. The king was compromised but not yet murdered. The countryside was likely trampled— warhorses, chariots. But maybe it wasn't blood-soaked, maybe it wasn't smoldering. Whatever. That's beside the point because Jeremiah knew— perhaps alone knew—that this was still no time to invest in the future because it wasn't clear there would be a future.

But he did.

What's more, he did it legally—and this is why we were made to sit through such details as to where exactly the witnesses were sitting in relation to the signing of the deed, and how exactly the open deed and the sealed deed were to be stored for safer days, and that the seventeen shekels of silver actually weighed what seventeen shekels are to weigh. This is why—because this would have been a perfect time to get a vineyard at a cut rate. But Jeremiah didn't. This would have been a great time to go light on the law. But Jeremiah didn't. Because, you know, when the law of the land has been suspended by the rules of war, it's a great time to take advantage. When the society that honors and upholds the law has been subsumed by chaos, it's a great time to make a killing in real estate. But Jeremiah didn't.

Had he never heard of looting?

Did he not know the time-honored tradition of getting while the getting's good?

I seem to remember a *Saturday Night Live* skit that involved a man in the market for various things. Sales people did what they do: "I'll give it to you for $200. That's a real steal!" And he'd come back: "I'll give you $400 and not a penny less." That's Jeremiah. And it's all the more impressive when you consider that Hanamel seemed eager to sell his field. He might have even been desperate to do so. He really meant it when he claimed the right of redemption belonged to Jeremiah. He needed to be redeemed. He needed to be bought out of a circumstance from which he couldn't salvage himself.

And that's what this reading is about: redemption. If you can boil a reading down, if you can boil a story as complex as this one down to a concept (something I'm not so keen on doing in general), then that's what this one is about: redemption. And, of course, Christians have tended to hear redemption as a spiritual concept—the salvific action of our redeemer, the saving power of Christ's life, death, and resurrection. By his blood, we are redeemed. In his offering his life as ransom to death, Christ frees us from the power of death. Spiritually speaking, Christ buys us out of circumstances from which we cannot save ourselves. And certainly this story of Jeremiah buying Hanamel's field has been heard typologically—as one that typifies Christ who was to come. It serves as a foundational story to the grander story that is yet unfolding; Hanamel's vineyard is literally the groundwork for the Christian idea of redemption. But let's not forget that it's a great story on its own. Let's not forget the power of what Jeremiah did simply by buying a piece of land from his cousin. Most of all, at least this morning, in our urge to see things spiritually, let's not overlook the power of money.

Christians have often got it wrong about money. Money is the root of all evil, we've been known to believe. Get rid of your money and become instantly righteous, we've proclaimed. And why shouldn't we think this? "Tell me what I must do to inherit eternal life," a man runs up to Jesus to ask him, a man who we learn later has many possessions. "You lack one thing: go, sell what you own," Jesus tells him. "Give the money to the poor, and you will have treasure in heaven. Then come, follow me."

This must have been a hard thing for this man to hear—and I don't mean the second part ("Sell what you own") but this first part, this insight: "You lack one thing." After all, he must have spent a lot of time acquiring, keeping. He *had* many possessions, the story notes; and he *kept* all the commandments, the translation states. (Other translations render this "obeyed," but this one chooses the more suggestive "kept.") So, he must have spent time and energy on acquiring and keeping; and now he learns that he lacks one thing. And I imagine it was hard to hear—that he could lack anything at this point.

Not long ago, someone came to my house for the first time. "This is a cute little place," she said. I don't have a lot of house pride, but I did feel diminished by her comment.

Longer ago, when I was first engaged to be married, an acquaintance noticed my ring. "I'd want my engagement ring to look like that," she said, thinking likely about her longtime boyfriend, "but I want mine to have a big diamond." I don't have a lot of diamond ring pride but I did feel cut down by this.

"You lack one thing," Jesus said, and it might have cut into this man in a particular way. The thing he lacked, of course, was treasure in heaven. The thing he was missing was participation in the kingdom of God. And here's why he lacked it, I imagine: he was so used to owning, but this thing that he now wanted (and *wanted* it he did, as evidenced in his running up to Jesus, *running* up to him), this thing that he now wanted isn't something you even can own; it's something you enter. He lacked it, I imagine, because he was so used to possessing, but this thing that he now wanted isn't something you possess but is something to which you give yourself that it might come to possess you.

Because something will, you know. Something will possess you—and I'm not thinking about *The Omen* here. I'm not thinking about *The Exorcist*. All those scary movies that I didn't see as a kid and yet that scared me anyway, all those scary movies with extreme visions of what demon possession looks like, all those scary movies that were but the wild fantasy of some Hollywood higher-ups, they had at least this right—that we do become possessed. The question is, by what?

By what spirit will we be possessed? By what spirit will *you* be possessed?

This man who ran up to Jesus—ran up to him!—is the only person in all the gospel narratives that Jesus is said to have looked at and loved. We can *imply* love in a lot of Jesus' responses to a lot of different people. We certainly do interpret love into much of what he did with his life. But this man is the only person of whom the narrative voice is clear to tell us: "Jesus, looking at him, loved him." Yet in spite of this—in spite of this man's own enthusiasm, having run up to Jesus; in spite of Jesus' response to him, having looked at him and loved him—the man went away grieving, for he had many possessions.

Or, you might he say, his many possessions had him.

Which is, perhaps, why Jesus advised him as he did. Because it's significant that Jesus didn't say this to every rich man he came across. This great challenge—"Sell everything you have and give the proceeds to the poor"—isn't something he said to everyone with wealth whom he came across. Not even the disciples were required to sell everything they had. Yes, they left their nets, their boats (as Peter in particular was eager to point out later on); but they didn't sell them off. Yes, they left their homes, their families; but they didn't disown them, nor were they (as far as we know) disowned by them. It's just this man to whom Jesus is remembered to have issued such a dramatic challenge.

We might wonder, why?

Here's what I suppose, that for this man worldly wealth and eternal life were indeed mutually exclusive. For this man *having* in this world and *participating* in God's kingdom were truly and terribly at odds with one another.

Perhaps they are for everyone, and so it is true indeed that only God can save us. (But, then, why should we even bother to try? Rich as we all are [let's not deny it], why should we even bother try to do right with our wealth?) Or perhaps these two—worldly wealth and kingdom living—were more at odds within this man than they are for most.

I've seen this. I've known people ensnared, imprisoned in their wealth. I've known people and even liked (and might have loved) people of whom I've had to realize I can't reach because they're protective, defensive of their wealth. They're not necessarily the richest among us, and it's not that they're greedy. It's that they hide in their wealth as if suspicious that this is the only thing about them that has worth, and that they hide their wealth as if suspicious that this, their wealth, is the only thing about them that other people are after. I've known people like this. I recognize them now by how they make me feel. Trying to be friends, I'm left not angry or envious but frustrated and sad.

And so it was. So it was that this man went away grieving, and perhaps Jesus did too. So it was that this beloved man was a camel and the way into the kingdom was narrower even than the eye of a needle. So it was, at least for now, at least as of this moment, when the man went away and returned to the embrace of his possessions, though I doubt that he *ran* to them.

But, you know, we aren't privy to what happened to him next. So who knows what coming months might have witnessed him doing? Who knows what opportunities coming years might have presented him with? Perhaps a vineyard in the middle of a war zone. After all, war was coming. Mark's gospel was written in the middle of one. Maybe that man with many possessions decided to "invest" it all in a vineyard.

It's a familiar image during these years following the great recession: people who are "underwater" with their mortgages, people who owe more money on their home than their home is worth. There are fewer such people these days than in the years closer to 2008, but they're still out there. Maybe you're one of them. If so, then redemption is no mere spiritual concept held wishfully for some far-off time. It's a hope that perhaps keeps you up at night. It's a need that perhaps presses on you with painful persistence. If so, then you know what redemption actually is. You understand uniquely what Christ accomplishes.

My son has been saying a lot lately that when he grows up, he's going to invent a law that makes it so no one can use money. I can relate. No, I can remember. I said this very same sort of thing to my father when I was Tobias's age. His response to me: money is good if you want to buy things. It saves time, and it establishes fair play in the marketplace. I'll say as much to Tobias, but I'll also say this: money is good if you can find a way to use it for good. To rescue some sinking situation back to secure footing, to ransom some apparently lost cause back from total loss: this is what makes money valuable, not the money itself but its potential to be spent on that which has value, that which feeds life and restores hope.

But it can only do these things if its possessor is willing to let it go.

What's your money worth?

I ask myself that every day.

Thanks be to God.

Wrong Bird
An Aside

THERE'S A HEN IN the fox house.

That's what Jesus seemed to imply.

Some people came and told him, "Get away from here, for Herod wants to kill you," and he told them, "Go, and tell that fox . . ."

What they were to tell "that fox" is that Jesus wasn't going to stop doing what he was doing—healing the sick, blessing the unclean—until this work of compassion was finished, until it all was complete. No amount of intimidation from the tetrarch was going to sway him. No threat, not even a most dire one and issued from a ruler who had the power to make it happen, was going to make him stop. Instead, he meant to fulfill his heart's desire, to gather the people of Jerusalem together "as a hen gathers her brood under her wings."

A hen.

I wonder how that sounded to the disciples who heard him say it. I figure they might have expected Jesus to choose a mightier bird, perhaps an eagle. That's a favorite in the Old Testament for giving an image to God. The books of Moses often hear God as likening himself to an eagle. The prophets often understand God as such: a bird of power, a bird of prey.

What good could a hen do?

We might wonder the same. A hen in the fox house: What good would that do?

That's only any good if there are lots more hens than foxes, and even then it's a troubling notion. One thing's for certain, I'd rather not be the hen trying to gather in that brood. But then, sometimes history makes demands of us, as does any given day.

Gaming for Good

The next day he saw Jesus coming towards him and declared, "Here is the Lamb of God who takes away the sin of the world! This is he of whom I said, 'After me comes a man who ranks ahead of me because he was before me.' I myself did not know him; but I came baptizing with water for this reason, that he might be revealed to Israel." And John testified, "I saw the Spirit descending from heaven like a dove, and it remained on him. I myself did not know him, but the one who sent me to baptize with water said to me, 'He on whom you see the Spirit descend and remain is the one who baptizes with the Holy Spirit.' And I myself have seen and have testified that this is the Son of God."

The next day John again was standing with two of his disciples, and as he watched Jesus walk by, he exclaimed, "Look, here is the Lamb of God!" The two disciples heard him say this, and they followed Jesus. When Jesus turned and saw them following, he said to them, "What are you looking for?" They said to him, "Rabbi" (which translated means Teacher), "where are you staying?" He said to them, "Come and see." They came and saw where he was staying, and they remained with him that day. It was about four o'clock in the afternoon. One of the two who heard John speak and followed him was Andrew, Simon Peter's brother. He first found his brother Simon and said to him, "We have found the Messiah" (which is translated Anointed). (John 1:29–41)

AS THE HEAT OF World Wars I and II cooled and the chill of the Cold War fell over the Northern Hemisphere, the fields of game theory, computer programming, and evolutionary biology cross-fertilized to produce a harvest that is to the good of society at large. Interesting, but long, is the story of how there came to be a computer game tournament that illustrates how nice guys came into existence and, though fraught with near misses and harrowing escapes, survived.[1]

I'll try to keep it short.

The fact of nice guys is a thorn in the side of strict Darwinian theory, that is, the theory of the survival of the fittest. Nice, after all, isn't fit. Indeed, unless everyone decides to be nice, being nice seems a liability. And yet nice exists.

How?

---

1. I'm paraphrasing Bass, in his article, "Forgiveness Math," para. 4.

This is a fact, a begged question, that haunted Darwin. Not only did he dread to think of living in the world that he seemed to have discovered, he was aware that creatures do actually help one another even at great cost to themselves. Baboons do it. Bats do it. Bacteria do it. There's an amoeba that will group together with others of its kind to become one larger organism, 20 percent of which will then die while allowing for the others in their group literally to find better pastures. Darwin was fully aware of this as a great mystery. Actually, he was aware of it as the greatest mystery. And if he couldn't answer it, then his theory in his own estimation wasn't worth anything.

This fact doesn't haunt Steven Dawkins enough. Though a strict Darwinian (not to mention a vocal so-called atheist), he isn't strict enough to be similarly haunted. He propagates the idea that nature is brutal—so brutal as to be fully dependent on the fit taking life from the unfit. And so it has become a common assumption that we live in an irredeemably brutal world—irredeemably so because this brutality in fact serves the purpose of life. Nature forces us to consider the suffering of the weak as good, as right.

Cue the Nazis. Cue the Stalinists. We're ready for their close-up.

Well, after they had their day, and Berlin was left a burning pile of rubble, and eastern Europe was left a mass grave, and the Soviet Union was left by those who could get out, gamers and theorists began to play. Actually, like us on certain Sunday mornings, they played with a story, one called the Prisoner's Dilemma.

Here's how it goes.

Two prisoners face incarceration for a crime they committed together and for which the police have arrested them and are now questioning them—separately, of course. They each face a choice. If neither rats out the other, their alibi will hold and they'll both be released after a few months in jail. If each rats out the other, they'll each get a longer sentence, but not as long as if they hadn't turned state's witness. If only one rats out the other, that one will get off while the other serves the full sentence alone. With an aim of getting the most points, the gamers assigned a name and point value to each of these. If both cooperate, neither ratting the other out, they would get three points each. If both defect, both ratting the other out, both would get one point each. If only one defects, and the other doesn't, the former would get five points while the latter would get zero.

So, I wonder, what would you do?

If you weren't in church, and it wasn't your pastor who was asking, what would you do?

It's hardly a dilemma, in spite of the game's name. You'd defect. Think about it. If you defected, the least you would get is one point, which your opponent would also get, and the most you would get is five, while your opponent would get stuck with nothing. In other words, the worst you would do is tie with your opponent and the best you would do is beat the sucker.

Duh.

But this story is too simple to shed much light. As a model of life, it fails to take into account the possibility that you know your opponent and that you'll come against this same opponent again. Remember, in the world of politics, especially cold war politics, you wouldn't face the prisoner's dilemma once; you'd face it over and over again. And cold war politics, remember too, was the context of this developing game.

So it was made more complicated, as to reflect life. And here, believe it or not, is where good news begins to dawn. In his article "Forgiveness Math" in *Discover* magazine, Thomas Bass writes:

> When you play repeated rounds of the prisoner's dilemma, the game is completely different. The most surprising fact is that the competition no longer has a single strategy that is better than all the others. The game becomes contingent, chancy. Everything depends on whom you are playing at any particular moment.
>
> . . . [In repeated rounds of] prisoner's dilemma, there is no best strategy, and it is impossible that a single one could ever be found. You can always encounter situations where it's better to switch strategies. It all depends on what kind of player you're partnered with.
>
> Consider the following example. If you meet a relentless defector, you should always defect. If you meet an all-out cooperator, you should also always defect. But if you meet a grim retaliator— someone who cooperates until his opponent defects and from that moment on never cooperates again—you should cooperate.
>
> Two mad-dog defectors hammering each other without surcease will pick up only 1 point per round, while two cooperators . . . will earn a steady 3 points per round. We begin to see how cooperation can pay off, and in the long run, with the arbitrary values we have assigned to the game, 3 points is the highest average payoff anyone can expect to earn per round.[2]

2. Ibid., paras. 13–16.

AND SO IT WAS for decades that mathematicians, game theorists, biologists, and now arms negotiators debated which strategy was best for playing repeated rounds, until Robert Axelrod, a political scientist at the University of Michigan, decided to settle the matter once and for all with a computer tournament. Researchers around the world mailed Axelrod fourteen different computer programs, to which he added one of his own and played all of them against each other in a round-robin tournament in 1978, the winner of which was the simplest program, Tit for Tat. This featured players that cooperated in the first round and then imitated whatever the other player did. Going up against a hard-line defector, Tit for Tat would defect. Going up against a cooperator, Tit for Tat would cooperate. And so, Tit for Tat—pragmatic, reflexive—would win.

But not one to leave well-enough alone, a couple years later, Mr. Axelrod introduced another factor—that the winner of each round would be rewarded with offspring, two or three made in the likeness of that one. Unsurprisingly, once again Tit for Tat was the winner. Indeed, in answer to the question, "Can cooperation thrive in this horribly hostile world?" Mr. Axelrod observed that, if you have enough cooperators and they have enough chance of meeting each other, then they can actually invade and take over the world, even if the world starts out horribly mean.

Yet now Tit for Tat won only for a time, for now a flaw in the program became apparent, a fatal flaw as it were—the fact that it has no tolerance for error. Tit for Tat has no room for misinterpretation, for miscommunication. In Tit for Tat, there may be echoes of cooperation, but there are likewise echoes of retaliation. Peacemaking can reverberate in Tit for Tat, but so can violence. And if the act that provokes a violent response is an act misunderstood—is taken as aggressive when it is meant as conciliatory—the reverberations are tragic. Of course, this is all of little concern in a computer-simulated game, in which actions are straightforward and reactions are too. It's of tremendous concern, however, when dealing with human beings—powerful as we are, prone to error in judgment as we are.

* * *

I love the above scene from John's gospel because it's so strange. No one imagined here is behaving in a way that makes much sense. John is standing somewhere amidst some crowd of people and catches sight of Jesus who is apparently just walking by. From where, to where, why? Who knows? John takes this as a chance to declare to no one in particular and apparently to no one's hearing: "Here is the Lamb of God who takes away the sin of the world!" Not even Jesus seems to have heard him.

Awkward.

You know, this is such a far cry from the way the other gospel narratives introduce Jesus as the Christ to the world—recalling Jesus at his baptism when the Holy Spirit descends on him and, like a dove, alights on him, while a voice from heaven speaks, "This is my son, the beloved, with whom I am well pleased." By sorry contrast, here is John yelling out, "Hey, everybody. Here's the Lamb of God."

The next day, he would try again. As before, Jesus is walking by. From where, to where, why? Who knows? As before, John exclaims, "Look, here is the Lamb of God!" But this time, someone hears him—two of his own disciples who turn now to follow Jesus. Jesus notices them and asks, "What are you looking for?" And they answer, oddly, "Where are you staying?" Jesus says, "Come and see." And they do. And they stay where he was staying for the day. And then they go out and tell their friends, "We have found the Messiah."

One wonders what they saw in Jesus' hotel room to lead them to this conclusion. Or was it his dorm room? Or his apartment? Where was Jesus staying, anyway? And what was there to lead these two men to such sudden conviction? Because, come to think of it, no one had suggested to them that Jesus was the Messiah. All they'd been told is that he's the lamb of God who takes away the sin of the world. And, speaking of which, what does that mean?

Well, as it turns out, not what we think.

This is one of those phrases from Scripture whose meaning we think we know and about which we're wrong. Jesus spoken of as a lamb is to call to mind the practice of blood sacrifice as a means of atoning for sin and being made right before God. Lambs were often used as such a sacrifice, were indeed mandated for such a purpose in the Law; and Jesus is seen to step into this system as the ultimate such lamb.

But to understand Jesus as such would mean that he is the lamb of people offered to God. What, though, does it mean to declare him the Lamb of God sent to the world to take away the sin of the world?

I think this: it's to understand that it isn't God who mandates violence in order for us to be acceptable in God's sight, but that it's we who require violence in order to feel safe, saved. No, it isn't God who spills innocent blood in order to restore order, in order to establish justice and ensure tranquility and generate unity. That's us.

We do it quite unconsciously, though, so it can seem spirit-led. We also do it collectively so it comes to us as a gift while the unity it generates is so sweet we take it to be a gift from God. Most of all, we do it so fundamentally that it is the very sin that God offered himself in Christ to take away—that we might no longer live in the kingdoms of this world whose currency is blood spilled under the auspices of social cohesion but that we might live (truly live the life that truly is life) in the kingdom of God whose currency is love.

This, of course, is where Jesus was staying. His hotel room that so convinced the disciples was the kingdom of God in which he dwelt and which dwelt in him. His dorm room that convicted the disciples that they'd found the Messiah was this—the kingdom of God which was his abode. No mere apartment that he kept in the city, the place where Jesus was staying is the Greek word *meno*, which appears so often in the Johannine tradition—the letters and the Gospel of John. Translated "abide," "dwell," "endure," "remain," "stay," *meno* signifies God's dwelling in Jesus, Jesus' dwelling in God, and the dwelling place that Christ himself prepares amidst the Father for each of us.

Wonderful, right? Doesn't it sound wonderful?

But we should make no mistake. The Johannine testimony doesn't amount to merely castles in the air. This is happening, even now, even among us.

* * *

Mr. Axolrod, a year later, developed what he called Generous Tit for Tat in order to address the tragic echoes that were the fatal flaw of Tit for Tat. This new player, Generous Tit for Tat, always met cooperation with cooperation; but when facing defection, rather than mimicking the move of the defecting opponent, the player would forgive on average one out of every three times.

The result was surprising. For one hundred generations, the Always Defect strategy dominated the population with what looked like inescapable ferocity, while a beleaguered minority of Tit for Tat survived on the edge of extinction. But then the defectors had no one left to defect on, and so the game reversed. Tit for Tat sprung to life while the Always Defectors weakened and died out.

But, there's more—for Tit for Tat was not the strategy that ultimately won the game. Eventually its fatal flaw of mimicking the opponent's behavior had it losing out to its more forgiving cousins. And it was these who were the ultimate winners—these, the forgiving cousins, the one-out-of-every-three-times forgiving cousins.

In sum, after one hundred generations, the game swings from defecting and death-dealing to tit for tat, taking an eye for an eye as it were. But after three hundred generations, it swings again as Generous Tit for Tat so firmly establishes itself that no aggression can invade the game.

To put it another way, after one hundred generations, the winning strategy is "an eye for an eye," and after three hundred generations, the ultimately victorious strategy is turning the other cheek at least one out of three times—not repaying evil for evil but overcoming evil with good.

Mr. Bass writes this conclusion, "Tit for Tat is not the aim of evolution, but it makes it possible. It is a kind of pivot." And through it all, though much "policing" is necessary—that is, the doling out of justice tit for tat, an eye for an eye, punishment fitting the crime—in the end, claims Mr. Bass, our science writer mind you, there is a "final apocalyptic outbreak of good feeling."[3]

You hear me say from this pulpit a lot that mimetic behavior is our basic creaturely building block. Unlike other animals, we've lost our instincts, evolved past them. Instead, we imitate. We imitate behavior from the first moment after we're born. We imitate desire, learning what's desirable by seeing what another finds desirable. We imitate values, establishing our own based on what we've caught from our culture. And this can have some positive effect—as we'd see in watching Tit for Tat play against itself, conciliation met with conciliation. But this can also have a disastrous effect—as we'd see in watching Tit for Tat misunderstand the opponent's response and so spiral downward into a mimetic crisis. "You did it to me, so I'll do it to you." "Well, you did it to me, so I'll do it to you."

A mimetic crisis. When you enter war preemptively in order to disarm an enemy who could well mean, though unprovoked, to attack you, you've fallen into a mimetic crisis. When we've seen the enemy and it is us, we've fallen into a mimetic crisis. When no amount of battling back can reestablish social order, no amount of scapegoating what seems wicked in our midst can bring about a sense of sacred unity among the "good," no amount of casting out others can tranquilize those safe inside; the grappling hooks

3. Ibid., para. 4.

of mimetic crisis have got us. And the only way out is this: "Peace be with you." A radical break from what's come before: "Peace be with you." To turn a downward spiral into a still point and then a rising up, to introduce a note of peace into an echo chamber of violence: "Peace be with you. As the Father sent me, so I send you."

These, of course, are the words Jesus offered the disciples following his crucifixion, amidst now his resurrection: "Peace be with you. As the Father sent me, so I send you." He said these words to those who defected on him, to those who betrayed him, denied him, abandoned him—"Peace be with you." And thus he gives us something life-giving to imitate. Thus he puts our mimetic nature to the purpose of good.

Could it be? Really, could it be that the aim of evolution is the aim of Christ? An apocalyptic outbreak of conciliation?

Well, if so, to whose benefit comes such conciliation is a question evolutionary gamers and the church will answer differently. The former will claim this as good news for those lucky enough to be alive when peace is won. The latter, the church, in faithful anticipation of a universal resurrection, proclaims this as good news for all that will have lived. (How I do love the future perfect tense!)

But that is then. This is now. And to live as if it were then could well cost now. We should understand this. Generous Tit for Tat sometimes gets played for a sucker, sometimes gets defeated and even killed off. Christ, we know well, gets crucified.

Likewise, and for this very reason, we should know that not everyone will join us—maybe not even any number of us at any given moment. There will be people who defect, even at every given chance. There will be those who work for justice, policing wrongdoing and doling out punishment to fit the causal crime. There will be people who forgive just one out of three times instead of seventy times seven, as Jesus tells us to do.

Fine. Let it be so for now. But also know this, know this in faith, that God is working God's purpose out, such that the only question for us is, where are *we* staying?

Thanks be to God.

Laugh It Up

"But to what will I compare this generation? It is like children sitting in the market-places and calling to one another, 'We played the flute for you, and you did not dance; we wailed, and you did not mourn.' For John came neither eating nor drinking, and they say, 'He has a demon;' the Son of Man came eating and drinking, and they say, 'Look, a glutton and a drunkard, a friend of tax-collectors and sinners!' Yet wisdom is vindicated by her deeds." . . .

At that time Jesus said, "I thank you, Father, Lord of heaven and earth, because you have hidden these things from the wise and the intelligent and have revealed them to infants; yes, Father, for such was your gracious will. All things have been handed over to me by my Father; and no one knows the Son except the Father, and no one knows the Father except the Son and anyone to whom the Son chooses to reveal him.

"Come to me, all you that are weary and are carrying heavy burdens, and I will give you rest. Take my yoke upon you, and learn from me; for I am gentle and humble in heart, and you will find rest for your souls. For my yoke is easy, and my burden is light." (Matthew 11:16–19, 25–30)

THE LIST OF THINGS pastors wish they had learned in seminary but didn't, is long. How to do a funeral, how to deal with an ornery bishop or congregant, how to do a capital campaign, how to maintain a big, old building: these are all factors in congregational life that you don't learn in seminary. Too busy learning the urgent things—biblical languages or medieval theology or atonement theories—you simply don't have time to study up on the finer points of pipe organ bellows rebuilding or snaking a clogged toilet on Easter morning at 9:56.

As for my list, it's not too long. I loved divinity school and loved learning what I learned, so I could forgive all that it was not. There is one thing on it, though. There's one thing on my list: I think every budding pastor should learn the art of lightening up.

We're an earnest lot, we pastors. We're the sorts of people who would have you explain that joke you just told. We might then have you justify it: Is that really the sort of thing we should be laughing about?

Of course, we pastors aren't alone in this. Churchgoers can be an earnest lot as well. And why not? We're so aware of all in the world. We're so aware of sin and suffering, of injustice and untruth. We contemplate the persistence of such things in the world on a weekly basis, perhaps on a daily basis. And in face of such things, in reistance of such things, we want to do what's right; we *need* to do what's right in order to answer the call of the gospel, in order to be the people God wants and needs for us to be.

And with that, things get very serious.

I know more than a few pastors who seem to perceive their congregations as never working hard enough, never changing fast enough, never being focused enough and on the right things. I know more than a few pastors who seem to take no enjoyment in their congregations. It's all disappointment. It's all resentment.

They're a drag, these pastors.

Studies show that raising happy children is almost every parent's concern. Studies show this by there being so very many studies on how to raise happy children, and then so very many analyses and articles and blog posts on how to understand the studies on how to raise happy children. These studies show, if nothing else, how obsessively concerned we are about raising happy children. Apparently, slightly dissatisfied children is the great scourge of our time.

I tend not to tune in to these discussions. But it's not that I'm against happiness—in my children or in anyone else. I just think happiness rarely results when it is itself the goal. Happiness, it seems to me, is a by-product: it comes into your life through the side door. But even I "clicked" on a happiness blog not long ago, and this was a good one.[1] To raise happy children, this one writer said, parents might allow for enjoying their children. Stop worrying about their happiness and start laughing at their jokes. Stop worrying about their success and try tickling them instead. Have some fun. Lighten up! Kids are fun, and funny, so enjoy them! Laugh!

It seems to me the same goes for pastors and congregational life. To participate in an effective church, try enjoying yourself in church. Indeed, to worship rightly, laugh loudly.

Never, never miss an opportunity to laugh.

(You know, I actually laughed a lot in divinity school, so I guess I did learn this there.)

Jesus, of course, seemed to be enjoying himself, and this was a problem. It was a problem for John, his cousin, and it was a problem for the crowd that Jesus had been attracting.

---

1. A good one—though I can't find it now. I couldn't find it again when writing this sermon, or now when preparing this sermon for publication. Maybe it wasn't a memory but a fabrication, a wish fulfillment.

To be fair, the people seemed quite fickle on this point, objecting to John's asceticism—living in the wilderness, wearing rough clothes, eating bugs and wild honey ("He's got a demon!"); and then objecting to Jesus' indulgences—eating and drinking, and with tax collectors and sinners ("Glutton! Drunkard!").

To be fair, too, this wasn't *all* Jesus was doing; he wasn't *only* having fun. In fact, where we catch up with him this morning, he has just gathered and then charged the twelve disciples, and in recent verses Jesus has had some quite sobering words: "See, I am sending you out like sheep into the midst of wolves . . ." "[Y]ou will be hated by many because of my name . . ." "Do not think my coming will bring peace to the earth; for my coming will not bring peace, but a sword . . ." "Whoever loves father and mother more than me is not worthy of me . . ." Makes for tough listening, all of these.

But Jesus did also enjoy himself—and with the wrong sorts of people, which seems to be central to other peoples' objections. Consider that the final disciple Jesus called, according to this gospel, was Matthew, a tax collector whom Jesus found sitting in his tax booth. Jesus approached him, told him, "Follow me," and so Matthew did—Matthew and apparently many others as well.

This is apparent because later, at dinner, Jesus was noticed to be eating with "many tax collectors and sinners," which the Pharisees questioned, asking the disciples, "Why does your teacher eat with tax collectors and sinners?"

And, "of course," you say. "Of course, the Pharisees noticed this and commented on this and likely objected to this. Of course," you say, "for the Pharisees were always objecting to everything." The interpreters of the Law, the sometimes enforcers of the Law, they were a perfect storm of religiosity, legalism, and policing. "Now, *they* were a drag," you say.

But it wasn't just them who objected; it was also John. Jesus' own cousin, the one who was to go ahead of Jesus—in life and (as it happened, sadly) in death—so to prepare a way for Jesus and his messianic work, John also objected, or questioned, at least. After all, it was John's disciples who, provoked by that same dinner that had the Pharisees so provoked, approached Jesus and asked him, "Why do we and the Pharisees fast often, but your disciples do not fast at all?"

John's disciples were surprised, I imagine, to find themselves sharing more in common with the Pharisees than with the one whose cousin they were following as students. If they were to find themselves on any team, I imagine they'd have thought they'd be on team Jesus and not on team Phari-sees. And yet here they were, sitting out the same dinner parties that the Pharisees sat out but which Jesus not only attended but became central to.

Why?

Jesus' answer to these questions is typically criptic. To the Pharisees he said, "Go and learn what this means, 'I desire mercy and not sacrifice,' for I have come to call not the righteous but the sinners." To the disciples of John, he said, "The wedding guests cannot mourn as long as the bride-groom is still with them."

And perhaps these answers satisfied for a time—satisfied at least John's disciples. Perhaps this eased John's disciples' anxiety that Jesus wasn't living up to his promise—that he was the beloved Son of God to whom people should listen. Perhaps this quieted their concern. But it didn't for long, for just one chapter hence, John is said to have heard, though in prison as he was, what Jesus was doing, what *the Messiah* was doing—heard in prison, which means his disciples must have come and told him. And so he sent those disciples back to Jesus to ask him, "Are you the one who is to come, or are we to wait for another?" This was, of course, to ask him, are you the Mes-siah? Are you, in all your eating and drinking and cavorting, the *Messiah?*

As you may know, the Messiah was a title that came with many expec-tations. The Messiah was expected to come to daughter Zion triumphant and victorious, and to bring to daughter Jerusalem dominion from sea to sea. The Messiah was to be the king to cut off the chariot from Ephraim in the northern kingdom of Israel, and to cut off the war horse and battle bow from Jerusalem in the southern kingdom of Israel. Really, the Messiah was to come mighty and powerful, as warrior and judge and savior and Son of God, commanding peace to the nations who, now dominated by the ultimate dominating force, would dare not refuse.

What's more, these were things needed to be done. This wasn't just some arrogant desire on Israel's part to be top dog in the ancient Near East. The people Israel and Judah were suffering—*suffering*—under Roman oc-cupation. Some scholars assert that this region at this time was the bloodi-est in human history until twentieth-century Europe. James Carroll in his book *Constantine's Sword* claims that to read the gospel narratives without consideration of the extreme violence of Jesus' socio-political context is as to read *The Diary of Anne Frank* with no consideration of the Holocaust.[2] These were times of crisis for Jesus' people. To live at this time was to live

2. Carroll, 90.

ever under the threat of terror and torture—and even more so at the time of the writing of this gospel, likely forty or so years after Jesus lived. Indeed, when Matthew wrote his gospel text, the temple had already been sacked, the city had already been destroyed, the people were running scared in every direction, and the vicitms of crucifixion loomed beyond the city walls by the hundreds.

So a Messiah at this time would have been a most welcome thing. The anointed one of God, the Messiah, the Christ: this would have been welcome, needful, deperately needful.

We're *waiting*.

Meanwhile, Jesus was enjoying himself. The Pharisees noticed, John's disciples noticed, John himself noticed, and most recently the church has noticed—its theologians and scholars and preachers too. Actually, there's quite a lot of hand-wringing done over this, worrying over Jesus' apparently enjoying himself. There's quite a long history of Christians attempting to justify Jesus' merriment, claiming, as has been done, that he did so because of recent success in his ministry. He had just gathered all his disciples. He had just sent them out with sound instructions. He managed to gather crowds wherever he went, crowds who came near and listened. He raised the dead and healed the sick, made the blind to see and the lame to walk. So, many conclude, Jesus was eating and drinking because things were going well for him and his mission. He had conducted an evaluation of his ministry (gathered data and analyzed it) and concluded that he was really getting somewhere. So now he could relax. He could enjoy a night out with some sketchy friends.

But all of this is to overlook the simple possibility that the promise and presence of God is itself a joyful thing. All of this is to dismiss the possibility that the sure reality of God-with-us—of which Jesus was keenly aware, of which Jesus was the manifestation—is itself a source of joy. Yes, all of this is to dismiss the fact of God's faithfulness and immanence as itself cause for rejoicing.

Forget for the moment that, actually, Jesus' accomplishments weren't all that great. Forget for a moment that, compared to what was expected of him as the Messiah, his accomplishments to date were a little disappointing. Forget that he had not, in fact, come to Zion triumphant and victorious, and that he would not, in fact, bring to Jerusalem peaceful dominion from sea to sea. Forget that he had not single-handedly brought all wrongs to right, all wrongdoing to justice, all rebellion to judgment. Forget that at his command, the nations of the world did not surrender their arms and make lasting and just peace. Most of all, forget the terrible truth that Jesus would become best known for having later been betrayed by one of his friends, arrested by his own people, tried like the common criminal he was taken to be, crucified like so many others, deserted, left for dead, and then buried in a borrowed tomb. Forget that his "success" is dubious indeed.

Forget all of that because that whole project serves the assumption that enjoyment must be justified, must be contextually approriate. Forget all that because that whole project of trying to justify his joy undergirds the assumption that rejoicing is an allowance you must earn, rather than God's ultimate reality, which is but breaking in—even here, even now.

The truth is that Jesus enjoying himself is itself the good news that he was sent to reveal, is itself the life lesson that he was sent to teach. And I love that he doesn't shame John for John's living an ascetic life, for John's and John's disciples resembling the Pharisees more than they resembled Jesus. I love that, though John doubts Jesus' way, Jesus doesn't doubt John's—because if the ascetic life is how God manifests himself to you, then that is right; and if enjoyment in eating and drinking among the outcast and hated is how God manifests himself to you, then that is right.

So, truly, that Jesus was enjoying himself in spite of so many reasons to fear and to despair, to live a life that is ultimately one long sickness unto death, is the good news, indeed is the gospel: this promise revealed in the word of God made flesh, not that mercy will come after a lifetime of labor, but that mercy is now in laboring for God; this promise revealed in the word of God made flesh, not that joy will come after a lifetime of trials but that joy is now, even amidst such trials, because of the ever presence of God.

Truly, as in all good literature in which form and content are in communion with one another, in which form and content indeed are one, that Jesus enjoyed his mission and ministry in this fallen world, according to the Gospel of Matthew, in spite of his having come and lived during difficult, even deadly, times, is the gospel of God-with-us.

Yes, of course, the joy of Jesus is the point. And it's a point missed by the wise and intelligent, the proud and the pious; missed by the religious professionals who were then literal in their reading of the Law but illiterate in their understanding of the Spirit and the religious professionals now whose earnestness is so heavy a yoke and so great a drag.

Might we instead, then, be infants in this regard—those little ones who rejoice for God knows what? The immediacy of life? The raw and surprising pleasures of embodiment? Laughing at their own toes, these little ones. De-lighting in their own subjectivity, these babes.

A few weeks ago in a sermon, I listed off many of the problems in our world right now and encouraged us to consider which of these we each mean to spend our lives in helping solve. "There's a lot to do," I implied. "So let's get to work." In a sermon more recently, I listed the many tasks this congregation needs to attend to and asked us to consider which, if any, of these we might set our hands and minds to doing. "Let's get to work," I likely *more* than implied.

But what I didn't tell you is that a couple of weeks ago the Old Testament reading was from Genesis, the moment when Sarah laughed at the three strangers having come to her tent and received of her hospitality and then announced that she would become the mother of a son. She laughed. She *laughed*, people—a momentary loss of control, body overcome by some delightful surprise or striking joy, the breath of life come double-shot.

We often hear it otherwise. We often assume she scoffed, some dismissive, defensive expulsion of air. That's what's implied, anyway, in so much shaming of her, in her own self-shaming. ("I didn't laugh," she says, though that's not true.) But the story claims she laughed, and the son to come claims also that she laughed—the son whose name, Isaac, means laughter. And *this* implies that God, far from faulting her for her reaction of laughter, instead perhaps used such laughter as a means, an opportunity.

I think Sarah's laughing was the moment of Isaac's conception, the moment when she first conceived of this promised one who was no longer some general notion, some impersonal "nation," but was something suddenly more specific, some*one* suddenly more specific. I think it's by this sudden laughter that God's promise is fulfilled. It's by this gift of laughter that God's covenant with Abraham is realized.

Do you hear what I'm saying? In our life together as a people of God, in our covenant with one another as children of God, laughter is a foundational act.

None of this I told you then. But I'm telling you now.

Rejoicing isn't something we get to do once we've finished our chores. Rejoicing is the thing by which all good work is done. Enjoyment isn't something we earn the right to do, but is the thing by which godly living is realized. To live in joy amidst this world that God so loves—though it is teeming with troubles, though we ourselves might be suffering such troubles (cancer, schizophrenia, depression, grief, to name just a few that are among us now in this very room)—to live in joy amidst such toubles is to live as God's commissioned people.

You know, this could have been a much shorter sermon. Really, this could have been it: lighten up, people. It's a beautful day. It's Tanglewood season; the Boston Symphony Orchestra is in town. It's the season of fresh vegetables and fifteen hours of daylight.

Go this week, then, to Jacob's Pillow, to their Inside/Out stage—free but world-class dance concerts! Go this week for a hike to Bash Bish Falls or Umpacheene Falls. Watch the World Cup, or don't, as you prefer. Go to karaoke at Rumpy's in Lenox. (This and every Thursday, 9:00 p.m.) Hear our new piano, and Gabi's gorgeous playing of it.[3]

As for how to sustain yourself through this thicket of wondrous joys, well, here we have set before us the joyful feast for the people of God. So let's eat and drink as Jesus once did, in joy unjustified, joy instead graciously and gratuitouly poured out for us.

Thanks be to God.

3. One of our many wonderful musicians who plays for us on Sunday mornings is Gabriella Makuc. At twenty years old, she's already a phenomenal pianist.

Control is Fool's Gold

An Aside

I'M THINKING NOW OF Tobias's birth, my first.

He wasn't eager, apparently, to part ways with me. (Eleven years on, he still isn't.) For several hours he was stuck in the birth canal, leaving the doctor and nurses largely unable to help. He was too far along to be born by C-section, but not far enough for intervention on the other end. Large head, wide shoulders, and elbow up because he was sucking on his hand: it was a close call for both of us, and a brutally painful one. He came out crushed, head misshapen, screaming. And I was only and hardly able to take it all in because of an epidural (okay, two) and because of the old story of Eve and what birth pains she would suffer. This is why that story is still with us, I realized—not because it speaks correctly of God's intention to punish but because it speaks honestly of this undeniable fact, that birth is a mind-bending agony for both mother and baby, an out-of-control experience that is also frighteningly powerful.

I know there are women who object to medical intervention out of hand as they plan for their birth process. It's called "natural," or even "normal," birth—not to have medicine. In fact, not long after Jack, my second, was born, I found myself on the receiving end of a lecture about all this. (Or was it a sermon? She was, after all, a colleague.) Pregnant and due very soon, she wasn't going to have an epidural for her birth because she didn't like the prospect of being out of control of her body. She saw this as a feminist issue.

As it happens, so do I. I appreciate that women have choices when faced with what might be the biggest trial they've ever had to face. I also appreciate that, while it was once the church that took a punishing approach to the pains of childbirth and to the earliest midwives whose aim it was relieve some of that suffering, there's been something of reversal here. Many midwives I know reject medicine out of hand, while I, an ordained minister, would tell women everywhere, have mercy on yourselves when you're in labor. Make use of what tools, by God's grace at work in history, are now available. Or don't. You choose.

I see it also, though, as a theological issue.

There's a difference between power and control. There's a distinction to be drawn here—because, of course, the reason a woman giving birth is out of control of her body isn't because an epidural has been applied; it's because of the birth. The rolling (not to mention terrorizing) contractions that just keep coming and more frequently, the inability to speak, to move: it's because of that coming baby. It's because of this that you're completely out of control. And yet you're participating in the most powerful thing you'll perhaps ever be a part of.

Or at least that's how it was for me. And it reoriented my faith along with my whole life. God isn't a God of control. God is a God power. God calls us not to be a people exercising control. God calls us to be a people participating in divine power—a building up of the beloved community that, by the power of the Holy Spirit, might be made real even in our midst for its flowing not to us but through us.

So, please, everyone for whom birth is crucible ahead, which is to say pregnant women, Christians, and people of hope everywhere, let's not settle for fool's gold. Let's go for the real thing.

Promise and Compromise

They went to Capernaum; and when the sabbath came, he entered the synagogue and taught. They were astounded at his teaching, for he taught them as one having authority, and not as the scribes. Just then there was in their synagogue a man with an unclean spirit, and he cried out, "What have you to do with us, Jesus of Nazareth? Have you come to destroy us? I know who you are, the Holy One of God." But Jesus rebuked him, saying, "Be silent, and come out of him!" And the unclean spirit, throwing him into convulsions and crying with a loud voice, came out of him. They were all amazed, and they kept on asking one another, "What is this? A new teaching—with authority! He commands even the unclean spirits, and they obey him." At once his fame began to spread throughout the surrounding region of Galilee. (Mark 1:21–28)

I'M READING ARI SHAVIT'S book *My Promised Land: The Triumph and Tragedy of Israel*. Shavit writes as a third generation Israeli, the son and grandson of Zionists. He loves his home but recognizes it as tragic—tragic in that one long-ago well-meant move unfurled a series of actions and reactions; and these have been mind-bendingly destructive for so many people of so many sorts; and yet that original move might also have resulted in the continued existence, indeed the thriving, of a people once threatened with extinction; tragic in that there's no one really to blame.

Now, there's a statement: "a people once threatened with extinction." And I don't mean the extinction part, though that is a lot to take in. I mean the "a people" part. Can it even be said that there's any such thing as a people?

How fixed, how enduring, are the lines that help us sort and catalog human beings? What's a Jew—and what isn't one? What's a European—and what isn't one? What's a Palestinian, or are they all Arabs? What about a Moroccan Sephardic Jewish immigrant now living in a society dominated by once-European Ashkenazi Jews? Is he black, African? Is he an immigrant, or more native than those third generation Israelis yet making Hungarian food for dinner and listening to Bach's piano concertos in the evening? It's the edges of these groups that are fuzzy. It's the details that make the story a complex entanglement.

But now that we're at it, what about racial lines? Another book I just read is Nell Irvin Painter's *The History of White People*. In it, she tells the story of how white people came to be. And let's be clear, the book is social history not natural history since whiteness is a social construct not a natural one.

So I recommend the book—both books, actually, but now I'm back to *My Promised Land*. I recommend the book, but only if you can handle ruminating on an issue that begs you to take sides yet without taking sides. Of course, trying evenly to consider all sides of this century-long, generations-deep unfurling is itself a stance that many will find offensive. So this I say in warning: don't read this book for answers. Don't read this book if you mean to figure out who did what wrong, who did the most wrong, who started it, who will finally end it, and how. Don't read this book it you're looking for clarity, if you're looking to have your ideology confirmed as correct.

But to be clear, I wouldn't fault you if this is what you're looking for in life. I wouldn't blame you. After all, that urge is a strong one. I'll admit, before I started to read it (required as I am for my book club meeting this evening), I put it off. I stalled. The whole thing made me want to shout, "Just stop it! Just stop your fighting!" As if getting the boys to lay off their bickering, their mimetic rivalry, I could see both sides and I just couldn't stand the conflict anymore. "Don't trace it back. Don't tell me who did what. Just stop it. Just start from zero, from here and now."

It works in regard to the boys. Why not in regard to geo-politics?

To be correct, to have things cleared up, cleaned up: that urge is a strong one. In regard to the Middle East, that tiny strip of land whose name we can't even agree on; in regard to life in general: the urge to clean lines, to clear moral standing, is a strong one.

I have to say, Jesus doesn't help in this regard.

There's a word left out in the rendering into English of the passage above. It's probably left out because it doesn't make much apparent sense in this context. Plus, it's one of Mark's favorite words; it shows up a lot in his gospel. So maybe those at work on translating this from its original Greek figured that to drop one wouldn't do too much damage.

Euthys is the word, a drumbeat throughout this book. *Euthys* becomes in English "immediately," "suddenly," "at once," "just then." This passage, if *euthys* were included, would read, "They came to Capernaum; and suddenly when the Sabbath came, he entered the synagogue and taught." And this is a little awkward, right? It's a little strange. It seems to imply that the Sabbath came suddenly. But how could this be? The Sabbath comes when it comes, quite predictably, after six ordinary days.

Of course, when I first became a pastor, about a year in, a colleague asked me what I was finding to be the biggest challenge in the work. "How frequently Sunday morning comes," I told her. "It's, like, every three days." But I doubt that's what Mark was driving at here. I think what he meant to give word to was the effect of Jesus' presence in Capernaum, in the synagogue, on that Sabbath. It was sudden. It was immediate. There was no mistaking this for a regular Sabbath. Something about this one was different. But what made the difference wasn't obvious, was mysterious.

Bible scholar Matt Skinner has this to say of Mark: "This gospel doesn't devote energy toward establishing a clear Christology, an understanding of Jesus' nature(s)."[1] This is largely John's concern, and to a lesser degree Matthew's concern, but for Mark, Jesus is important as "the one uniquely authorized, commissioned, or empowered to declare and institute the reign of God."[2] In sum, Jesus *is* the reign of God. Whatever will be the felt experience of our ultimate end in the presence of God, whole recreated creatures amidst a whole recreated creation, perfected by God's presence and sustenance and redemption; whatever felt experience that will be is what Jesus brings when he walks into a room to everyone in that room.

I grope for an example here, but I find I can't find one. There's no equivalent. Think about it, when Jesus groped for an equivalent—"The kingdom of God is like when . . ."—he had to tell a strange, suggestive story in order for his hearers to enter into some likeness of a state with which no one has any full, conscious experience of.

But I can tell you this, which I've told you before: something is immediate if it has no medium for our then-experience of it. Thinking literally, something is *im*mediate if it's not being mediated, which, in our age of so much that is mediated, is worth meditating on.

What in our lives comes to us without any sort of mediation?

What in your life is immediate, felt—viscerally felt, cellularly felt?

What answer you came up with comes close to the felt experience of Jesus that Mark means for us to take away from his gospel narrative.

And it's just this that made that Sabbath feel sudden, and Jesus' entry into and teaching in the synagogue feel sudden. But it doesn't end there. Jesus as immediate, felt presence and experience isn't the point of Jesus among us: it's the mode or perhaps the evidence.

1. Skinner, "Commentary," para. 11.

2. Ibid.

The point of it all, though, is this: when Jesus entered the synagogue, it would be better rendered that he occupied it or that he possessed it or made it busy, alive with his presence. And this explains why Jesus said to the spirit, "Be silent and come out of him." In contrast to the room being filled, busy, alive with the Holy Spirit in Jesus Christ, the unclean spirit is to be silent. In the same way, when the unclean spirit that occupied the man, convulsing him, now left him, it would better be rendered that the spirit "un-occupied" him, "un-possessed" him, became "un-busy" about him. Jesus' coming near makes unclean spirits take flight. Jesus' approach spurs unclean spirits to retreat.

Consider, the unclean spirit asks Jesus, "What have you to do with us?" But it's an idiomatic phrase, hard to translate. Its rhetorical effect is this: "Why are you picking this fight? Why not just leave well enough alone?"

And it's a good question, if you ask me. After all, many are the times when I decide to leave well enough alone. I actually regard this as a sign of my maturity, as a sign of my growing understanding that I can't fix everything and that, in many, perhaps most, cases, I shouldn't even try. I should just accept things as they are and try my best to respond in grace and pray deeply that the situation is well in God's hands—well and not just well enough.

But this is just it in regard to Jesus. He's not merely one of us; he is also of God. And so leaving well enough alone is literally, and essentially, something he cannot do. Like oil and water, like soap and grease, Jesus cannot negotiate with what's destructive; he cannot compromise with what's evil. His presence means evil's taking flight. His occupying a space means evil's ceding, its retreat.

This is why Jesus doesn't need to destroy the unclean spirit, as the unclean spirit suggests he means to or assumes he will do. "Why are you picking this fight? Have you come to destroy us?" And of course evil would assume destruction. Its own mode, evil would assume and assert this as the go-to mode for everyone and everything. No surprise then that Jesus doesn't, that he hasn't—hasn't come to destroy this or anything. He merely sets evil to flight.

I remember pointing out one Sunday morning that Mark's gospel is less concerned with sin and more about God's creation having fallen into enemy hands. I remember I implied that Mark's Christ is less about saving us from sin and more about freeing the creation from enemy occupation. I remember it so well (even as I forget a lot of what I've preached) because

I'd never noticed that before, hadn't even noticed it then, but had it pointed out to me by a lectionary podcast I listen to out of Luther Seminary in St. Paul.[3] And it's amazing to me that I missed it because it makes so much sense now seeing it.

These exorcism scenes make for tough preaching because they're so wildly out of step with our modern context, and even a postmodern context for those who've already left the modern era behind. So with this in mind, preachers have tried to cast this in language that speaks to us today. We might say, those said to be demon-possessed in the New Testament bear symptoms that resemble epilepsy or various mental illnesses. But in doing so, we're disposed to think either that the New Testament writers were quaint and erroneous because we have better ways of treating epilepsy, so the story and its significance dissolve to nothing. Or we diagnose a mental illness, which leaves those today struggling with illnesses that cause enough suffering as it is to wonder if perhaps they've got a demon, which adds yet another layer of dread and suffering.

But to understand Mark, and Mark's Jesus, as understanding the world as having fallen into enemy hands is to understand these scenes of cleansing and demon "un-possession" in a way that yet speaks. To understand Jesus as one who has come to a creation that has come to be occupied by an enemy presence is to open up a whole new way of relating to this Christ who is, yes, brother and friend, but also stranger and disturber of the peace.

And yes, it's a peace that isn't absolute. But it is functional, serviceable. It works for me. So couldn't he just leave well enough alone?

A least favorite notion from Scripture is this one: that the fear of the Lord is the beginning of wisdom. It's a least favorite, but a most persistent one. It shows up a lot, and it's tough to take. The one time I preached on it, a parishioner got up and left in the middle. Yet, here I go again, and because it's just this that I think is fearsome about the Lord—just this, that God is not here to endorse the world as it is, which we've managed for the most part to make function well for us, or at least well enough. No, God doesn't come to us in order to inhabit and ordain the shelters that we've constructed for self-protection and self-preservation, even if (regrettably) not everyone can come in. God hasn't come to us and to the world in order to negotiate a better arrangement, a *slightly* better arrangement. No, of course, God has come to establish God's reign, which is absolute in goodness, absolute in grace.

3. "Sermon Brainwave."

And this is fearsome, because it means that our constructions and machinations will fall away; it means that our apparent control of ourselves and our circumstances is all appearance, is illusory and fleeting. This is fearsome, but it's also where wisdom begins—with this truth, with this simple, humbling, painful, undeniable truth. We can only manage things for so long.

Hear that again, though: the fear of the Lord is the beginning of wisdom. The fear of the Lord is the *beginning* of wisdom, which implies to my hearing at least that this fear, though wisdom's beginning, is not where wisdom ends. Really, in my experience, the final insight of wisdom is not fear of the Lord but faith in the Lord, not fear of the Lord but desire for the Lord. Yes, the fear of the Lord is the beginning of wisdom, but its end is faith and hope and peace.

Somewhere in the middle is where we might be. Somewhere in the middle, between the world having come to be occupied by an enemy presence and the world as filled with the good and gracious spirit of God, is where we are.

Somewhere in the middle: you are here; we are here.

And let's be clear, this is no easy place, for we are not God and we are not Christ. We *do* negotiate with evil. We *do* compromise for a better way and we do settle for good enough.

We tack into headwinds, life a series of course corrections. If Christ walks a straight path even across stormy waters, we tack into headwinds in the faith that by zigzag we'll reach our straight-ahead goal.

So, yes, I'm sorry to say, sometimes wisdom dictates that we leave well enough alone, for when we get into a stubborn mindset of no compromise, no negotiation, that's when we become uniquely dangerous.

There's hardly a more dangerous idea among humankind than the idea of purity.

There's hardly a more destructive notion than this one, which so often springs from godly faith—that we must be pure and so we must eradicate evil in our midst. The urge to rid the world of what's unclean has been historically, I'd say, the most destructive urge. And it's an urge that finds reason in religious faith, which is why people so easily assert that religion itself is evil, that religion does much more harm than good.

But this urge isn't essential to religion. It's essential perhaps to human beings and so finds expression and fuel in religious faith. But it isn't essential to religion itself.

On the contrary, I believe that the Christian faith read rightly testifies to something quite different: the promise that, in Christ, there is a time and there is a means by which the world will be free of that which seeks destruction; that we journey through life in the light of this promise to that time; and that meanwhile we pray for grace to act for the sake of the gospel, we pray for forgiveness for when we thwart the gospel, and most of all we pray for faith that God acts even when we fail to act or we counteract or we act out.

The good news today comes with a heaped helping of news quite a bit harder to take. But there is good news in it, and this is it: that though we might feel ourselves to be living in tragedy, to be enduring tragic circumstances through which we can hope only for good enough, something serviceable and provisional and that gets us through, this isn't the end of the story. The end is God's good and gracious end.

But there's more: that we don't have simply to wait for the end to experience God's good grace; that we don't merely have to endure occupation all the while promise dwells in some distant, unfelt future. No, for it's breaking even now, breaking in even here. Christ's coming to the world shows us what it looks like; Christ's coming reveals what will have us recognize it. When evil is put to flight simply by presence, when destruction is silenced by an authoritative word spoken in fierce compassion, when love is lived: the end is now.

History unfurls, circumstances seem dire, then love speaks, love acts: and the end is now.

Thanks be to God.

Working It Out

As he walked along, he saw a man blind from birth. His disciples asked him, "Rabbi, who sinned, this man or his parents, that he was born blind?" Jesus answered, "Neither this man nor his parents sinned; he was born blind so that God's works might be revealed in him. We must work the works of him who sent me while it is day; night is coming when no one can work. As long as I am in the world, I am the light of the world." When he had said this, he spat on the ground and made mud with the saliva and spread the mud on the man's eyes, saying to him, "Go, wash in the pool of Siloam" (which means Sent). Then he went and washed and came back able to see.

The neighbors and those who had seen him before as a beggar began to ask, "Is this not the man who used to sit and beg?" Some were saying, "It is he." Others were saying, "No, but it is someone like him." He kept saying, "I am the man." But they kept asking him, "Then how were your eyes opened?" He answered, "The man called Jesus made mud, spread it on my eyes, and said to me, 'Go to Siloam and wash.' Then I went and washed and received my sight." They said to him, "Where is he?" He said, "I do not know."

They brought to the Pharisees the man who had formerly been blind. Now it was a Sabbath day when Jesus made the mud and opened his eyes. Then the Pharisees also began to ask him how he had received his sight. He said to them, "He put mud on my eyes. Then I washed, and now I see." Some of the Pharisees said, "This man is not from God, for he does not observe the Sabbath." But others said, "How can a man who is a sinner perform such signs?" And they were divided. So they said again to the blind man, "What do you say about him? It was your eyes he opened." He said, "He is a prophet."

The Jews did not believe that he had been blind and had received his sight until they called the parents of the man who had received his sight and asked them, "Is this your son, who you say was born blind? How then does he now see?" His parents answered, "We know that this is our son, and that he was born blind; but we do not know how it is that now he sees, nor do we know who opened his eyes. Ask him; he is of age. He will speak for himself." . . .

So for the second time they called the man who had been blind, and they said to him, "Give glory to God! We know that this man is a sinner." He answered, "I do not know whether he is a sinner. One thing I do know, that though I was blind, now I see."

They said to him, "What did he do to you? How did he open your eyes?" He answered them, "I have told you already, and you would not listen. Why do you want to hear it again? Do you also want to become his disciples?" Then they reviled him, saying, "You are his disciple, but we are disciples of Moses. We know that God has spoken to Moses, but as for this man, we do not know where he comes from." The man answered, "Here is an astonishing thing! You do not know where he comes from, and yet he opened my eyes. We know that God does not listen to sinners, but he does listen to one who worships him and obeys his will. Never since the world began has it been heard that anyone opened the eyes of a person born blind. If this man were not from God, he could do nothing." They answered him, "You were born entirely in sins, and are you trying to teach us?" And they drove him out.

Jesus heard that they had driven him out, and when he found him, he said, "Do you believe in the Son of Man?" He answered, "And who is he, sir? Tell me, so that I may believe in him." Jesus said to him, "You have seen him, and the one speaking with you is he." He said, "Lord, I believe." And he worshipped him. (John 9:1–21, 24–38)

IN THE BEGINNING: EVEN in this biblically illiterate age, most people know this as the first line of the Bible, the first line of Genesis; most people know this is how it all begins, most even know what unfolds from here, seven days during which God made all that God made and then at last came to rest. What we do with that is another matter. Whether we regard it as scientific (I don't), or as somehow prescriptive (I don't), or as poetic, a suggestive story that points to and plays with the mysteries yet beyond our knowing (I do)—all that is another matter. But regardless of where we go from here, we all know how it begins: in the beginning.

I imagine John relied on people's familiarity with this. It made his departure from what's familiar that much more striking—or rather his stalling out. Whereas the writer of Genesis imagines the word of God, "Let there be light," and the creation of light as but the first step in a long series of steps that gets us to where we are in history, the writer of the Gospel of John imagines this and no more: "In the beginning there was the Word" by which came life and light. No second day, to say nothing of six more days; certainly no seventh day for rest. John imagines things as just getting started.

And so perhaps they were; they *are*.

Did you notice how passive the man born blind was? Unlike those healed elsewhere, this man born blind didn't ask for healing and played no part in it. Think of the others: demoniacs following Jesus, calling his name; a woman with a hemorrhage sneaking up from behind just to touch his cloak; another blind man somehow sensing his presence and his promise, and calling out to him that he might he healed; a paralyzed man whose friends lowered him on his mat through a hole they'd made in the thatched roof, so crowded was the house in which Jesus was teaching. Unlike any of these, really unlike any others, this man didn't have such faith as to make him well, didn't have such friends to push his case for him, didn't have want of healing perhaps at all. Really, he was little more than an object made useful to the disciples for a lesson in morality and theology: "Rabbi, who sinned, this man or his parents, that he was born blind?"

I'm not thrilled about that.

Here he was, we might suppose, sitting in a doorway or in a rare spot of shade, covered in dust and begging of passers-by, all as usual. Here he was, perhaps content or at least familiar with his routine, and adapted to what little he might expect of life, which isn't such a bad thing. Not all of us need to be go-getters. Not all of us need to strive for a better life. Sometimes there's blessing in being content with what you've got, even if what you've got is not a lot.

But then came Jesus—Jesus, whose interest wasn't really in this man but in the larger point he meant to make about God. Yes, here came Jesus who recognized in this unassuming man a chance for God's works to be revealed in him. And suddenly this man's life, familiar, if not entirely comfortable, was no longer *his* life but belonged to all sorts of people who meant to make a point of him.

We might wonder whether he went on to be happy with his new life. We might wonder whether, when all was said and done, the man born blind was now happy with sight. After all, his blindness might have been his livelihood. His blindness might have been the thing about him that made others have mercy on him and so act with charity in his regard. His blindness might have made his begging somewhat more profitable. What's more, there are contemporary stories of people born deaf getting cochlear implants or people without sight getting ocular implants. These stories don't always have the happy endings we want. Some people never can adjust to the jangling world of hearing, the glaring world of seeing.

We might wonder, was he happy?

Our writer, John, would have us know. We just have to work for it.

There was some confusion as to whether the supposedly healed man was the man who'd once been blind, or if perhaps he was someone else and the (still) blind man was now missing, nowhere to be found. Maybe this hadn't really been a miraculous healing, people on the street supposed, but a case of mistaken identity. The neighbors and those who had seen him before as a beggar began to ask, "Is this the man who used to sit and beg?" to which some answered, "It is he," and others said, "No, but it is someone like him." So much confusion! But all the while, there was one clear voice speaking up, the voice of the man himself. He kept saying, "I am the man," or, in Greek, "*Ego eimi.*"

These are powerful words in the Gospel of John. Reminiscent of the name which God uttered for himself: "YHWH" or "I am than I am" or "I am that which is," *ego eimi* should grab our notice. Here it should all the more so because this is the only time these words refer to anyone other than Jesus. Everywhere else in this gospel, it's Jesus who says this and it's Jesus to whom it refers. "I am the bread of life." "I am the light of the world." "I am the gate for the sheep." "I am the good shepherd." I am the resurrection and the life." "I am the way and the truth and the life." "I am the true vine." "I am he, the Messiah." The fact that here it's *not* Jesus but a once-blind man saying this should pique our hearing. Transformation happened here, and awesome as it is to give sight to a blind man, this is actually the least of what's gone on.

So was he happy with what happened? Who can say? Are you made happy by your faith, and by all it would have you see and know?

Is happiness really what this is all about?

One thing seems certain; he was made a full human here. Though at first approached as an object, he comes into full subjectivity. Notice, please, that he is the only one in the whole story to speak in terms of the first person singular. He's the only person to speak in terms of "I." The Pharisees are "we." The man's parents are "we." Both cast him as "you," so to be separated out from "we." But only he speaks in terms of "I." And I think there's such power in this: to know yourself, to speak for yourself.

I'll admit I'm not a joiner. I'm my father's daughter in that regard. I don't tend to join groups. I've seldom been successful on a team. I couldn't even cope with summer jobs that involved a uniform—and by uniform I mean guidelines as lenient as khakis and a blue shirt. So maybe this is some neurotic tendency of mine that I've spun self-servingly into a courageous stance. But I do think there is such power in speaking in clear terms of "I" and moreover in terms of "I am."

Danish existentialist and sometimes theologian Soren Kierkegaard suspected that most people are less afraid of being wrong in their convictions than of standing alone in their convictions, and I suspect the same thing. Of course, he was speaking to a church that had become wholly civilized, wholly taken into civil life and governance as to have nearly nothing agitating to say to the world. The state church of Denmark was a comfy place of well-mannered conformity, and Kierkegaard couldn't stand that— a feeling that I imagine fast became mutual. Of course, also, this isn't a problem we face in the American church. We're not publicly funded; we're not slowly dying of an entitled lack of mission. But people are people, and people in groups tend to go slack.

The struggle between the individual and the collective, this most important struggle in the world, according to anti-Communist crusader William F. Buckley, is also an ancient one. God called (and still calls) people into community, and God spoke (and still speaks) to us and through us in terms of "I am."

You know, Jesus came back for the now-seeing man when he heard that the Pharisees had driven him out. This singular "I" now had no one with whom to be "we." One morning last week, as usual while walking the dogs, three strays that we adopted, I was listening to music, and a song came up, "Walking In Your Footsteps," by the Shout Out Louds. In it, the lyricist speaks of feeling like a stray, following someone he perceives to care.[1] And as I listened, I stopped and turned, and there was Daisy, our smallest and strangest looking, right at my heels and now looking up at me, her underbite especially jutting. Her tail twitched and I leaned over to pet her. She was nervous at this, my height coming down on her. A threat? A treat? A treat! Kind words and stroking! "It's like the church," I might have said to her. Jesus has gathered a bunch of strays and called us lovely, beloved friends.

As to why the now-seeing man was cast out, I think there are two reasons.

First, prior to his healing, the man born blind was an uneasy but accepted presence in the Pharisees' proximity. Now, though, as they were

---

1. I can't print the lyric here because I couldn't get permission. But it's a great pop song so find it on the Internet and give it a listen.

pressing him, "How then do you see?" he came too close to them, came even to identify with them: "*We* know that God doesn't listen to sinners, but he does listen to the one who worships and obeys him." This had the Pharisees react. "You were born entirely in sins, and are you trying to teach us?" And at this, the story goes, they drove him out.

Do you see? He'd come too close to them. He'd spoken in terms of we. And whether by we he'd meant himself and the Pharisees or himself and Jesus, either way this outcast had forgotten himself (if only for the moment), had forgotten that when it comes to himself there is only himself. Outcasts aren't supposed to create communities, yet they're also not supposed to be individuated, self-differentiated. They're supposed to be grateful, snivelingly grateful, for whatever attention they get, and otherwise are supposed to be invisible, unseen and unseeing.

A second reason for their driving him out is that to do so would solve the problem of their having become divided amongst themselves. Remember, they'd argued. Some of the Pharisees had said, "This man is not from God, for he does not observe the Sabbath," while others had said, "How can a man who is a sinner perform such signs?" And so they were divided, which they but couldn't let stand for long. It's not for nothing that Jesus says elsewhere, "A house divided against itself cannot stand." As it happens, though, there is one reliable solution for the problem of division among ranks: a mutual enemy, an agreed upon outcast to drive out. And so they drove him out.

And so Jesus came back to claim him—this now completed bit of creation.

The mud, this mud, this *adamah* which Jesus used to the heal the man born blind: this is the very stuff of which Adam in the beginning was made—*adam,* which is "man," and *adamah,* which is "dust of the ground," sharing the same Hebrew root. Jesus rubbed *adamah* and saliva on this *adam's* eyes, and so healed him, completed him. And, of course, this is what Jesus meant when he claimed that this man was born blind not because of sin but so that "God's works might be revealed through him."

"Why?" the disciples had asked. "Why was he born blind? Who sinned, this man or his parents, that he was born blind?" And Jesus' answer might seem callous, might sound dismissive of the real pain this real human subject might have suffered—indeed it did to me as of just a few minutes ago. "Neither this man's parents nor he himself sinned; he was born blind so that God's works might be revealed through him." But it's important to note that there are several ways to understand cause, that there are a few ways to understand Jesus' saying "so that."

One is that God purposely has left things incomplete *so that* Jesus will work a miracle and God will be glorified. This certainly seems to match this gospel's main agenda. John seems principally interested in getting people to see, to recognize and embrace Jesus as the Son of God.

But, of course, God intentionally allowing people to suffer in order to get glory for himself once the suffering stops is a problematic notion. It actually sounds a lot like the Stockholm Syndrome, wherein hostages fall in love with their captors. So here's another way to imagine this situation and Jesus' response to it, a framing that would have been more noticeable in Aramaic, the language that Jesus spoke, than it is in English, our very cause-and-effect language. The fact of this man's blindness presents an opportunity for Jesus to do the work that was his work to do. The fact of this man's being not yet complete, almost fully made but with yet unseeing eyes, presents itself as an opportunity for Jesus to put on the finishing touches, for Jesus to perfect and complete.

Can you hear the difference? The former ascribes intention to the state of things: God meant for suffering, God meant for imperfection in order to be glorified himself. The latter merely accepts things as they present themselves, as yet imperfect, as yet incomplete, and responds accordingly.

I have to say, this is one of my favorite ways to approach a day: "Let's see what happens." This is one of my favorite ways to approach my own work, either here among you all or with my children or whatever: let's see what presents itself and I'll hope to respond rightly. You know, there's all this literature about church leadership that puts such emphasis on the importance of planning, strategic planning that is, in the church world, called "envisioning." Congregations should plan and strategize, then program and evaluate. And I'm sure such things have their place. I'm sure there are congregations that, big as they are and so budgeted as they must be, benefit from visionary leadership and strategic, data-based decision-making. But I'm also sure there are congregations in which all that would be stifling, foreclosing, of what opportunities the Spirit might present. The Holy Spirit, after all, in my experience at least, is nearly always surprising and moreover delightful, the very stuff that cannot be planned for and, worse, the missing of which drains all the fun out of being people of God.

So how about we just take this as it comes?

Jesus' answer to the disciples certainly seems to imply the theological truth in such a way forward: "Neither this man's parents nor he himself sinned; he was born blind so that God's works might be revealed through him." Jesus' answer seems to be saying that the assumption of the disciples ("Who sinned . . . ?") isn't at all the right way to come at understanding God and God's creation—for God doesn't punish sin. God works it out. Literally, God works it out—a potter working with air-pocked clay, a baker working with dough that it might rise. And it was this work, this ongoing yet unfolding divine work, that Jesus meant to reveal, meant to perform. This is what he meant: God is yet creating and Christ is yet with God creating. The man born blind wasn't born so because he was sinful or because his parents were sinful but simply because the creation is yet incomplete, is yet imperfect.

And so we see Jesus performing such work even on the Sabbath, working the works of him who sent Christ rather than resting as if the work were already complete. The reason there is no Sabbath rest in John's "in the beginning" is because the God's work of creating is not yet complete. According to John, we're yet amidst those first six days.

This gospel would also make the bold, if puzzling, claim that all would at last be complete in the cross, in this ultimate act of self-giving love, Jesus' dying words according to John being these, "It is finished." But as it is, we're only halfway through, in the ninth chapter of twenty-one chapters. And this lands us here, on this Lenten morning. Easter is yet ahead, the revelation of the cross that is the end—when love has won, when self-giving has proved saving, when life (and not death) has come to sustain life, and when Christ rests at the right hand of the Father for the world is filled with the knowledge of God as the waters cover the sea.

Yes, Easter is yet ahead. Meanwhile, we of the church are charged as Christ was charged to do the work of him who sent him, as Christ then charged the man born blind, the man made to see, to wash in a pool of Siloam (which means Sent).

Yes, meanwhile we are to see and to be sent, for there's work to be done and (good news!) it's ours to do.

Thanks be to God.

What Grows at Gould Farm
(Should Also Grow in Church)

They came to the other side of the lake, to the country of the Gerasenes. And when he had stepped out of the boat, immediately a man out of the tombs with an unclean spirit met him. He lived among the tombs; and no one could restrain him any more, even with a chain; for he had often been restrained with shackles and chains, but the chains he wrenched apart, and the shackles he broke in pieces; and no one had the strength to subdue him. Night and day among the tombs and on the mountains he was always howling and bruising himself with stones. When he saw Jesus from a distance, he ran and bowed down before him; and he shouted at the top of his voice, "What have you to do with me, Jesus, Son of the Most High God? I adjure you by God, do not torment me." For he had said to him, "Come out of the man, you unclean spirit!" Then Jesus asked him, "What is your name?" He replied, "My name is Legion; for we are many." He begged him earnestly not to send them out of the country. Now there on the hillside a great herd of swine was feeding; and the unclean spirits begged him, "Send us into the swine; let us enter them." So he gave them permission. And the unclean spirits came out and entered the swine; and the herd, numbering about two thousand, rushed down the steep bank into the lake, and were drowned in the lake.

The swineherds ran off and told it in the city and in the country. Then people came to see what it was that had happened. They came to Jesus and saw the demoniac sitting there, clothed and in his right mind, the very man who had had the legion; and they were afraid. Those who had seen what had happened to the demoniac and to the swine reported it. Then they began to beg Jesus to leave their neighborhood. As he was getting into the boat, the man who had been possessed by demons begged him that he might be with him. But Jesus refused, and said to him, "Go home to your friends, and tell them how much the Lord has done for you, and what mercy he has shown you." And he went away and began to proclaim in the Decapolis how much Jesus had done for him; and everyone was amazed. (Mark 5:1–20)

LAST SUNDAY MORNING, I took the dogs on a walk as usual—on a three-mile there-and-back through state land between the river and the railroad tracks. And, as usual, Lucy and Gus found an exciting trail to follow that led them out of my sight. Also as usual, Daisy, the little one who'd get lost easily in the thickets and woods and tall grass, stayed close by. She'd make a good snack, she seems to know.

We've been kicked off nicer walks than this, and due to bad behavior. There's a lovely meadow near St. Helena's chapel, a circle tended by people in the parish. It's called the Meditation Meadow. But it's devolved into something of a dog park recently, so its keepers earlier this spring sent out a gently worded letter asking all dog-walkers to use leashes because the neighbors had begun to complain of wanderers and trespassers.

This was a deal-breaker for me, and moreover for Lucy. Before we adopted her, she had been a street dog whom I imagine loved the freedom of it. To be on a leash, then, during her walk would defeat the purpose of the walk, of the run, of the mad-fun dash. When we put in an electric fence around the house and yard, she seemed genuinely depressed by it, staying inside and on the bed for nearly a week. I imagine also that she didn't mind the begging her prior life of freedom had cost her—begging for food, begging for shelter in rain. She has a winning way about her. Ugly as she is, people tend to find her adorable.

She went missing on Sunday morning. I heard wailing in the distance, but it was deep so I thought it was Gus. I turned toward it—the wailing, ran toward it though not sure where it was coming from. The woods, the thick bramble: how would I find it? I called his name—"Gus! Gus!"—and it seemed he would answer. I'd call and there'd be a howling response. Caught in thorns, caught in a beaver trap, caught in something sharp and scary and painful. "Gus! Gus!" I ran and got closer to the sounds, and then I was getting father away, or they—the sounds—were getting farther away from me. Between them and me were brambles so thick I knew I wouldn't be able to push my way through them, to say nothing of what Daisy could manage. Then there was the fact that I had to get to church. I was running out of time.

I took out my phone and called Jesse, still in bed at home. "I need your help," I said short of breath, short of emotional reserves. And I knew he'd be electrified out of bed at this, moments only before he'd be at the trailhead, now scared himself. So I ran toward the trailhead, away from the howling, Daisy at my feet, me trying not to kick her in the face. I turned a corner, from woods to meadow, and there, wagging and jolly if a bit confused, was Gus.

Oh my God. It had been Lucy. But it hadn't sounded like Lucy.

Oh my God. Coyotes.

I haven't seen her since, except in the many pictures I've posted on Facebook, on my wall, on the walls of rescue agencies, on the walls of friends who've shared the photo. One person commenting on the Lee/Lenox Animal Control page wished us the best. "I'd be beside myself," she wrote.

Funny. That was the very phrase that came to me in Bible study at Gould Farm on Wednesday when we read this story.[1] We're reading through the Gospel of Mark, the earliest gospel and also the shortest, which makes it a good choice for reading aloud as a group over however much time it takes to get through it. It's also action-packed, brief and dense. It keeps you moving. Having that phrase—to be beside oneself—come to mind in that gathering and then again on my Facebook wall as regards my missing Lucy spurred me to depart from the lectionary and go with preaching on this.

You could argue that it wasn't such a great decision. After all, we only a few weeks ago heard this story, though according to Luke so it was only a few weeks ago that I preached on this—the encounter between Jesus and the man in Gerasa with the legion.

Then, I made a lot of the fact that this so-called demoniac was possessed by many demons, which called themselves "Legion." I made a lot of the fact that legion is a military term, was then a term used to name a Roman military dispatch. I claimed this man was occupied in the same way the region of Gerasa was occupied, in the same way the whole Middle East was occupied. The Roman Empire had extended its reach far and wide—and this was both blessing and curse. *Pax Romana*: there's a lot to be said in favor of peace through strength. But Jesus' healing of the demoniac seems to imply that he's more in favor of peace through peacemaking, peace through healing, peace through mercy and vulnerability and forgiveness. His driving out the demons so named Legion seems to imply that the sort of peace empires offer is cheap and tragic compared to the sort of peace the gospel intends and inspires.

It was a good enough sermon. I stand by it. I'm going to preach a different sermon now.

We don't ever hear this story according to Mark. We don't ever hear it according to Matthew, though it does appear in each of these, too. This

---

1. I lead a spirituality group, which is sometimes in the form of a Bible study, at Gould Farm each week. Though the farm is an unlocked facility where the guests are free to come and go, it can be difficult to get rides in our car-reliant town to groups like the one I lead. So I go to them. I also have lunch there, where the food is terrific and where I might even be able to sit with my husband, who is Gould Farm's prescribing psychiatrist.

is somewhat rare. Not very many are the stories that appear in all three synoptic Gospels, Matthew, Mark, and Luke. And it's hard to know how to interpret the fact of those that do Are we to take such stories as especially important, especially telling or emblematic? Or is it that such stories spoke to the situations of each of the three communities for whom these gospel writers wrote their narratives, in ways either particular or universal? Or is it that these stories by some accident of history were more widespread, more enduring, though not necessarily more important? We don't know. We *can't* know. In the case of this story, though, the lectionary resolves the question by including it just once every three years, during Luke's year, Year C. This is the year in which we now find ourselves. But during Year A, when Matthew is our guide, and Year B, when Mark is, the Gerasene demoniac is uncharacteristically quiet.

What made him otherwise so noisy is a question for debate. It's most easily thought that what was once believed to be demon-possession we now know as mental illness. Certainly the symptoms might suggest this, the howling, the cutting, the suffering. Also the remedy is reminiscent of the way people with mental illness were treated before medicines were common—to be chained up, to be locked up—God be praised that we're largely past this. No, as I've said before, I think it's problematic to consider mental illness as a modern-day equivalent to being possessed by an unclean spirit.

On the other hand, there's so much we don't know about mental illness, and the sad fact is that the people who suffer live often as outcasts, even as the living dead.

This man of ancient Gerasa was very much so. Living among the tombs, his only company was the dead.

And so it was with such tender caution that I read this story with the Gould Farm spirituality group. Not everyone in the Bible study has mental illness, just as not everyone at Gould Farm has mental illness. But certainly the proportion of those who do is greater than in your average Bible study. "Who has felt a multiplicity of selves within themselves?" I wondered as we considered this story. "Has anyone here ever felt at conflict with yourself about something, at odds with yourself, out of your own mind?"

I wasn't being coy. No, for I think it's likely that we all have. Considering how many phrases we've got for this phenomenon, this experience—to be of two minds about something, to be out of your mind, to be beside yourself—it's likely that everyone knows this experience to one degree or other.

Here's something: in this gospel, when Jesus had performed several healings and so had begun to attract huge crowds; when he then returned to his hometown and his family heard that he was back, they went to get him, to try to restrain him for people were saying he was out of his mind or, as might be transliterated from the Greek original, people were saying he had "gone outside."

Going outside is big in this gospel. Jesus is often seen going out—*out* to pray all alone, *out* to be tempted in the wilderness, *out* of homes and villages and towns. When Jesus steps out we should hear it as a risky thing, as a trailblazing thing. *In* is where you're safe, where you're seen after. *In* is the structures we build to give us shelter, shade in the summer and warmth in the winter and no rain on your head when it's raining out. *In* is the society by which we are known, are indeed knowable. *In* is a holding environment—our homes and families, our villages and tribes, the cultures we establish so as a people we might thrive. *Out* is chaos, wilderness, death.

Or is it?

The further out Jesus goes, the further out he brings God's light and life. The more often Jesus goes out, the more he reveals as provisional these things that we've taken as absolute. The final thing out of which Mark remembers Jesus to have gone is the tomb, as if even death's containment is just for a time. And whenever Jesus goes out, he collects more outcasts to be his friends. The more often he goes out and the longer he travels on this ministry of in and out, the more people there are who gather around him—now himself a center, a still point, the focus and aim.

The church is said to be a community of outcasts whose center is the ultimate outcast. The church is *meant* to be a community of outcasts whose center is the ultimate outcast. But this isn't always the reality. Some churches are much too upstanding to stand for that. After all, the crucified as Lord: how crazy is that?

This weekend Gould Farm celebrates its 100th anniversary. One hundred years of picking up strays, taking in lost causes, harvesting hope for recovery where others can promise only a cycle of loneliness and locked units—Gould Farm does better than most Christian congregations I can think of at being a community of would-be outcasts amidst whom there is salvation, inexplicably, and against great odds salvation, healing. And mind you, it's hard. I'm very aware that it's hard. Ask anyone who participates in the life of Gould Farm—guest, volunteer, staff member, board member—and you'll hear of any number of ways in which it's hard. And that's important talk; that's important to consider.

But so is this: I'm better for having Gould Farm in my life, a better pastor, a better person. And I know I'm not alone in receiving such benefit; indeed, I'm not the foremost in receiving such benefit. And there's this: the church in Monterey is alive for having Gould Farm as a partner in the work of the gospel and a wellspring of faithful souls trickling or flowing into what might otherwise be a backwater congregation. And there's this: the town of Monterey is more real for having such a farm in its midst. We harvest all sorts of things in Monterey—second homes, recreation and relaxation, high culture and folk art; hay and syrup, vegetables and flowers; and, by virtue of Gould Farm, hope. Has there ever been a more essential crop?

"Has anyone here ever felt a legion within yourself—a whole sackful of jangling drives that compel you in all directions and no direction?" I wondered of the group. For it's this scattershot consciousness that I think Jesus means to heal us of. It's this that I think Jesus means to save us from. That we might not disintegrate into all these jangling drives but have integrity in our desire—a desire for God; that we might love the Lord our God with all our mind, heart, soul, an strength—this God who is the Lord, who is One; that we might be one focused on the one who is One. In this our souls might find rest and so it is this that Jesus intends, as for the Gerasene demoniac, so for us.

"Has anyone here ever had such a legion within them?"

I have, I said, leading the way into the thicket of such thinking. This week, my dog went missing, I explained, and I've been a distracted wreck. My mind is always partway with her, wherever she may be. Hurt? Scared? Trapped? Or having a blast, running with a coyote or two, or after deer or two? I keep thinking I should be at that trailhead waiting for her to come happily or guiltily around the bend, late as she has been many times before, but never this late. Or I should be at the copy shop making posters and then out posting them. Or I should be on the phone calling shelters and rescue leagues and vets. Or I should be searching the woods for signs of struggle and searching the sky for circling birds of prey. I'm very exhausted because I've got this split down the middle of my being, this splintering of my attention and awareness.

Well, a lost dog is a pretty good problem to have. I know this. So when Jesse, "Dr. Goodman," my husband, came home from his workday at Gould Farm on Wednesday, and he showed me what the clinical team had done for me—made posters by cobbling together pictures and information about Lucy that I'd posted on Facebook—I came a bit undone. They'd done this because I hadn't managed to put together posters yet and the people who'd been at the Bible study mentioned our loss. They'd done this so now we'd have something to pin up around the neighborhood. They'd done this for us.

How is it, I wondered—and I think I even asked Jesse—that these people engaged in the urgent work of recovery, and from most devastating illnesses, have time for my lost dog and my wandering, searching, outside?

The work done at Gould Farm is the work of a Savior who holds close those who might as well be living among the tombs that they might now come to be clothed and in their right minds. This happens at Gould Farm for those with major mental illness and for those with run-of-the-mill human predicament stuff. And it's a process, a sometimes hard process. We are none of us the Savior; we are none of us the Christ. But we are *all* of us just this, or so we might be. We are *all* of us just this: saving, healing, redeeming.

That's what we've been told, anyway. That's what Jesus promised. By the presence and power of the Holy Spirit, we might be the very body of Christ. And there are good and valid reasons why such overtly Christian rhetoric cannot be proclaimed at Gould Farm. Though the farm did spring, a century ago from the imagination of a man informed by the gospel and the church, Will Gould, there are good and valid reasons to speak now in different terms. We cannot risk alienating by rhetoric those who need good care.

But here, it's a different matter. Here, in this place, among this people, we can say that Gould Farm's mission is as Christ's mission. And so I say quite frequently, thanks be to Gould Farm, though not quite as frequently as I say this:

Thanks be to God.

An Easy One

Just then a lawyer stood up to test Jesus. "Teacher," he said, "what must I do to inherit eternal life?" He said to him, "What is written in the law? What do you read there?" He answered, "You shall love the Lord your God with all your heart, and with all your soul, and with all your strength, and with all your mind; and your neighbor as yourself." And he said to him, "You have given the right answer; do this, and you will live."

But wanting to justify himself, he asked Jesus, "And who is my neighbor?" Jesus replied, "A man was going down from Jerusalem to Jericho, and fell into the hands of robbers, who stripped him, beat him, and went away, leaving him half dead. Now by chance a priest was going down that road; and when he saw him, he passed by on the other side. So likewise a Levite, when he came to the place and saw him, passed by on the other side. But a Samaritan while travelling came near him; and when he saw him, he was moved with pity. He went to him and bandaged his wounds, having poured oil and wine on them. Then he put him on his own animal, brought him to an inn, and took care of him. The next day he took out two denarii, gave them to the innkeeper, and said, 'Take care of him; and when I come back, I will repay you whatever more you spend.' Which of these three, do you think, was a neighbor to the man who fell into the hands of the robbers?" He said, "The one who showed him mercy." Jesus said to him, "Go and do likewise." (Luke 10:25–37)

THIS ONE'S EASY. "Go and do likewise."

Thanks be to God.

Actually, wait. Of whom are we to go and do likewise? After all, lots of people in this story have gone and done. Whose going and doing are we to imitate?

Well, that's easy too. The Samaritan's, of course—this is the one whose actions should be our actions. He's the "good" one, after all. It says so right in the title of the story: "The Good Samaritan."

I know, that's not the actual title of the story. That's something convention has tacked on for the sake of convenience. But why not? It's a good title. It is, after all, what the story is about: a Good Samaritan. I mean, what else could we call it? "The Bad Thieves"? That's too obvious; it has no "punch." The "Compromised Clergymen"? That's just picking the low hanging fruit. "The Vulnerable Pilgrim"?

Hmm.

* * *

I've said it before and I'll say it again: parables aren't allegories, and they're not fables; they're not "moral of the story" stories.

An allegory is a story that offers a one-to-one correlation—its characters to the real world. *Pilgrim's Progress* is an allegory. It features characters with names like Pliable, Timorous, Hopeful, Prudence, and the star of the show, the pilgrim of the title, Christian. One of the places Christian stays on his journey is House Beautiful, which sounds a lot like the ideal church and its congregation. That's an allegory, which is not a parable.

A fable usually features animals acting as people, and they typically either attempt an explanation for some natural phenomenon or an exhortation for caution or courage or curiosity or some other virtue. "Little Red Riding Hood" is a fable. The talking wolf, the innocent in the woods, the protective woodsman, the high-stakes threat of death, and the low-stakes assurance that everything turns out alright in the end—the fable warns that there are dangers out there and that innocence is a mixed blessing. That's a fable, which is not a parable.

A "moral of the story" story, not a technical term, is a story that has a clear moral revealed at the end. Parables typically have no moral to the story; they might even be said to be amoral.

This story that Jesus told, though, comes close to having moral, right? "Go and do likewise," is one way of saying, "And the moral of the story is . . ."

The difference is, the snag is, that Jesus doesn't say of whom the lawyer should go and do likewise.

Welsh New Testament scholar C. H. Dodd defines a parable as "a metaphor or simile drawn from nature or common life, arresting the hearer by its vividness or strangeness, and leaving the mind in sufficient doubt about its precise application . . . " And what a parable is *for* is "to tease the mind into active thought."[1]

Southern preacher Fred Craddock claims, "The parable as such would be contradicted and destroyed by being explained and applied."[2] In other words, if you can explain the parable, you've killed the parable. More troublingly, if you can apply the parable, you've missed the point.

1. Dodd, *Parables*, vii.
2. Craddock, *As One*, 54.

But, listen, the man was asking for what he must *do*. "What must I *do* to inherit eternal life?" He wanted action steps! He wanted direction. No, he wanted *directions*.

("Carry no purse, no cloak, no sandals," I seem to remember Jesus just having said.)

So I'm frustrated, and not just on his behalf—the lawyer who got a parable instead of a moral or a lesson or instructions as to how to live. (Ten Steps to a Better You, Seven Steps to Happiness and Fulfillment.) I'm frustrated on behalf of me, on behalf of us. After all, isn't this why we come to church? Isn't this why we go to such bother to gather and to listen—that we might live, that we might know how rightly to live?

So people who know seem to know that the parables by which Jesus spoke and taught defy direct application. Yet Jesus did most of his speaking, teaching, preaching in parables. Moreover, Jesus himself *became* something of a parable. So, what exactly is this movement that he began if it has no direct application in life, in our lives? What exactly is Christianity, is following Christ, if it's not about right living?

* * *

Jesus told the man first to consider the law. When the lawyer approached Jesus, meaning to test him, "What must I *do* to inherit eternal life?" Jesus first had him consider the law. "What is written there? What do you read there?"

That the lawyer stood up to test Jesus likely has us skeptical about his motivations. After all, those who test Jesus are a questionable crew; those who are remembered to have tested Jesus aren't company we're likely meant to want to keep. Satan in the wilderness, some Pharisees, and this scribe, this lawyer—the ones remembered to have tested Jesus—aren't remembered to have done so in a generous spirit.

And I get this. Off the top of my head, I can think of a couple times when I felt people were testing me, questioning me as to judge the legitimacy of my being a pastor. Both times coming from more doctrinaire Christians than I am, I resented their testing me, I grew defensive at their questions. To one I even said, "I feel like you're testing me," to which she replied a forcibly casual and pleasant, "No, no. I'm just curious."

But recently I was listening to a podcast whose news host made this passing comment. To the point of how credentials in some fields are more important than others, he said, "I don't care if my clergy person just got his ordination over the Internet, but I'd like to know that the pilot flying the airplane I'm on has formal training." I'm the daughter of an airline pilot, as many of you might know. So this comparison hit a little too close to home. Of course, I want the pilot flying the plane I'm on to know what he's doing. But I want the person preaching at me to know what she's doing, too. I've never sat happily—in a pew, in a lecture hall, in a classroom—while the person up front demonstrates to me little or no authority. And I certainly don't want to put you in that position as this whole set-up is rigged to have me talk while you listen. The church is ill served by clergy who might as well have gotten their credentialing over the Internet. The gospel is ill served by leaders who seem not to know what they're doing and who moreover can't tolerate or withstand being tested on that question once in a while.

When Jesus lived, there were apparently lots of people promising lots of things—salvation, healing, wisdom, a better way. When Jesus lived there were messiahs on every street corner. So this lawyer stood to test Jesus. And, so, maybe we shouldn't shun him for that; maybe we shouldn't shame him for that. Maybe we should thank him, admire him for that. After all, Jesus could—indeed did—withstand it. "What is written in the law?" he responded to the test. "What do you read there?"

The law was the right place to start. For this lawyer looking for action steps, the law was exactly the right place to start. But what he found there isn't exactly straightforward: "You shall love the Lord your God with all your heart, and with all your soul, and with all your strength, and with all your mind; and your neighbor as yourself."

For what it's worth, what the lawyer recited is actually two laws, though well conjoined. The former is to be found in Deuteronomy 6 as part of the *Shema Israel*, which Jews are to recite twice daily, which they're to post in mezuzahs on their door frames and to teach their children, which they're to aim to have as the last words they shall ever speak in life. The latter is in Leviticus 19, to be found amidst a long list of commandments concerning moral and ritual holiness.

That the lawyer picked these two out of four law books in which there are a sum total of 613 commandments tells us something about this man and the tradition in which he was raised. These are supple commandments. As far as action steps are concerned, these are nuanced and challenging ones.

"You have answered rightly," Jesus said.

But wanting to justify himself, the lawyer didn't stop there. "And who is my neighbor?" That is, who is the one I am to love?

I suppose his hope was that the neighbor whom he was to love was nearby and would be somewhat easy to love. Not some foreigner, not some stranger, the one he was to love was, I suppose, someone (he hoped) he'd already managed to come to love. He was, after all, the story says, trying to justify himself. He was, after all, trying to prove to himself and likely to others that he was already fulfilling his duties as a child of God, that no more stretching and striving was necessary. And of course, we know that the gospel isn't about stretching and striving, that living in the light and life of God isn't about earning our place there. Living amidst the kingdom of God is about faith not works. And yet faith without works is dead: the gospel calls and we're to respond, we're to respond by *doing* something, *doing* something different.

"A man was going down from Jerusalem to Jericho . . ."

* * *

Jews and Samaritans were sworn enemies. Neighbors in the land—Jews on the west side of the Sea of Galilee and Samaritans on the east—Jews and Samaritans were similar enough that their differences meant a lot, a whole lot. Their cultic rituals shared an aim, the Living God; but they differed in means. Their cultural and social bonds shared a similar framework, a law code; but the laws themselves differed a bit. They were similar enough; they were as siblings. But you know how siblings are. I, for one, love my sister, am more dedicated to her than I am to nearly anyone else, as she is to me; but there's no one on earth who gets to me the way she does.

A couple chapters earlier in this gospel, the disciples were traveling with Jesus through Samaritan territory. Jesus had just set his face toward Jerusalem; that is, he'd set his aim as the city where he knew his ministry would culminate, likely in catastrophe. And on his way there, he and his disciples found themselves needful of a Samaritan village for a place to stay. But the village refused to receive him, refused to receive them—and because they were headed to Jerusalem, the cultic center of the Israelites. Jesus and his disciples were of their deadly rivals, and they were heading into the heart of their deadly rival. So they refused to receive them. As to the disciples' response to this? "Lord, do you want us to command fire to come down from heaven and consume them?" to which Jesus replied, "No," rebuking them and simply leading them to another village for the night.

Meanwhile, there was, quite the opposite of any and every Samaritan, a priest, whom every Jew would have known was a good guy. The lawyer listening to Jesus tell this story would have known it; the disciples perhaps listening in would have known it too. Everyone would have known that the priest was the good guy.

And yet the priest passes by the beaten man on the other side. And who knows why? It might have been for concern of becoming ritually unclean. It might have been for fear that the robbers who'd done the beating were still around, were looking for other victims; or for fear of merely being on this road, this road that was indeed a dangerous one. It might have been that he was busy and in a rush to get to Jericho. (Peter Gomes played with this idea. Worried as all preachers are as to how we come across in this story, Rev. Gomes of Harvard's Memorial Church at Harvard thought perhaps this clergyman was on his way to a meeting to discuss how to make the highways safer for pedestrian traffic.)

Meanwhile also, there was, quite the opposite of any and every Samaritan, a Levite, whom every Jew would also have known was a good guy. The Levite as one who answers to an even stricter law code than normal Jews of the time, he might have held particular standing in this lawyer's mind. He might have been someone this lawyer held in special esteem.

But he, too, passed by on the other side. (Perhaps hurrying to that same meeting?)

Then came the Samaritan, the "good" Samaritan, the one of whom we're to go and do. (That's settled, right?) Though likely shocking to the lawyer, to the disciples, to the earliest hearers of this story, it's so obvious to us, so clearly the case. There's even a hymn that accepts this interpretation as the only interpretation: "I know who's my neighbor and whom I should love, for whom I should do a good deed; For Jesus made clear in the story he told, it's anyone who has a need, yes, anyone who has a need."[3]

Odd that the preacher didn't choose this hymn for us this morning.

* * *

It's funny how universally we've accepted the role of the one who shows mercy as the role we're to fill. It's striking how universally we've rejected the role of the one who is vulnerable, beaten, in need of mercy as the role we're to fill.

---

3. Wesson, "They asked," 541.

"Which of these three, do you think, was a neighbor to the man who fell into the robbers?" Jesus asked the lawyer. In other words, which of these three is the one whom the commandment "Love your neighbor as yourself" would have you love? Which—the priest, the Levite, the Samaritan—is the one whom you are to love?

The question isn't who is the one you're to *be*; the question is who is the one you're to *love*. In other words, assumed in the story is that you are the one vulnerable, beaten, and in need of mercy.

Jesus means for the lawyer to love the one who showed him mercy. Jesus means, by extension, that we're to love those who show us mercy. This story doesn't indicate that we are to be merciful (though we certainly are). This story indicates that we are to love those who show us mercy, which puts us in the role not of the Samaritan, who in this story has a tremendous amount of power, but of the one beaten and left for dead and in need of mercy, the one whose travels leave him vulnerable and whose circumstance casts him powerless.

"Blessed are the merciful," Jesus said according to Matthew, "for they shall receive mercy." I wonder if he'd also have said, "Blessed are those who receive mercy, for they shall be merciful."

* * *

A conversation I had with a colleague about this story had him claim, laughingly, that he'd never refuse help from anyone who had it on offer when he had a need. If he needed help, it wouldn't matter to him who was offering it. The assumption was that we were in agreement on this point: if we're in need, there's no one whose help I would refuse.

And this is true of me on one level, I think, as it is likely true of all of us. If I needed help, I wouldn't refuse such an offer based on the potential helper's ethnicity or group identification. I wouldn't refuse help based on that. But I would refuse help. There are times, there are circumstances, in which I would refuse help, I have refused help. And it's never out of some formality; it's never out of, "Oh, no, please, allow me." It's always out of a primal, tearful need not to be in need; and it always takes me by surprise.

The offer for help is too sweet; I can't manage it.

My need for help is too immediate; I can't take it.

The moment of need and mercy is so small and sudden that it reveals something deep and always true—and I don't want it to be true.

"No, I've got it," I say, begging. "I got it," I say with now more force, such that sometimes the mercy I end up receiving is the other pretending along with me that I don't need help, that I've got it all under control.

I've refused help in circumstances like that. Have you?

* * *

It's funny how universally we've accepted the role of the one who shows mercy as the one we're to fill. It's striking how universally we've rejected the role of the one who is vulnerable, beaten, in need of mercy as the one we're to fill.

* * *

We are all traveling the road from Jerusalem to Jericho. We are all pilgrims on a journey that could land us in need at any time. We are this as individuals; we are this as a nation. We are this as families and households; we are this as congregations. As often as we might be helpful, merciful, we are in need of help, in need of mercy. Or we are to be such things, at least. To "go and do likewise," is to say that we should proceed into the world, proceed into the day, as vulnerable as we are forthright, as circumspect as we are self-assured. ("Carry no purse, no cloak, no sandals," I seem to remember Jesus just having said.) We will balk at this. We will recoil from this. We'll arm ourselves against this and defend ourselves against this. We'll stand our ground. We'll preempt.

Or we won't. And it will be a sweet surprise, too touching to manage, too moving to hold at arm's length—the mercy that God has sent out in Spirit, sent out by way of Samaritans whose sweetness surprises.

Which will it be today?

Thanks be to God.

Surprise Parties

Let mutual love continue. Do not neglect to show hospitality to strangers, for by doing that some have entertained angels without knowing it. Remember those who are in prison, as though you were in prison with them; those who are being tortured, as though you yourselves were being tortured. Let marriage be held in honor by all, and let the marriage bed be kept undefiled; for God will judge fornicators and adulterers. Keep your lives free from the love of money, and be content with what you have; for he has said, "I will never leave you or forsake you." So we can say with confidence, "The Lord is my helper; I will not be afraid. What can anyone do to me?" (Hebrews 13:1–6)

On one occasion when Jesus was going to the house of a leader of the Pharisees to eat a meal on the Sabbath, they were watching him closely . . . When he noticed how the guests chose the places of honor, he told them a parable. "When you are invited by someone to a wedding banquet, do not sit down at the place of honor, in case someone more distinguished than you has been invited by your host; and the host who invited both of you may come and say to you, 'Give this person your place,' and then in disgrace you would start to take the lowest place. But when you are invited, go and sit down at the lowest place, so that when your host comes, he may say to you, 'Friend, move up higher;' then you will be honored in the presence of all who sit at the table with you. For all who exalt themselves will be humbled, and those who humble themselves will be exalted."

He said also to the one who had invited him, "When you give a luncheon or a dinner, do not invite your friends or your brothers or your relatives or rich neighbors, in case they may invite you in return, and you would be repaid. But when you give a banquet, invite the poor, the crippled, the lame, and the blind. And you will be blessed, because they cannot repay you, for you will be repaid at the resurrection of the righteous." (Luke 14:1, 7–14)

THE TEMPLE OF POLISHED marble that is One Liberty Square in the financial district of Boston had a couple of strange visitors the other day. It was otherwise picture-perfect. The white marble floors and white marble walls of the lobby gleamed, so smooth. Men in gray suits and women in gray suits walked with purpose, heels clicking. But outside the bathroom door, to the left of the bank of elevators, leaning against the drinking fountains—which were shining silver and oddly dry, making one wonder whether anyone ever drank out of them—were a couple of scooters, one a Razor scooter, the other a Whiplash scooter, both favorites among the middle school set.

As for me, I stood in the high-ceilinged hallway waiting for the boys, my two sons, who were indeed in the bathroom, making use of it before we climbed in the car to head back home. Three floors beneath this temple lobby we'd parked our car for its proximity to South Station. We'd spent two days in Boston before having to get back to school. We'd spent this day down by the harbor and then in the financial district, me on foot, our friend and houseguest Petr on foot though now ready to board a bus from South Station, and the boys on their scooters racing, careening, setting pigeons to flight and pedestrians to stand aside.

It turns out the financial district is ideal scootering terrain. Who knew? Wide and mostly depopulated plazas, smooth flooring inside and out, revolving doors: the boys were in heaven. Most other creatures of this pinstriped ecosystem ignored them, as if they were not only unnoticed but unrecognizable—but by one man. We saw him a little later in the morning—he who was an anomaly among his kind for wearing no jacket as he made his way down the street, but just his suit pants and a white shirt and tie. He was an anomaly also for moving not crisply. The wind rumpled him like it didn't seem to anyone else. He looked up at the plaza in front of Bank of America, with its fountains and its security guards and its matching trees and now with its T-shirted boys scootering and yelling, "Arriba!" whose meaning they clearly didn't know. He looked at them, smiling and puzzling this over. Then he saw Petr and me, also clearly not of this place. I asked the man "Do you remember being that free?" "I wish," he said, and I believed him.

Back in the lobby of One Liberty, though, the man approaching the bathroom had even less to go on. He'd come clicking around the corner from the grand main lobby into this side hall leading to the elevators, the bathrooms, and the drinking fountains. He'd come knowing what to expect. Tall, good-looking, he was a master of his universe. At the sight of the scooters, though, unmanned and at rest, he might as well have been looking at a couple horses parked there, braying, kicking the ground, ready to go. He might have wondered, he might have turned to look suspiciously at the security cameras, "Am I being punk'd? Am I on *Candid Camera*?"

The boys coming out of the bathroom settled the question for him, but not entirely.

Surprise!

* * *

Did you know that the Greek original rendered in English as "hospitality" is *philoxena*? That is literally "love of the strange."

I'll admit that the book of Hebrews is one of my least favorites of the Bible. Strange to say, it's just too preachy and high-minded for my taste.

The Letter to the Hebrews is included among the letters in the New Testament—letters to specific congregations and mostly written by Paul, some undoubtedly so and some under dispute. But it's an anomaly among its kind because no authorship is claimed and no specific people are addressed. It's an anomaly also because this is less a letter than a collection of essays or perhaps sermons. This is to say that its commonly conceived title, the Letter to the Hebrews, is wrong on both counts. This is neither a letter nor is it necessarily to the Hebrews.

Discuss.

All that said, there are a few gems here. This collection of sermons does have quite a few gems on offer.

There is this, the definition of faith that still rings true even now, 2000 years later: "Now faith is the assurance of things hoped for, the conviction of things not seen."

And there is this, the litany of those who "by faith" prevailed: "By faith, Abel offered to God an acceptable sacrifice . . .," "By faith, Abraham obeyed God . . ." "By faith, Moses led the people . . ." "By faith, the people followed him through the Red Sea."

And there is the way in which this litany concludes, with words of encouragement to a people weary of waiting: "Therefore, since we are surrounded by so great a cloud of witnesses, let us also lay aside every weight and the sin that clings so closely, and let us run with perseverance the race that is set before us, looking to Jesus the pioneer and perfecter of our faith, who for the sake of the joy that was set before him endured the cross, disregarding its shame, and has taken his seat at the right hand of the throne of God."

And finally there is this, this grab bag of wisdom and guidelines for living as Christ would have the church do: "Let mutual love continue. Do not neglect to show hospitality to strangers, for by doing that some have entertained angels unawares."

Surprise!

This, of course, is thought to be a reference to the three strangers whom Abraham and Sarah welcomed into their tent by the Oaks of Mamre. These strangers, as you might remember, would be one more voice of promise that Sarah, though old, would soon bear a son. And remember, too, that Sarah laughed, laughed in the tent where she was preparing a welcoming meal, which the strangers heard and which Sarah denied, but at which she did indeed become pregnant to bear a son whom she and Abraham would name Isaac, which means "son of laughter." In sum, we might say that the angels she entertained were not mere messengers of a promise; they were a means of grace. Yes, if her son Isaac was indeed a son of laughter, then among his parentage was in some way the Spirit by which such laughter is possible.

But entertaining angels unawares might also be the Pharisee who'd invited Jesus to the Sabbath dinner. The fact that the lectionary has these two readings paired together is coincidence. We've been making our way through Luke's gospel these past four months, and we've been hearing the greatest hits from the Letter to the Hebrews these past four weeks, which is to say this pairing is not on purpose. But the shared theme of hospitality is worth noticing.

What's also worth noticing is how strange indeed Jesus was at this otherwise decorous feast.

This should come as no surprise to us by now. Neither the fact that he's about to eat nor the fact that he was strange should come as any surprise to us by now. Luke's gospel does, after all, remember Jesus as eating a lot. Really, as Luke tells it, Jesus was either always on his way to eat, was eating, or was just leaving the table—and yet never as the host but always as the guest. So, too, Jesus is ever defying expectations, healing people on the Sabbath, paying attention to women, claiming children as ones who will most easily enter the Kingdom of Heaven. Really, Jesus, in this as in all four gospels, is indeed very strange, might even be regarded as rude, offensive.

Last time I preached on this text, this is what I supposed. And I wasn't necessarily wrong. After all, at this particular Sabbath meal, Jesus is remembered to have told three stories (though we only hear two as we follow the lectionary), all three of which imply some criticism aimed toward others at the meal.

The first seems aimed at the guests: "When you are invited by someone to a wedding banquet," Jesus said, "do not sit down at the place of honor, in case someone more distinguished than you has been invited by your host."

Well, this isn't a wedding banquet, but Jesus' comment does come into the room a little too closely.

The second seems aimed at the host: "When you give a luncheon or a dinner, do not invite your friends or your brothers or your relatives or rich neighbors, in case they might invite you in return, and you would be repaid. But when you give a banquet, invite the poor, the crippled, the lame, and the blind." Well, this isn't a luncheon the host has thrown, but it is a dinner, the Sabbath dinner. So either the host has failed to live out Jesus' instruction or he has succeeded at this, and the guests should know themselves to be the poor, the crippled, the lame, the blind—those unable to repay the host for what he's given them.

The third, which we didn't hear but is of a piece, is also the most peculiar of all, featuring a host who invited many people to an upcoming, but apparently unscheduled, dinner party. The would-be guests perhaps responded that they would come, but when the dinner was at last ready and the slave was sent out to tell the people that now was the time, they each had had other things come up. One said, "I have bought a piece of land, and I must go out and see it; please accept my apologies," while another said, "I have bought five yoke of oxen, and I am going to try them out; please accept my apologies," and still another said, "I have just been married, and therefore I cannot come"—all valid excuses for their having now to refuse the invitation.

Consider: these would-be guests were important people in society, and their conflicts are proof of that. These weren't "I changed my mind, I don't like the others invited, I have to wash my hair" kind of excuses. These were people living up to their responsibilities. Rather than going to a dinner party, they were doing what they ought to do in order to keep society going. In fact, you could argue that the fault of the stalled-out dinner party falls on the host, who had kept everyone guessing as to when it would be until he announced, "Everything is ready *now*."

So out goes the slave to round up a second-string group of guests—the poor, the crippled, the blind, the lame. And, lo and behold, they're free to come just now. But why wouldn't they be, for they have nothing else to do. They're the ones who stand on street corners and sit on stoops waiting for something to happen—for work to find them or for help to come or for a passer-by to take some interest and start up a conversation. They're the ones who wait for life to find them rather than those who have the wherewithal to go out and make their lives happen. And yet they're the ones who will taste the great host's dinner.

Offensive, these stories!

Rude, this storyteller, this provocateur!

Or perhaps just strange, surprising. Who's to say that some of those around the table weren't delighted by these strange stories?

We've recently hosted a houseguest, Petr, who was visiting from the Czech Republic, come all this way to attend Film Night at Tanglewood. A twenty-three-year-old man (he arrived on his birthday), he was born a year after the Velvet Revolution that turned Czechoslovakia, a Communist state, into the Czech Republic and Slovakia, both now democratic states. It took some time, though, for technology and the arts to arrive from the West. Petr was eight years old when he got his first audio CD. It was of John Williams's music, themes from *Star Wars, Indiana Jones, Superman,* and the like. He was enthralled. At twelve, he received a Casio keyboard whose demo reel played the *Star Wars* theme song, and by it he learned to play the piano, first playing along to the demo reel, then playing along when seeing Williams's movies on TV, then venturing off on his own, composing his own tunes. He is now a graduate student in music composition, and he's really talented. So to come to Film Night at Tanglewood, perhaps even to meet John Williams—this was what his summer has been all about.

He stayed with us for a week, we managed to get him a few moments with John Williams, and Film Night was a crowning affair. But the thrill for *me* was having a stranger in our midst and to be a stranger to someone else. To be certain, he was sweet, a thoroughly easy guest. But he was also strange. Sometimes we couldn't understand each other (though, to his credit, his English is a lot better than my Czech). More often, though, his attitude and manner were just slightly out of place, while, to hear him describe it, what made America strange were the small details, every single one of which was different than in "CZ." Most surprising of all, how much I now miss him.

Bible scholar Erik Heen thinks twice about the exhortation of the writer of Hebrews to the Christian community that they practice hospitality, and he recognizes, "At one level it is astounding that this beleaguered, suffering, and vulnerable community—one that had experienced the *loss* of property . . .—is asked to open itself up as a patron to strangers."[1] But then he considers it from another angle: "Many ancients were locked into lives

---

1. Heen, "Commentary," para. 10.

of routine and did not stray far from their places of birth. Life was difficult and mobility was limited. . . . Hospitality was provided, then, by those who had 'love of the strange,' by those who were curious about the wider world. . . . [And in this] was a kind of marvelous exchange, . . . of mutual benefit between host and guest. The guest received protection (inns were dangerous places), food, and company. Hosts were led out of themselves and their 'little' worlds. . . ."[2]

Last time I preached on this text, I thought on the challenges of hospitality—that to open yourself up to guests who might conform to your expectations of behavior and demeanor, or who might not, is a gracious art; that to open your life and your home and your table up to people who may or may not be as you anticipate they will be is a strain, a risk. But it's one that Christ would have us do.

And that's a good lesson for the church. That's a good reminder, for some congregations more than others. "All are welcome," we proclaim. But do we really mean it? What expectations do we hold even as we say, "*All* are welcome"?

But here's the same exhortation from another angle, again from Professor Heen, "Rather than an obligation, 'love of the strange' . . . provides the opportunity to be blessed by exposure to the wider world that God cares deeply about. . . . In the church's 'love of the strange' one actually encounters Christ [who is himself strange, a stranger] . . . Hospitality, then, is a gift that feeds and nourishes *us* as well as our guests."[3]

Well, the end of summer takes away many of my sources of strange. Houseguests have come and gone. The children are back in school. One of our three dogs remains missing, which makes the house that much less chaotic and explosive and bizarre. Happily, I still have this little church I serve. And I've said it before, but I'll say it again: when we open our doors on Sunday morning, that right there is a very strange thing because we never know who's going to come through them. Of how many other buildings can that be said? (I can tell you this, the buildings of the financial district do not adhere to the same convention. We were "excused" from the plaza out front of the Bank of America, asked to stand on the opposite side of the street if we were going to stand nearby at all.) But here, in this building, the doors open, and anyone can come on through. And, of course, we can usually predict who all that will be. We just as easily know where almost

2. Ibid., para. 11–12.
3. Ibid., para. 14.

everyone will sit. But just as usually, there's someone here who comes as a surprise, who comes as a stranger. To them I say, "Come, eat; and tell us a story of who you are that we might know the Lord's creation all the better."

Hey, I wonder how you guys feel about surprise parties—because you're at one.

Thanks be to God.

And Speaking of Power
An Aside

I FIND MYSELF IN a foreign place in my life. As a mother of two growing sons, I find myself thinking of power in a new way, or at least more frequently than before.

I come from a girl-world. With a sister, with female cousins, with a strong mother, and two very strong grandmothers, I realize now that the boys I knew early in my life were few and the men were mild mannered. I realize that the games I played or heard of others playing were seldom about power, were more about relationship, and that the assumed aim in life was seldom about having power or gaining power, but about being in relationship.

But now I have it all around me, and, while I don't want to overdraw the gender difference, I have to admit I am struck by it. Tobias and Jack are interested in power, as are their friends with whom they mostly play games of power. They are interested in becoming men of power: they dream of inventing things that solve big problems; they dream of discovering things that excite and inspire. They dream of governing, and in such a way that makes wrongdoing illegal; they dream of policing, and in such a way that makes wrongdoing impossible! They dream of exploring and laying claim to; they dream of spying and saving the day. They envision themselves being strong and confident, supermen really. They imagine themselves having six-pack abs, and they don't even know what a six-pack is.

Of course, they're playing out a larger cultural fantasy. Or is it a human fantasy—for haven't we long imagined and hoped for such things? From the ancient Greek concept of the *deus ex machina*, the god who rushes in from offstage to rescue those in distress, to the contemporary myths of superheroes that crowd the screens of multiplex after multiplex, we humans fantasize of beings whose power is invulnerable, yet whose goodness is unassailable and so who will keep themselves in check. I mean, the one licensed to kill never goes on a shooting spree. The one who broods over the city by night never has his way with a citizen or two. The one who can see through everything but lead never becomes a Peeping Tom. Like the long-ago Israelites who demanded a king, we yet dream of someone who will be mighty and good, all-powerful and all good, ever protective and never exploitative—all fine things to wish for, but only with a close eye on what we do with those wishes.

Meanwhile, many in the church eschew power as itself an evil. Though the word "power" is woven into our liturgy ("the power of the Holy Spirit" "the kingdom, the power, and the glory, forever") many in the church, as I know it at least, disavow power as if this is good and right to do.

But as I watch my sons and their friends play, I begin to question the wisdom of such disavowal because the truth is, I want them to be men of power. I'll say more: that they become men of power is a prospect in which I find grounds for hope. After all, we've got problems in need of solving, and they're big ones that demand boldness in our response—the sort of boldness I see them playing out every day.

So, be men of power, I tell them; I tell them in both word and deed—as I rise to my own power (rowing again and racing and writing a book!)

I also tell them, please don't be gym bunnies. Please don't mistake muscles for strength.

And remember that power dwells in its readiness to serve. Strength is self-giving.

Really, what I hope I'm telling them in all sorts of ways, even as I tell myself, power exists not for its own sake but in its availability to be poured out for the sake of something greater and grander and far more glorious than any one of us.

I say this as a woman who was once a girl who played at being in relationship; I say this to boys who will become men who will have once played games of power. I say this also as a preacher for God's sake. Power-in-relationship is, I believe, both our means and our end. To leave out relationship is to risk becoming brutal, cruel. But to leave out power is to doubt and to undermine our good purpose; to leave out power is even to commit violence against those whose well-meaning will to power is crucial to our collective success.

There was once a time when I might have shamed those whose will to power is a primary drive in life. I'd have been wrong to do so. Now is a time when, with one eye on my boys, I'd instead say, "Go for it. Actually, let's go for it together."

You Can't Do That

Isaac prayed to the Lord for his wife, because she was barren; and the Lord granted his prayer, and his wife Rebekah conceived. The children struggled together within her; and she said, "If it is to be this way, why do I live?" So she went to inquire of the Lord. And the Lord said to her, "Two nations are in your womb, and two peoples born of you shall be divided; one shall be stronger than the other, the elder shall serve the younger."

When her time to give birth was at hand, there were twins in her womb. The first came out red, all his body like a hairy mantle; so they named him Esau. Afterwards his brother came out, with his hand gripping Esau's heel; so he was named Jacob. Isaac was sixty years old when she bore them.

When the boys grew up, Esau was a skillful hunter, a man of the field, while Jacob was a quiet man, living in tents. Isaac loved Esau, because he was fond of game; but Rebekah loved Jacob.

Once when Jacob was cooking a stew, Esau came in from the field, and he was famished. Esau said to Jacob, "Let me eat some of that red stuff, for I am famished!" (Therefore he was called Edom.) Jacob said, "First sell me your birthright." Esau said, "I am about to die; of what use is a birthright to me?" Jacob said, "Swear to me first." So he swore to him, and sold his birthright to Jacob. Then Jacob gave Esau bread and lentil stew, and he ate and drank, and rose and went his way. Thus Esau despised his birthright. (Genesis 25:21–34)

"DISRUPTIVE INNOVATION" HAS BEEN the subject of much media chatter lately. This is the catchphrase of Harvard Business School professor Clayton Christensen—disruptive innovation. Christensen is known for his interest in why companies fail, and he wrote a book in 1997 called *The Innovator's Dilemma*. This explored the possibility that established companies in established fields had little incentive to innovate, had incentive in fact *not* to, and so innovation often came from outside, and sometimes came then to devour those established companies and even those established fields.

Consider your iPhone and all its apps. How many industries have such things undermined?

Now this idea has taken hold in much the same way these innovations do. It started small, but now it's everywhere, most recently in the pages in the *New Yorker* magazine, Jill Lepore having taken it up in last week's edition. "Ever since 'The Innovator's Dilemma,' everyone is either disrupting or being disrupted," she writes.

> There are disruption consultants, disruption conferences, and disruption seminars. This fall, the University of Southern California is opening a new program: "The degree is in disruption," the university announced. "Disrupt or be disrupted," the venture capitalist Josh Linkner warns in a new book . . . in which he argues that "fickle consumer trends, friction-free markets, and political unrest," along with "dizzying speed, exponential complexity, and mind-numbing technology advances," mean that the time has come to panic as you've never panicked before. . . . Much more disruption, we are told, lies ahead."[1]

It's not uncommon that something takes hold, becomes fashionable, becomes ubiquitous, then falls under critique and is declared passé before I become aware of it, if at all. I'm often late to the party (except to actually parties, to which I always seem to arrive early, once even a week early). And so it has happened with disruptive innovation. Jill Lepore takes long and well-researched issue with this thing that I only discovered as compelling. And while all the hype and fury around this concept seems comical to me, the idea underlying it strikes me as useful.

Lepore is less convinced. "Every age has a theory of rising and falling," she writes, "of growth and decay, of bloom and wilt: a theory of nature. Every age also has a theory about the past and the present, of what was and what is, a notion of time: a theory of history." And she traces these changing theories through time: "Theories of history used to be supernatural: the divine ruled time." But then "progress" came to dominate the narrative of history. Starting in the eighteenth century, "The idea of progress—the notion that human history is the history of human betterment—dominated the world view of the West between the Enlightenment and the First World War. It had critics from the start, and, in the last century, even people who cherish the idea of progress, and point to improvements like the eradication of contagious diseases and the education of girls, have been hard-pressed to hold on to it while reckoning with two World Wars, the Holocaust and Hiroshima, genocide and global warming."[2]

And thus we reach the age of innovation—this notion that, according to Lepore, "skirts the question of whether a novelty is an improvement. . . .

1. Lepore, "Disruption Machine," para. 4–5.
2. Ibid., para. 8, para. 10.

[Innovation, then, is] the idea of progress stripped of the aspirations of the Enlightenment, scrubbed clean of the horrors of the twentieth century, and relieved of its critics. Disruptive innovation goes further, holding out the hope of salvation against the very damnation it describes: disrupt, and you will be saved."[3]

It's a foolish faith, she seems to believe, this faith in the power of innovation to save—foolish because it's all based on a book (Christensen's) whose evidence the author apparently cherry-picked (though people critiquing Lepore's critique claim she's done the same in return), foolish moreover because it claims to be not only descriptive but also predictive, promising that its adherents will be able both to look back and notice the innovations that have brought us to this place, but also to predict what innovations are to come (and therefore which to bank on). "Faith in disruption," Lepore writes, "is the best illustration, and the worst case, of a larger historical transformation having to do with secularization, and what happens when the invisible hand replaces the hand of God as explanation and justification."[4]

It's here where I part company with Lepore. I'm with her, on the platform, while the bandwagon of innovation gallops its way, reckless, into every facet of the future. (Does anyone ask the difference between disruption and destruction?) I stand with her watching while people unquestioningly call every novelty revolutionary, and then invest in it maniacally. But as far as her claim that today's innovation is the project of a God-starved world, I stand apart from her. As far as her claim that "faith in disruption" is a strictly secular enterprise (and which she seems to think is a tragic flaw), that to believe in the promise of innovation is to believe in "the invisible hand" and is not to be believe in a provisional, providential God: I say Lepore doesn't know her Bible.

To be fair, Lepore doesn't claim to know her Bible. I, however, do. This is what I bring to the table.

Rebekah gets a bad rap. For her favoring Jacob, she gets a bad rap. And for her machinations to establish Jacob as the patriarch who would carry on the mission of this people—that they become a great family whose members numbered more than grains of sand in the desert—she gets a bad rap. We see her sly hand at work less in this scene than in one yet to come. But the seeds of her work are here, in her favoring Jacob. And can't

3. Ibid., para. 10, para. 13.

4. Ibid., para. 30.

you just hear the chorus of criticism? Can't you just join it? "Mothers aren't supposed to have favorites."

It's worth wondering, however, why she does so.

As it happens, I am the mother of two boys who, though companionable, are very, very different from one another. And if I lived in a society in which the first-born son was expected to carry the mantle of leadership into the next generation, expected without question, I'd be tempted to do what I could to free Toby from such an ill-fitting fate and to free Jack to rise to where he really, really needs to be.

Toby is a content child; Jack is ambitious. Toby likes the outdoors and free time to make up play; Jack is verbal and social, though he doesn't know his own age. Jack can get a paragraph into the space between Toby's words. Toby's a love; Jack's a thrill-ride; and as such, I'd venture in saying that if anyone in my family is going to be president, it's not likely to be Toby; and if anyone is going to tend carefully to his relationships and home life, it's less likely to be Jack.

All of this is to say, I can easily imagine Rebekah considering her two sons—the older a wild man of the hunt, and the younger a quiet man of the tents; and then considering her tribe's traditions of the first-born son having to carry the culture forward into the future; and finally coming to the conclusion that this old formula simply is not going to work, not with the new challenges that lay ahead.

And of these new challenges, they meant that too much was at stake for just going along to get along. Too much was at stake with this generation. The stakes were the same as in the generation prior—that this people was to become *the* people to carry this notion and experience of God into the future; that this people was to be *the* people to move from relating to the divine and the world in terms of household gods and tribal gods to relating to the divine and the world in terms of a universal God whose eye is on all, whose creative work is revealed in all, and whose presence is available to all. The stakes were the same as when the call rested upon Abraham and Sarah; it's just that the circumstances were different, the challenges different. Then, the challenge was whether Sarah and Abraham would have a child through whom the people would become a great family spanning the world over. Now, the challenge was whether this people could move from subsistence to sustaining, from a hand-to-mouth existence to one that was invested and well founded.

Esau showed no signs of being able to manage that move. This is clear in the story that we just heard. That he was willing to sell his birthright for some stew; that he was so short-sighted as to see no value in his status as eldest son—to say nothing of a sense of responsibility; that he even despised such things because he was *that* hungry: Esau showed no sign that he could make the move from subsistence to sustaining.

But, you know, this might well have been evident of him from the beginning, from the moment when he first began to reveal himself and to be known. Really, this is a fact of him that Rebekah might long have known. You know that marshmallow test—the one in which a young child is put in a room to sit at a desk on which sits one marshmallow? Left alone now, the child has been told that he or she can either eat the one marshmallow now or wait about fifteen minutes at which time the child can have two marshmallows. I imagine Esau as one of the children who ate the one marshmallow just as soon as he got the chance. And I imagine Rebekah as a mother who might notice such a tendency.

"Let me eat some of that red stuff, for I am famished!"

Robert Alter is a professor of Hebrew and Hebrew literature whose commentary on this story is helpful.

First, Alter translates it thus: "Let me gulp down some of this red red."[5] And he notes that, although in the telling of these ancient stories the voices of the characters as they're quoted in speaking is usually the same as the overall narrative voice, here the voice in speech is quite degraded. That is, "the writer comes close to assigning substandard Hebrew to the rude Esau. The famished brother cannot even come up with the ordinary Hebrew word for 'stew' and instead points to the bubbling pot impatiently as 'this red red.'"[6]

What's more, "the verb he uses for gulping down [this red red] occurs no where else in the Bible, but in the rabbinic Hebrew it is reserved for the feeding of animals."[7] Of course, this linguistic trend takes place long after this story was so written down, so we should be careful to read this evidence in the right direction. The word choice might indicate that the writer saw Esau as bestial, but it also might indicate that Esau came by tradition to be seen as bestial and so the writer's word choice came to have that ring to it. More complicating yet is the fact that Esau's name came to be the name

5. Alter, *Five Books*, 131, n. 30.
6. Ibid.
7. Ibid.

of Israel's perennial enemy, Edom, and that this enemy is said to suffer the same crude impatience as Esau did.

But trying to peel back all these layers of implication and aspersion, I wonder if we can remember Jacob and Esau as two men, two boys, a pair of brothers. Whether or not they have such historical reality, I wonder if we can suppose for a moment that they do—that they were real, that they were complicated, and that they were both created by God to serve in their generation for purposes that God would gather in and make God's own. Whatever shortcomings each had—Esau and his appetites and need for instant gratification, Jacob and his trickery and calculated getting ahead— could come to be incorporated into the larger story of God-with-us.

Here's what Esau may well have managed to do—to keep his family and household somewhat well fed while the society transformed from hunting and gathering to more settled and invested farming. (And this is no small thing. Really, many Americans could attest to how the megatrends of history can leave crushed those caught in the day-to-day dwindling of resources and opportunity.) And here's what Jacob may well have managed to do—to usher in a new mode of living for his people and (if we take this story as emblematic) for all of human history, a mode based on the delay of gratification, on investment for the sake of future generations, of planning and storing and meting out. (And this is no small thing, as in just the next chapter it's said a famine has come to the land—the very sort of thing that separates those living by subsistence from those living more strategically.)

I feel cautious about preaching a sermon that seems to vaunt white, middle-class American values as the best values by which to live, indeed as God-intended and God-blessed. And I feel wary that this is what this sermon is suggesting. But then I hold in mind such underdeveloped places that have whole swaths of the citizenry living very vulnerable lives—namely, women and children, vulnerable to violence and rape, starvation and exploitation; and I hold in mind that some such places have been saved from chaos by someone establishing there a bank, a place where people can entrust their earnings, which then incentivizes investment, which then stabilizes the whole society. And then I wonder, were I not to vaunt the sort of values that nurture my life and the lives of so many I love, would this would be one more way that my privilege remains privatized?

I remember a conversation I had with a classmate in divinity school. She said she wanted to go into the ministry, but she also wanted to make a good living, to make good money. I said, "Oh, you shouldn't make money the guiding principal in your life." She, a Hispanic-American woman from Los Angeles, said to me, "You've never been poor." She was right.

Well, there's a lot I don't know. But here's one thing I do know: God wants God's creation to live and all in its midst to thrive. What's more, the way forward at the point in history when Jacob and Esau are said to have lived seems to be a way of settling down and getting established, of planning ahead and (yes) delaying gratification. God wanted God's people to live and to thrive, planning ahead and delaying gratification were the means by which they would do so, and Rebekah was perhaps the first person to understand this and to innovate that this might come to pass.

Did you notice, though, this thing that Rebekah did—this, which I'm calling a disruptive innovation—is not *necessarily* something she did out of a secular worldview? Yes, it's possible she feared that God's promise would not come true, and so she had to take matters into her own hands. But it's also possible that she knew God's promise would come true, and moreover by the means of God-with-her disrupting convention. Yes, it's possible that she knew God's promise would come true—would do so through her confidently breaking with convention and finding a better, more sensible way for society to move forward so to sustain life.

In sum, Jill Lepore's take that disruptive innovation happens apart from God strikes me as the very same secular move that she decries in the culture of innovation for innovation's sake; for it's just as possible that God—God himself, God herself, the God we meet in Scripture and tradition—is the ultimate disruptive innovator.

Virgin birth, anyone? Talk about disruption of more conventional means!

The project of disruptive innovation has become quite goofy, and in some cases full of false promise. But the hope that, by our minds and imaginings, and then by our labor, we might forge a new future for ourselves and for God's whole creation isn't goofy. It's the gospel—persistent and faithful.

The events of Jacob's generation of the people of God are never said to have involved that hand of God at work. The story itself never explicitly confesses that all of these events are "God's plan" or "God's doing." No, instead they're said to have come about through the machinations and manipulations of regular old people—flawed but faithful to the promise, hapless but hopeful that God was providential and providing for them.

And so God was. That these stories became scriptural stories, that these people and events became folded into the grand story of God-with-us:

this is all to look back and to see, in the herky-jerky movement of history, God at work indeed—yet not controlling, but responding to events as they unfolded on the ground and providing in the midst of ever-changing circumstance.

Well, these people are our ancestors, and their project is our project. The details differ, but the challenge is the same as it ever was. Much of what has worked for us in the past isn't going to work for us much longer, and we can't go back. Much as we might want to, desperately as we might try, we can't go back. So, it's time for something new.

You know, I often wonder who is somewhere right this minute coming up with the latest pivotal offering.

Blessed be that garage lab, or that basement studio or study. Blessed be that tent-city schoolhouse or that tenement rehearsal space. Blessed be those who disrupt a status quo that is perhaps good enough but isn't in any absolute sense good.

Let's not stop—not here, not now. Let's keep going.

Thanks be to God.

Cheek

"You have heard that it was said, 'An eye for an eye and a tooth for a tooth.' But I say to you, Do not resist an evildoer. But if anyone strikes you on the right cheek, turn the other also; and if anyone wants to sue you and take your coat, give your cloak as well; and if anyone forces you to go one mile, go also the second mile. Give to everyone who begs from you, and do not refuse anyone who wants to borrow from you.

"You have heard that it was said, 'You shall love your neighbor and hate your enemy.' But I say to you, Love your enemies and pray for those who persecute you, so that you may be children of your Father in heaven; for he makes his sun rise on the evil and on the good, and sends rain on the righteous and on the unrighteous. For if you love those who love you, what reward do you have? Do not even the tax-collectors do the same? And if you greet only your brothers and sisters, what more are you doing than others? Do not even the Gentiles do the same? Be perfect, therefore, as your heavenly Father is perfect." (Matthew 5:38–48)

IF ANYONE STRIKES YOU on the right cheek, turn the other also. If anyone wants to sue you and take your coat, give your cloak as well. If anyone forces you to go one mile, go also the second mile. These are Christianity's greatest hits. We know them well.

What's more, we know how they so often play out—and it's not pretty. Those saintly ones who turn the other cheek and who give not only their coats but also their cloaks and who go the extra mile, those saintly ones who "give 'til it hurts," eventually coil back and turn passive-aggressive. Giving 'til it hurts becomes killing with kindness. And, of course, the church is full of such people and personalities. The rest of the Western world, though, has moved on, "therapized" out of such masochistic madness.

This is all when the words of Jesus are actually taken to be commanding. But there are as many Christians who hear these not as commanding but as merely aspirational. We should *aim* to turn the other cheek; we should *aim* to give not only our coats but also our cloaks; we should *aspire* to go the extra mile. But, of course, we won't be able to, not all the time, not even most of the time. No. So that will be for Jesus to do, and in his so doing our failure so to do will be revealed that much clearer, and so we sinners will be driven into the arms of grace. Blah, blah, blah.

Ugh. Let's talk about something else.

Did you watch much of the Olympics? We Goodmans did, every evening, skiing, snowboarding, figure skating. Amazing! We saw the bobsled, the luge, the skeleton—each one more crazy-risky than the last. As always, I found it all so awesome. But, I have to say, as a nonathlete, I have found just as interesting the unfolding story about Johnny Weir and Tara Lipinski. Have you followed this at all?

Johnny Weir never medaled in the Olympics for his figure skating, but he's had an illustrious career, winning medals in national and world competitions, and taking fifth at the 2006 Olympics and sixth in 2010. Born in Pennsylvania, he's twenty-nine now, and, with Tara Lipinsky, he was one of two teams of on-air commentators for the skating events in Sochi, Russia.

Tara Lipinski, of course, is also a skater, a medalist, in fact. She won the gold in 1998, in something of an upset when she beat out favored Michelle Kwan. She earned quite a few "haters" for that, I half-heartedly among them.

But she persevered in the skating world, as did he. They also became, apparently, good friends. And then they became a team of commentators, though the junior varsity team, so to speak. Their events were aired live from Sochi, which is to say in the morning here, when only a narrow slice of America is watching. The prime-time viewers heard tape from the more seasoned Scott Hamilton and Canadian pairs skater Sandra Belzic, older and more experienced and so trusted with a much wider audience.

But, in true Olympics tradition, there was a bit of an upset. Johnny and Tara sort of stole the show. Not only were they well spoken, and even kind, compassionate, in their commentary (when Gracie Gold fell during her free skate program, all they said was a pained "ouch"), they were also a sight to behold, dressing like a skating pair—sequined or shiny or pink or gilded, and always matching.

Very cheeky they were for network sports anchors.

Cheeky indeed. Weir is gay and, though only recently out (as of 2011), he's never appeared to try to hide the fact. By contrast, Russia under Vladimir Putin is quite the homophobe, in the last six months ushering in all sorts of laws to crack down hard on homosexuals there. One allows police officers to arrest tourists and foreign nationals they suspect of being homosexual, lesbian, or pro-gay, and to detain them for up to fourteen days. Another reclassifies "homosexual propaganda" as pornography, such propaganda being any media coverage of homosexuality that doesn't condemn it. Consider that "the media" includes television broadcasts, newspapers, and online social networks such as Facebook and Twitter. Consider that "pornography" is a punishable offense, an offense that theoretically could land you in prison. Consider, then, that anyone who might attend something like an Olympic event in which someone gay or suspected of being gay participates, and then goes on to broadcast, post, or tweet about this: any such person is subject to arrest and punishment—all of which is to say that anyone could break this law at any time doing the most benign of things, like commenting on an event while wearing something flamboyant.

Johnny Weir is, publicly anyway, almost always wearing something flamboyant. That he did so on TV in Sochi earned him quite a few haters, as well—and I'm not talking about Vladimir Putin and his accomplices. Some supporters of LGBT causes in the US condemned Johnny for taking part, for not advocating a boycott of the Olympics. The online comments following a *New York Times* story from October largely defend him—for doing his job, for not politicizing the Olympics, and for not personalizing them. But there were more than a few detractors, calling him vapid, cowardly, and even a collaborator. Hitting closer to home, though, was his own husband, a first-generation Russian-American: he wanted Johnny at least to speak out, "to be more on the side of the gay team."[1]

But then came February, and Weir did his thing, coiffed, compassionate, articulate, and expert. And it earned this response from blogger Shaunna Murphy of Hollywood Life, a website that is itself quite flamboyant: "Johnny Weir's Olympic Fashion: The Perfect Pro-Gay Putin Rebellion."

She knows that Weir knew what was at stake. "I risk jail time going there," he told the *New York Times.*[2] But he also had an appreciation for what the Olympics mean, not least for the Olympians: he pointed out, also according to the *Times,* "that his parents emptied their bank accounts to pay for his coaching, his costumes, and his travel for him to reach his Olympic goal."[3] Not to have that come to fruition because of a political stance would have been a tragedy to him, and so he imagines it would be for other Olympians. But his worry was less for himself. In an interview with *Philadelphia* magazine, he said, "I'm not trying to be funny here, but Elton John got in and out of Russia for a performance recently. And he dedicated his entire concert, very bravely, to a young gay man in Russia who lost his life recently

1. Macur, "Outspoken Weir," para. 13.
2. Ibid., para. 7.
3. Ibid., para. 10.

by a beating. So I think the problem here is more what's going to happen to the Russian community [than to me]."[4]

At this, Shaunna Murphy wonders, perhaps herself trying to be funny, "[What's Putin] going to do about it? Arrest Johnny for wearing leggings?"[5]

Well, that *would* have been funny, and pathetic: big, tough, bare-chested Putin, in charge of a most beautiful and brutal culture, in charge of a most severe and punitive legal system, marching onto the NBC set to arrest the reigning queen of Olympic commentary all for wearing pink and sequins and make-up but *not* while performing a figure skating routine. It would have been funny—how little it takes to threaten a big tough guy.

Murphy imagined the mantra of Weir's rebellion: "I'm here, I'm queer, I look fabulous in vintage Chanel," while Putin just looks goofy bare-chested on his horse.[6] Now that's cheek.

I looked it up. No one—no one from *Webster's Unabridged* to the on-line Urban Dictionary—seems to think that the mostly British concept of "cheek" and "cheekiness" comes from the Sermon on the Mount. But, you know, Walter Wink might have thought otherwise.

Theologian Walter Wink, recently deceased, has a persuasive understanding of this section of the Sermon on the Mount. It begins with his study of this phrase rendered in English: "Do not resist an evildoer," a phrase too easily heard as encouraging Christians just to take it and take it. Think of the steadfast battered wife. Think of the happy obedient slave. Wink says this is expressly *not* what Jesus was saying. The word rendered "resist," based on its usage elsewhere in Scripture, means not simply resistance but violent resistance, revolt or armed insurrection. Similar to the way some states have construed "stand your ground," it has come to mean, "Shoot first; ask questions later." For this reason, Wink recommends the Scholars Version of the Bible in translation, which renders this, "Do not react violently against the one who is evil." In sum, according to Wink, "Jesus is not telling us to submit to evil, but [also not] to oppose it on its own terms."

"If someone hits your right cheek," Jesus said. But why be so specific? Why the *right* cheek? Here's why. To be hit on the right cheek is to be hit with a backhanded slap. No one in the ancient Near East would have hit someone else with anything other than the right hand. But to hit someone

---

4. van Zuylen-Wood, "Johnny Weir."

5. Murphy, "Johnny Weir's Olympic Fashion," para. 7.

6. Ibid.

facing you with your right hand and to have it land on the other's right cheek is to hit backhandedly and to have been hit backhandedly—and this was a gesture meant not to injure but merely to humiliate, to degrade. With a backhand slap, there's no respect for the other as an equal. This is merely a put-down and stay-down.

So to turn the other cheek is to demand of the one doing the hitting something of a promotion. It's a defiant turn, an empowering turn. According to Wink, "The left cheek now offers a perfect target for a blow with the right fist. But only equals fought with their fists . . . and the last thing the master would wish to do is [to cooperate in establishing] the underling's equality. [Therefore], this act of defiance renders the master incapable of asserting his dominance in this relationship. He can have the slave beaten, but can no longer cow him."[7]

"If anyone wants to sue you and take your coat, give your cloak also." Indebtedness was a "plague" in first-century Palestine, according to Wink; it led to the gross but commonplace exploitation of the poor. In this scene we witness it played out. "A creditor has taken a poor man to court over an unpaid loan. Only the poorest of the poor were subject to such treatment . . . [What's more] the debtor had no hope of winning the case; the law was entirely in the creditor's favor. But the poor man [transcended] this attempt to humiliate him."[8] By offering the creditor not only his coat but also his cloak, he stripped himself bare; and the shame for nudity fell not on the one who was nude, but on the one who sees him nude. The shame born of this scenario—and shame was a weighty thing—fell entirely on the creditor. Moreover, the now-naked debtor has exposed the system's "essential cruelty and pretensions at justice."[9]

"If anyone forces you to go one mile, go also a second mile." The Roman army was ever on the move. Ranking legionnaires employed beasts of burden—slaves and animals—to carry their packs. But most rank-and-file soldiers were on their own to lug their gear—unless they came upon someone in the street whom they could conscript into service, just as Simon of Cyrene was conscripted to carry Jesus' cross. The one limit: they couldn't force anyone to walk more than a mile, and if they did, they themselves were subject to punishment. Just so, Wink would have us notice: "Jesus does not encourage Jews to walk a second mile in order to build up merit

7. Wink, *Powers*, 102.
8. Ibid., 103-104.
9. Ibid., 106.

in heaven, or to [be pious], or to kill the soldier with kindness. He is help-ing an oppressed people find a way to protest and neutralize an onerous practice"[10] or in other words to "take the power back."

Really, in general over the course of this reading, Wink would have us understand: "[Jesus] is formulating a worldly spirituality in which the people at the bottom of society . . . learn to recover their humanity. . . . To those whose lifelong pattern has been to cringe before their masters[their slave masters as the one being slapped, their economic masters as the one being sued, their military masters as the one being conscripted], Jesus of-fers a way to liberate themselves from servile actions and a servile mental-ity. [What's more] they can do this before there is a revolution. . . . They can begin to behave with dignity and recovered humanity now . . . Jesus' sense of divine immediacy has social implications. The reign of God is already breaking into the world, and it comes, not as an imposition from on high, but as the leaven slowly causing the dough to rise . . ."[11]

This is all good news. Mohandas Gandhi thought so—impressed by Jesus' Sermon on the Mount and putting to good use Jesus' counsel. Martin Luther King thought so—also employing the principles here and so changing the world. But what's truly astonishing is that Jesus isn't merely interested in liberating the slaves; he's also interested in liberating the mas-ters. Jesus isn't merely interested in revolution, a turning of the tables; he's interested in enlarging the table so that everyone has a place here. Else why would he say, "Love your enemies and pray for those who persecute you"? Else why would he say, "Be perfect as your heavenly Father is perfect"?

Mind you, perfection isn't flawlessness; it's wholeness. Perfection isn't that which is without blemish; it is that which is without partiality. To be perfect is to be complete, to have left nothing out. Our heavenly Father, who gathers all things, redeemed, unto himself, is so; and we are to be so as well—yet not because we *should* but because, by God's grace, we *can*. And there is joy in this.

Well, the world is a messy place. The world can be a cruel, brutal place. Sometimes the perfection, the wholeness, we seek to participate in will come easily. The sleights to be overcome will be slight; the offenses dividing us will be thin. But sometimes the wholeness we seek will be met with an armored tank singling us out and staring us down, crosses burn-ing on our lawns, dispossession and deportation, the threat of prison time

---

10. Wink, "Beyond Just War," para. 10 under subhead Go the Second Mile.

11. Ibid, paras. 10 and 12.

in some notoriously evil prison—and for crimes no greater than seeking merely to live out our humanity. When things get this extreme, there is something fabulous about the power of cheek to undermine all the terrible, self-serious dignity of dictatorship. I wouldn't wish such a need for cheekiness on anyone. But I pray that it might arise when needed and I rejoice in those times when it does.

Today is Transfiguration Sunday, the last Sunday of Epiphany, the last Sunday before Lent. Every year on this day, we remember Jesus ascending a mountain with a few of his disciples and transfiguring before them—accompanied by Moses and Elijah, which is to say all the Law and the Prophets, and becoming a shimmering glow of light. All three gospels feature this scene, so we hear it every year. But only seldom, very seldom do we hear so much of the Sermon on the Mount. This most well-known, and assumed to be well-understood, text is featured in the lectionary only every three years, and then only when Easter is late. This year, Easter will be almost as late as can be, in mid-April. But even still, we must leave off the Sermon here, just one chapter into its three-chapter span.

Time constrains us. That's one of its gifts. We must make choices. Today's choice was between two spectacles: one on a mountaintop and another rinkside, one of otherworldliness and the other very much here. Lent is some serious business, so on this Sunday just prior I went with cheek.

Thanks be to God.

Here's the Rub

In the time of King Herod, after Jesus was born in Bethlehem of Judea, wise men from the East came to Jerusalem, asking, "Where is the child who has been born king of the Jews? For we observed his star at its rising, and have come to pay him homage." When King Herod heard this, he was frightened, and all Jerusalem with him; and calling together all the chief priests and scribes of the people, he inquired of them where the Messiah was to be born. They told him, "In Bethlehem of Judea; for so it has been written by the prophet: 'And you, Bethlehem, in the land of Judah, are by no means least among the rulers of Judah; for from you shall come a ruler who is to shepherd my people Israel.'"

Then Herod secretly called for the wise men and learned from them the exact time when the star had appeared. Then he sent them to Bethlehem, saying, "Go and search diligently for the child; and when you have found him, bring me word so that I may also go and pay him homage." When they had heard the king, they set out; and there, ahead of them, went the star that they had seen at its rising, until it stopped over the place where the child was. When they saw that the star had stopped, they were overwhelmed with joy. On entering the house, they saw the child with Mary his mother; and they knelt down and paid him homage. Then, opening their treasure-chests, they offered him gifts of gold, frankincense, and myrrh. And having been warned in a dream not to return to Herod, they left for their own country by another road. (Matthew 2:1–23)

HERE THEY COME. ONCE again, here they come, every year.

We'd do well to consider them odd. We don't need to consider them three, though we likely will as we always have. They brought three gifts—gold, frankincense, and myrrh. But that doesn't mean they were themselves three. What they were, though, is odd. Like their gifts, they were definitely odd.

More than that, they might have been upsetting to those whom they met on the streets of Jerusalem, disturbing to those whose paths they crossed. They'd come out of the East, after all. They had come out of the East, like the Babylonians long ago, like the Assyrians less long ago. True, the Romans shook it up a bit by coming out of the West. But the East still emanated suspicion, threat. Who came out of the East but imperial forces with imperial aims? And maybe they were beautiful—richly appointed, ornately dressed, all glint and color-burst. But that could well have been one more way that they upset, disturbed. You're not supposed to dress like that.

And this is very much the point—that they were out of place, that they were out of place in this place among this people. Consider: into this unfolding of a Jewish baby born of Jewish parents to be king of the Jews as promised by Jewish prophets, and even now lying in this stable, in this outpost of the great city Jerusalem, in this land that had been the Promised Land to the Jews; into all this come the Magi. Consider: this is a thoroughly Jewish story—that is until the Magi arrive. And this is the point of their showing up, and of Matthew's remembering it: this King of Jews will have implications not only for the Jews; this Messiah will have reverberations not only as regards the Jews, and not even mostly as regards the Jews, but will draw the whole world into the story of the Jews.

Every Christmas Eve, we recite this hope, which comes to us from the prophet Isaiah: that, through this baby born, the Lord has multiplied the nation; that the Lord has increased its joy. I hear this to mean that God's intent all along has been to fold into God's embrace ever more people. God intends to enlarge God's people. God intends to reveal himself in and through history—God's immanence woven into, and transcendence spanning across, all time and territory, all to the end of gathering all people, all creation, to himself and by way of gathering us to one another.

And this is good news, right?

Certainly, Matthew's Magi would lead us so to believe. The coming together of these two worlds—the Jewish world and the Gentile world—is so seamless, so gracious, as only to be seen as good. What the Magi knew only made sense when mixed with what the scribes knew; and what the scribes knew only gained traction when mixed with what the Magi knew.

The Magi knew the night sky. They were astrologers and astronomers all in one. They knew the material world, the cosmos, the creation; they knew how to read and interpret these regular yet also ever-changing things. And their knowledge opened up to them the rough outline of a world-changing event—that a baby had been born to the Jews and his coming would change everything. A new star in the night sky had somehow led them to this conclusion, and so had led them to Jerusalem, which one could well assume would be the birthplace of such a baby. Jerusalem, the city of David, that great king of old who wrested the city back from the Philistines; Jerusalem, the city of power both politically and religiously—of course a king to the Jews would be born here.

But if what the Magi knew was the night sky, then what they lacked in knowing was the Jewish Scriptures. And why should they know them? Long, detailed, full of contradiction, the Hebrew Scriptures were dense even to those who staked their lives on them. And that, of course, is what the chief priests and scribes were for: to reveal as relevant and commanding those ancient texts, to make the Wisdom of old yet enlightening even now. A paid, professional clergy: such a thing is not to be scoffed at (or not *only* to be scoffed at). And so it was that they were called on—the chief priests and scribes for their knowledge of even the minor prophets, the likes of Micah, who long earlier had proclaimed not only the glorious impossibility that a shepherd would be born to Israel who was from ancient days, but also that this would come to pass in a humbly improbable place, Bethlehem.

And this good news, right? What the Gentiles didn't know, the Jews did; and what the Jews hadn't noticed, some Gentiles had. And this is good, even gracious, news that two distinct, even warring traditions had now together opened up a new way for God into the world, had moreover revealed the whole world as living out one grand story begun and made complete by the one God in whom all things are made one. It's just one big party, and everyone is invited. Everyone will be there! This is good news!

Right?

When Jesse and I were not quite newlyweds anymore, but also not yet parents, which is to say still quite young and just starting out, we made a trip to Paris where Jesse has a cousin. A professor in philosophy, she's a serious-minded atheist. As for me, I was then a new and therefore still eager-to-please pastor. I didn't want to be mistaken for one of those close-minded simpletons. I didn't want to be confused with the sort of Christian who would happily imagine so many people suffering eternal torment following the condemning judgment of a punishing God. We can all be friends, was my theological summation. It's going to be a big party—the here and now, and the hereafter. Everyone's invited and everyone will be there!

"Write me out of that narrative," was our cousin's flat response. "I want no part of your Christ."

"But he's a really nice one," I might well have said. Really, writing people out of the narrative is what we used to do, and people hated that about us. So, now we're writing everyone into it.

Which is good news . . . isn't it?

Yes, until you think about it for more than a moment. Then you begin to wonder, what does it mean for all people, all the world, to be written into one story? What would it look like for all cultures—so varied, so particular (not to mention all individuals, so varied, so particular)—to be written into one, singular narrative? How would that come to be? What would that look like? Yes, think about it for more than a moment and this good news comes to seem either folly or frightening, a sentimental pipe dream or a totalitarian terror-state.

Come to think of it, it might not be a coincidence that it was a Parisian who rejected such a theological stance. After all, totalitarianism is no mere political theory in Europe; it isn't even history for many, but memory, even recent memory. One book I read last year, *Savage Continent*, reminds the reader that the war, which Americans think ended in 1945, didn't end for much of Europe until 1989 when the Berlin Wall fell and Soviet Communism collapsed or retreated. Those wounds have been, in my lifetime, still felt. Those resentments yet burn, yes, slow, but also hot.

Incidentally, this was one of many books I read over the last year about totalitarian regimes. Maybe you noticed; maybe you remember. I began in the East with North Korea, and moved west, from Russia to Latvia to the Czech Republic. It was a slightly bizarre mini-obsession that I indulged, and one whose spur I couldn't quite place—until now, with the return of these oddities from the East. I think it was last year on Epiphany Sunday when I found myself holding in one hand Christ and in the other any number of dictators who meant to bring the world to heel. I think it was last year's Epiphany Sunday sermon when I found myself in this surprising place, where Christ and, say, Stalin seemed not unrelated. And, you know, usually I love it when writing a sermon is a process of discovery; usually I love it when I'm surprised by something a sermon unearths. But when the surprise is that Jesus and the likes of Stalin have quite a bit in common, it's less delight than dread.

It's a resemblance that our writer Matthew may have wanted to call to our attention. Really, this pericope—that is, this scriptural passage—could well be entitled "A Tale of Two Totalities" and might have been intended as a study in compare and contrast. Herod and Jesus: both would be king; both would mean to win the world. But Herod hovers over this story like a toxic cloud, lurks beneath the surface of this story like leviathan. His surfacing brings suffering so profound that it cannot be consoled. Christ, by contrast, is born into the story, a helpless child; no hovering, no lurking, just pitiful need and compelling loveliness. Herod wins subjects by fear and force; Christ wins subjects by vulnerability and grace. And so it is perhaps that Matthew intended to compel from us, his listeners, a decision: Which way will it be? Would we win people by fear and force, or by vulnerability and grace, by self-giving love?

Sad to say, of course, the church has often gone the wrong way, has often in history signed up for the wrong totality. And it's of little good to say, "Never again. We know better now." And it's of little comfort to look around and realize we couldn't achieve imperial power now even if we wanted to and tried really hard. Some people feared, when George Bush was president, that theocracy was a real threat. But ten years on, even the Evangelical church is shrinking; and as for America, we'll go to war for any number of things (I regret to say), but a twisted idea that we do so for Christ, I think, won't be one of them.

Here's something: the Magi returned to their own country, just by a different road.

Yes, let's think about that. The Magi had made this long journey, and they were overwhelmed with joy at the sight of the star coming to a stop over the stable. They were worshipful at the sight of the baby and his mother, and they were generous with gifts, odd though the gifts were, seemingly off the mark and yet also knowing. But then they returned to their own country, just by a different road.

Clearly, they'd been moved by this whole, strange experience. Perhaps they'd even been changed by this hard-won encounter—as signified perhaps that they returned *by another road*. This was to avoid Herod, yes, whose intentions they knew to hold in cautious doubt; this was for some practical purpose. But it also might have had poetic significance, that significance being that they were different now, and so journeyed in the world by a different way, in a different way.

And yet, they returned home never to be heard from again. Come, and then gone.

What is that about?

They might have stayed in Israel. They might have joined. They might have conformed, or at least tried to conform. But they didn't. They didn't become Jewish and they certainly didn't become Christian. Yet there's nothing in the telling of this story that would have us think they were wrong to return home, wrong not to stay and join and conform.

That the Magi come resonates with meaning, implies so very much. That they go might imply just as much.

What does it look like, this world that is held in God's embrace—and an embrace revealed as ever wider, ever increasing? What does it mean that everyone and everything is a member of this one whole, one gracious totality? It means not that everyone needs to become the same, but this much more challenging thing, that everyone needs to become themselves. It looks like not everything becoming uniform but everything becoming fully formed as they are—God-given, life-created, biologically determined, environmentally shaped. This is what the whole world is to become: ourselves.

And I realize that this will be an offense to some. That I can't—that *we* can't—write people out of this narrative: I realize this will be an offense to some. And I regret this. I regret that the world as I see it holds people who don't want to be held, embraces people who really don't need a hug. But what can I do, for to do any less would be to choose the wrong totality?

This tension, this struggle, these unanswered questions—these all mean that we haven't reached the end. The unresolved conflict means there's still much to work out.

The eager-to-please pastor will steer away from such things. The faithful know that where there's difference, there is life.

Thanks be to God.

Ruined

He put before them another parable: "The kingdom of heaven is like a mustard seed that someone took and sowed in his field; it is the smallest of all the seeds, but when it has grown it is the greatest of shrubs and becomes a tree, so that the birds of the air come and make nests in its branches."

He told them another parable: "The kingdom of heaven is like yeast that a woman took and mixed in with three measures of flour until all of it was leavened."

Jesus told the crowds all these things in parables; without a parable he told them nothing. This was to fulfill what had been spoken through the prophet: "I will open my mouth to speak in parables; I will proclaim what has been hidden from the foundation of the world." (Matthew 13:31–52)

I TEND TO AVOID confessional preaching, but not so today.

Brace yourselves.

I've been watching *Spartacus*, its most recent rendering, which is on cable TV and so doesn't conform to cultural standards of decency. It is so absurdly violent that it dwells in that strange land where you shudder, cover your eyes, and then laugh for some relief. And it's so sexualized that it really should make any self-respecting clergyperson blush.

And it does.

It also makes me think. I've never spent any time studying the Roman Empire, which, it's wise to remember, started out as a republic. And, of course, this TV show is something I probably shouldn't consider an introductory course. But it's still got me thinking.

Maybe you know the story of Spartacus. I didn't, in spite of the fact that it was first written down (to our knowledge) just one generation after Spartacus lived, over two millennia ago, and has been told many times since. Popular particularly since the nineteenth century, it has a surprisingly modern ring to it—this early tale of a slave successfully leading an uprising of so many slaves against so many masters.

A Thracian, which is to say a Greek, Spartacus was enslaved to Rome when his village was attacked by one of the empire's legion. It's unclear whether he was once a mercenary who fought for Rome and who turned then against them, or whether he was just a villager in this place that Rome would now take. In any event, he was made a slave and offered for sale at market, where a man named Batiatus bought him to train him to be a gladiator.

Batiatus ran a *ludus*, which was a school for gladiators, and so had many such slaves—these of high rank whose only service was entertainment. They'd fight to please the crowd in the stands who wanted to see a good, bloody fight. They'd fight to thrill the senators in the box seats who, smirking, would seem somehow above it all and yet were very invested in it all. They'd fight to bring glory and honor to their masters and even to themselves—for to own a champion gladiator was similar to owning the Yankees or the Packers, and to *be* a champion was similar to being a first-round draft pick. Conversely, to own a cowardly or reckless gladiator was to be put to shame, and to be a gladiator who shamed your master was to put yourself to death—death by things such as slaughter in the arena or, in special cases, crucifixion.

And in this way, being a gladiator differed from being a Green Bay Packer. Gladiators lived in cages. (Of great strength and skilled in fighting, they couldn't be let loose because they could overpower most people who stood in their way.) Sometimes enslaved for having fallen into debt, other times taken as war booty, they were occasionally volunteers, but only because they were otherwise outcasts with no means to live, no way in to society.

Now, of course, they'd be let in, but only in so far as the arena; and they'd be let out of their cages only to train and to fight.

There was, it seems, a certain discipline to it. But, at the end of the day, it was a discipline to their own deaths. A lucky gladiator would have a glorious death following a long run as champion—death in the arena at the end of a final, well-fought fight against a formidable opponent. Most would die ingloriously, anonymously—maimed, ripped apart, spectacularly let of so much blood, and then dragged away as food for wild animals or just to rot in the sun.

Meanwhile, across the empire, when Jesus said that the kingdom of heaven is like a mustard seed, his hearers would likely have leaned in to make sure they were hearing him right. "The kingdom of heaven is like a mustard seed that someone took and sowed in his field . . ."

We often focus on the fact of its smallness, as Jesus himself seemed to do: "[I]t is the smallest of seeds," he said, "but when it has grown it is the greatest of shrubs and becomes a tree, so that birds of the air can come and make nests in its branches." And in this, we assume, is the lesson; in this is the moral to the story. Good things start small, but can have yet great impact.

But a parable isn't a lesson. It isn't a story that has a moral. A parable is a realm you step into that, disoriented now, your senses altered now, you see and hear anew. A parable isn't a noun, it's been said; it's a verb. A parable isn't something we listen to; it's an action done to us. Jesus "parabled" his followers, and by this they were changed. Jesus parables us, and by this we're to be changed.

This is what he meant when, just moments earlier, he explained to the disciples, "The reason I speak to the crowds in parables is that 'seeing they do not perceive, and hearing they do not listen, nor do they understand.'" He was eager for this generation not to fulfill again the prophecy of Isaiah, who himself spoke to a generation that was so to be described: "You will indeed listen, but never understand, and you will indeed look, but never perceive. For this people's heart has grown dull, and their ears are hard of hearing, and they have shut their eyes; so that they might not look with their eyes, and listen with their ears, and understand with their heart and turn—and I would heal them." Jesus would then rely less on prophecy or plain proclamation and more on parable, that the way he described his disciples might become so: "But blessed are your eyes, for they see, and your ears, for they hear. Truly I tell you, many prophets and righteous people longed to see what you see, but did not see it, and to hear what you hear, but did not hear it."

The irony here is that the very things Jesus said in order to upset, and to reset, the hearing of those listening are now familiar to us, are to some of us so much so that they rarely upset us; they rarely reset our mindset. Those of us who come to church every week and have so for years; those of us who've listened to the words of Jesus to the degree that we can recite at least some of them; those who know very well that the meek will inherit the earth and that we're to pray for our enemies and that we're forgiven for we know not what we do (blah blah blah)—we are very easily like those who listen but do not hear and who look but do not perceive. We are very easily like those who long to see what Jesus means for us to see, but do not, and who long to hear what Jesus means for us to hear, but do not.

Okay. So what is it that we're to see, to hear?

The seed is small, yet becomes great. But even this greatness sounds a strange note. After all, the typical image of greatness in the Bible is the cedars of Lebanon. The go-to symbol of towering strength was these trees that were not just legendary but were so because they were the raw materials used to establish Solomon's temple. Yet with this familiar trope framing the disciples' expectation, Jesus' likening the kingdom of God to a bush would have surprised them and probably seemed a mistake. With the image of towering trees in their minds' eye, the image of even a mighty bush that somehow becomes a tree would have struck the disciples as falling comically short. And so it would have required a blessed sort of hearing; it would have required a blessed sort of seeing—the blessing being that the God the disciples had thought they knew was, yes, coming to the world, but differently now; the blessing being that the God whom we call almighty is, if mighty, then in a strange, even disturbing, way. Not towering strength, but tangled proliferation: this is the character of God-with-us.

And speaking of strange, disturbing, what about this? No one would sow mustard seed in his field, no one would plant mustard in her garden because it takes over! It's a weed. Like the goutweed that I can't seem to stop from taking over my pachysandra, mustard let to seed spoils everything. Yes, it will become a mighty shrub, and birds will enjoy it, but then it'll take over. Then it'll become the all in all. Nothing else will stand a chance. Everything, everywhere will be mustard, mustard.

Same with leaven in dough. Let's remember, the Jews were a people who prized unleavened bread. And in this vein, once a year Jews would (and still do) scrub their households clean of any leavening in order to keep kosher for Passover. Chametz is what the proscribed food is called, and now here it's praised in being likened to the kingdom of heaven. Religious tradition would have us know that just a little bit of leavening spoils everything. But now Jesus was saying that just a little bit of this same leavening makes everything to rise.

And that's not all. This yeasty, weedy kingdom is all the stranger to hear about, and still more to rejoice in, given the parable that Jesus told immediately prior to these—when the kingdom of heaven was compared to someone who sowed good seed in his field, but while everybody was asleep an enemy came and sowed weeds among the wheat and then went away. Well, of course, when the plants came up and bore grain, then the weeds did as well. And in our listening, we make the same assumption the slaves of the householder did—that the weeds should be removed so the wheat can be let to grow. Moreover, we assume that the master is either Jesus or God, right? When the master says that all must be left to grow together, and that they will be separated at the end of the age, we hear this (wink, wink;

nudge, nudge) as insight from Jesus/God; and we accept (smugly, if we're self-righteous enough) that in the end what's clearly good will be confirmed as good and treated accordingly, while what's clearly bad will be confirmed as bad and treated accordingly.

The problem with this conventional understanding, though, is that it fails to hear and take into account what comes next. It doesn't see that, in the very next story, the weed is cast as good.

Alright.

So we regroup.

And we wonder, what if the master in the story isn't Jesus, but is precisely as named, a slave master? And what if the enemy in this story isn't some shady enemy of God, set to thwart God's good intentions, but is the enemy of such human cultures as produce, for example, master-slave relationships? And what if the weed this enemy sowed isn't something that infects what is good with what is bad but is something that infects what is expedient with what's eternal? Yes, what if the field is the world, the enemy is the Christ, and the weed sown is the gospel that grows up among social convention and cultural norms—norms that serve the purpose of safety and security for their citizens (some of their citizens at least), that do indeed serve to sustain life (for a time at least, for some people at least), but that ultimately fall to their death-dealing ways.

I'll tell you this: the smack that Jesus was talking was a weed to the likes of gladiatorial Rome. The church that Jesus was beginning to generate was weed to the wheat of Rome's economic, political, and social structure. It would take over the good grain that would earn good coin in the arena, because the outcasts who'd make good gladiators might decide instead to follow Jesus. The kingdom that Jesus was even now inviting the people to see unfolding among them and to hear breaking out in their midst; the kingdom that Jesus was even now entreating the people to contemplate and to live among: this kingdom was indeed as a weed growing, undermining, choking out the good fruits of civilized culture, because those who'd otherwise have joined the economy, fueled as it was by their sweat and blood, might decide instead to join this proliferating whatever-it-was. And so, can't you just imagine all the people made secure within Rome's cast-iron culture thinking that this enemy, Jesus, or later on his followers, sowing bad seed among what's commonly recognized as good, really should be weeded out?

Now, I know I'm dealing with a roomful of farmers and gardeners. So I know the idea of the kingdom of heaven being like a weed is going to be a hard sell. But here's why I like it, my battle with goutweed notwithstanding. There's a lot about Western civilization that feels to be coming to an end. The ascendency of the East; the globalization of the economy; the crisis of the world's changing climate, brought about by our actions; as well as our country's more immediate difficulty in addressing the problems of unemployment and a shrinking middle class, its apparent inability to lessen the growing disparity of wealth among citizens and its national debt: these are all things that tempt us to despair.

I know they do me. For, while on some level I don't want to live amidst a mighty empire, in my weaker moments I wouldn't mind it so much. It's nice, after all, to live out your days secure in the illusion that you know what's good and what's bad, that you've indeed cultivated what's good and cast out what's bad. Yes, in my weaker moments I wouldn't mind it so much. After all, once you've been the most powerful player—the champion gladiator, as it were—it's hard to imagine how else to be, easy even to wonder whether you will yet continue to be.

Unless you imagine a realm of love that has the strange power of proliferation. Unless you see ever before you a kingdom of love that simply cannot be rooted out. There's something inevitable about the victory of God's way. There's something inevitable about the victory of freedom, of true relationship, of life, of love. This is the gospel that Christ not only proclaimed but also unleashed. This is the word that Christ not only spoke but also enacted. Once you see a slave as a human being, you can never go back to keeping him caged. Once you recognize beasts as living beings and so beloved of God, you can never go back to burdening them to death. You've been parabled. You've been gospeled. The empire will no longer have you, is no longer your home. You're ruined for it—ruined by what abides, which is to say faith and hope and love.

Happily, you're not alone. None of us is. There are other imperial castoffs—some by design, some by choice.

Maybe we could get together, be a force to be reckoned with.

Thanks be to God.

Now that "Parent" Is a Verb

An Aside

IT WAS A JUST a few days before I gave birth to our first child that my husband Jesse and I were at a dinner party—a small group of people a generation older than we are, all soon-to-be grandparents, as it happens. One of them, the man sitting next to me said something I think I'll never forget. "We've left behind God the Father," he said, and mournfully to my surprise. "We've left behind God the Father, and we've separated ourselves from Mother Nature. So now everything comes down to the mother, the birth mother, the actual mother. She has to do it all."

I didn't know this to be true then, but I know it now. Jesse and I find ourselves raising children in the age of "helicopter parenting." We don't fit the type, but we certainly feel the pressure. Or at least I do.

I had occasion to think about this in the context of church when, a couple years ago, I was preparing to baptize an infant on the last Sunday of the church year, Reign of Christ Sunday. It was an odd choice, made for scheduling reasons rather than theological ones, and I struggled to make it fit. Think about it: baptism is largely about beginning, Reign of Christ Sunday is culmination; baptism inaugurates a life of ministry, Reign of Christ Sunday points to the end—and not just an end, but *the* end.

Come to think of it, though, Reign of Christ Sunday isn't an easy fit for nearly the whole of the mainline church. The eschaton, the end of all that is—this is something we in the mainline have largely abandoned. Sure, we'll walk with Jesus in his earthly ministry, focusing on the gospel narratives. Sure, we'll commit ourselves to the Holy Spirit and the good works of the church. Absolutely, we'll be the voice of the prophets, holding forth hope of justice and speaking words of truth to a world so often enthralled to lies. But the end? The end of all things, history's consummation and final judgment?

Here's what we lose, though, if we go dark regarding the eschaton. That history has shape; that its every moment and jagged turn and random happening and jangling unfolding all, somehow, by some miracle of omniscience and embrace, participate in ultimacy; that nothing is lost or forgotten or left to waste, but that everything can and has and will be redeemed and revealed in the light of the end to have significance and purpose: the end of all as consummation, as final judgment, means the truth of all will be held in God's light, the significance of all will be brought to full recognition, and the promise of all will be brought to fulfillment.

I suppose "final judgment" sounds scary, but only if we assume the "judge" to be harsh and pleased to humiliate. What if the judge, though, is wise and pleased fully to recognize—and not only what we've done but also what we've been up against; not only what we've made of our lives, and of life itself, but also what handicaps and hardships we might have inherited or had conferred on us?

Yes, what if the judge can discern not only how we finished but where we began, not only our performance but also our motivations, not only what intentions we brought to the task of living but also the unintended effects we've had for good?

Truly, what if the judge were one who understood the complexities and vagaries and ambiguities at work in time and space, in history and living; and who looked upon our meager, if ambitious, attempts and offerings with love, with a heart for redemption, and with an overflowing of grace upon grace?

Holding this God close, then, here's what we would forfeit were we to forfeit the church's sense of an ending: the vision by which all life coheres into meaning and without which our lives are but atomized and far-flung.

I imagine that's a tough world to live in—random, pulled-apart. I imagine, also, it's a tough world to raise kids in—incoherent, unreliable, such that it all comes down to you, the mother, the father. It could keep you up at night, the anxiety and fear of all that could go wrong, even terribly wrong, if you even for one moment don't have your eye on all things. It could keep you from ever enjoying yourself and the gift of life you've been volunteered to steward and raise up. You might look out to the quavering mound of flesh and spirit, and feel never awe, never joy, only resentment.

To be baptized on the Reign of Christ Sunday, then, is to be baptized not only into the faith and family of Jesus Christ but also into a story that has an end, and moreover a joyful end by which the whole story of the whole of Creation is endowed with good purpose. And to be baptized as a young child on Reign of Christ Sunday is to assure the parents, and all parents, everyone really, that they're not in this all alone—made to stitch together meaning and value from scratch, forced to settle for busyness because coherence is too much to hope for.

This is true whenever baptism takes place, though—an affirmation that helicopter parenting isn't necessary, or even helpful, not when the whole high sky of the cosmos cradles us, our children, and all life.

Let God be the verb, then. Take some time to be a noun. Sit with your little nouns, whatever things are yours to nurture. Sit with them and let God do the work for a bit, as ever God does.

What a Shame

[Jesus said,] "When the Son of Man comes in his glory, and all the angels with him, then he will sit on the throne of his glory. All the nations will be gathered before him, and he will separate people one from another as a shepherd separates the sheep from the goats, and he will put the sheep at his right hand and the goats at the left. Then the king will say to those at his right hand, 'Come, you that are blessed by my Father, inherit the kingdom prepared for you from the foundation of the world; for I was hungry and you gave me food, I was thirsty and you gave me something to drink, I was a stranger and you welcomed me, I was naked and you gave me clothing, I was sick and you took care of me, I was in prison and you visited me.' . . . " (Matthew 25:31–46)

SHE HAD A NAME, but I don't know it. I think I did once, though. She wore a name badge at work, and I knew her from work—*her* work. She was a dining hall server at my high school, a boarding school, Phillips Exeter Academy. The dining halls were open from eight o'clock in the morning until eight o'clock at night, seven days a week; and most of the thousand students ate most of their meals in one of the two dining halls. A lot of people worked to make it all happen, and she was one of them.

I was a day student, and I remember bumping into her one summer day when most of the other students were scattered far and wide. I was with my mother, who worked in the library and so knew by face others on the (very large) campus staff. We both recognized her, so we said hello and explained how we knew her.

Homely and simple, she lit up at the mention of her work. She was so proud to serve in the dining halls. She was proud to work at Exeter and proud to know the students there. She knew it was an elite environment and she was proud to be a part of it. I found it very touching. I knew how she was often perceived. I knew what she was sometimes even called— "wombat." The dining hall ladies sometimes were called wombats.

This was a slur made slightly less nasty because it was nostalgic. It harked back to crueler days at Exeter, when it was all boys and when the faculty was formal in its role, cool and hands-off. So there was a time when the two dining halls were connected by tunnels, and the dining hall staff would often travel by these tunnels from one hall to the other and then emerge from underground like wombats. It was a smear not often in use when I was a student. It had mostly died out. But there were outbreaks.

I forgot about it, and forgot about her and my brief interaction with her, until earlier this month when an article in the *New Yorker* brought it all back—their food issue. A writer and foodie, Chang-rae Lee, was at Exeter in the early eighties, just prior to when I was. And of his memories of the dining halls he had this to write: "Let's be clear: I didn't love it—nobody could, unless you were clinically insane or had just been airlifted there from the Soviet bloc. The food was not good. But, then, it wasn't meant to be good, at least not by the standards of the outside world, and surely not compared with my mother's cooking . . ."[1]

He went on to complain that, with only one hot entrée per dinner, there weren't enough selections to choose from. At the same time there was too much milk: "You washed it all down with milk. Always plenty of milk . . ." And he concluded that "being catered to isn't the most satisfying thing."[2]

His sour attitude about a quite privileged experience goes on:

> We pulled our trays from the stack and shook off the excess dish-water; the tiled floor there got slimy by the end of the meal service . . . We moved down the line, wondering what the wombats would dole out to us. That's what the dining staff—all older ladies—were called, after the rotund, earth-burrowing marsupial. . . . Their repertoire, I came to learn, was classic . . . [and] the mains were always accompanied by a form of potato or other starch and a spent, long-suffering vegetable. . . . [When the entrée was cheeseburgers,] I always ate two . . . [but] I picked off the bacon, as it smelled exactly like the fetal pigs we dissected in biology class."[3]

This isn't true, by the way. The bacon didn't smell like the fetal pigs from bio. Similarly, the dining hall floors, though they could get slippery, weren't slimy. And as for the food, it was indeed meant to be good.

It's this that got me: his claim that it wasn't meant to be. It's this that had me—shaking, really, following my reading of it—remembering my brief conversation with that woman, that worker: his dismissive, entitled claim that it wasn't meant to be good. Did he imagine the staff spitting into the food that he was then made to suffer eating? Did he imagine them intending to make something that didn't satisfy his more individual and worldly tastes? "It wasn't meant to be good." This would have been news to that one server, so gratified by her work, so proud of it and grateful to us for

1. Lee, "Immovable Feast," para. 1.
2. Ibid., para. 5, para. 7.
3. Ibid., para. 3, para 4.

receiving it. Shame on him for not even entertaining that as an idea. Shame on him for not even imagining her as a person.

No, scratch that. It's too bad for him. He missed the party.

* * *

Matthew is on a tear. Matthew, our gospel writer, is on a tear—so much so, in fact, that I have colleagues who are parting company with him. This week, they're preaching on the psalm, on the epistle. After a full year of him, his voice and his remembrance of Jesus, they're parting company with him on this last week spent with his gospel.

Mind you, this is the last Sunday of the church year. Next Sunday we begin a new season, Advent, and a new church year, Year B; and so we begin hearing a new narrative voice, mostly Mark, my favorite. But they can't take even one more week of this. They can't take this final week and this final word for the liturgical year, this final gospel word (gospel, which is to mean good news): " . . . these will go away into eternal punishment, but the righteous into eternal life."

And I'm with them. It's a pretty sour note to end on, a pretty scary note to end on. What's more, we've endured a few weeks now of Matthew's take on Jesus—Jesus as harsh in his judgment of the people and moreover their leaders. Really, we've had to endure several weeks of parables and proclamations whose implications are quite dire—for some people anyway.

It's important to note that none of our other gospel writers remember Jesus as a judge so persistently harsh.

It's important also to hear these things in the context of Jesus' preaching and Matthew's remembering his preaching in the Sermon on the Mount. Here, Jesus sketched what the kingdom of God is like, what the church is to be, and what opportunity there is for the people to live by grace both in the hereafter but also in the here and now. Here, Jesus imagined the meek and merciful, the peacemakers and the poor in spirit as meant to be blessed. Moreover, here he imagined no such thing as damnation.

Then there's this: that Matthew was, quite likely, a committed Jew and so was especially incensed when the religious authorities did wrong by the people—which might account for his experience of Jesus as a harsh judge. Matthew counted himself as one of the people whom the religious authorities were meant to serve, so he felt especially betrayed by their duplicity and corruption, and so he all the more relied on the decisive judgment of a still higher authority.

And another thing: we're in the final week of Jesus' life. This reading comes to us from one of Jesus' final days, which he spent in the temple apparently provoking everyone he possibly could. The money changers and sellers of animals for sacrifice, the Pharisees and Sadducees and Herodians, the wealthy and the powerful: he was ticking everyone off. The pressure was rising, the time for the Passover sacrifice was nearing, the crowds in the city and the temple were swelling, the imperial authorities were making their policing presence all the more known; and whether Jesus was actively participating in the heat rising or was merely responding to it—touchy himself, anxious himself: he knew what was coming—is impossible to say. It's just clear that the tone of things has changed. "Blessed are the peacemakers . . ." has become talk of eternal punishment.

Finally, there's this: that the one to speak of eternal punishment in the not-quite-parable that Jesus has told is said to be the king. The Son of Man has come in his glory, and separated the people, righteous and unrighteous, as sheep from goats; and then the king has explained the fate of each group—the sheep entering eternal mercy just as they have shown mercy to others, and the goats entering eternal torment just as they have tolerated the torment of others. It was the king who promised such an ordering of things even in eternity.

And we know that kings in the Bible are not so straightforward a thing. We know that, while God is often considered king, and while Christ is often called king (as on today, Christ the King Sunday), and while God imagined a gracious king though of the human variety, there is the fact of mere earthly kings to contend with—earthly kings which the people asked for early on in their collective life as a people, and which God only reluctantly ordained, reluctantly because God knew that no earthly king could possibly rule in the way that God intended (and intends) for the people to be ruled.

God intends for grace to reign, while earthly kings rule by fear and force.

God intends for justice to be coupled with mercy and for peace to come by forgiveness, while kingly justice comes via some threat and earthly peace is most often established by military strength and well-defended borders.

In sum, it is indeed the case that a king would separate out the bad from the good—and would then safeguard and reward the good while casting out and punishing the bad. So Jesus in this story is saying what's actual.

This is indeed the way an orderly realm is run. But it's not necessarily how God's good realm is ever to be.

In other words, we can't be sure that the king in this parable is Christ or God. Parables aren't allegories, so there's no direct equation. We also can't be sure that this story is more prescriptive than descriptive, more saying what should be than saying simply what is.

But, you know, this is all really beside the point. (Sorry to go on about it, then.) Because here's the point: the irony woven into the story. Irony flips it, reverses it. As with so many parables, so with this one—that as soon as a parable's implications are made clear, the story turns inside out and its implications are inverted.

Consider: as soon as the bad are cast out according to the justice meted out that Jesus imagines, these cast-out baddies become the hungering and thirsting strangers whom Jesus means for his disciples to welcome in. As soon as the wicked are imprisoned in eternal punishment, they become the likes of those imprisoned whom Jesus meant for his people to visit.

Yes, consider: as soon as those deemed bad are tormented, they become the sick ones whom Jesus meant for the people to take care of.

Isn't this true, don't your sympathies flip as soon as someone you thought worthy of bad fortune lands in some bad fortune? Elsewhere than here, I worked with someone who made me nuts at every meeting—goofy, bloviating. Then he got sick, really sick, and he had to resign from the committee. I missed him. In all my frustration with him, I never meant *that*.

Truly, consider that parables are inconclusive: their conclusions are another look, their endings land you right back at the beginning. The therefore *in*-conclusion of this parable is that the ones punished, even rightly punished, become the ones to be shown mercy.

We can't ever rest assured that matters are settled, sorted out. We can't ever rest assured that things won't transform—become something else altogether, become something new. When it comes to the gospel and the God it reveals, we're climbing up a stairway as drawn by M.C. Escher and, with each story higher we climb, we land right back down on the ground floor—this ground of our being.

We can't rest assured. Of this, and only this, we can rest assured: we can't rest assured. God's not finished with us. God is never finished with us.

* * *

Not long after that article in the *New Yorker* came out, I was on the phone with my sister. I wondered whether she'd seen it. I wondered whether she remembered the author. Their time at Exeter might have overlapped. But she hadn't seen it. We didn't even talk about it. She was too wrapped up in the selling of her house—or rather the not selling of it.

They live in Denver—her husband and their two sons and her. But they were moving because her father-in-law was to move in with them and they needed a house with a different configuration of rooms.

They found one—and not far away, which is good because they like their neighborhood, Stapleton. This is a new part of Denver, a planned neighborhood with a population comparable to that of Lenox. It's built on the site of the old airport—this quite perfect grid of streets and homes and parks and a community center and, across a canal, about a half mile away, the state women's prison.

Well.

Fifty people—individuals, couples, families—came and went through their house, and fifty people objected to the fact that you can see the women's prison from one of the bedroom windows. You can't see the details of it. You can't see the fence or the razor wire. You can't see the sirens or the gates. You can just see the fact of it, the fact that it *is*—out one corner of one window of one bedroom.

As it happens, many of the most violent criminals in that prison are women who killed men who were abusing them.

As it happens, this prison is also the site of a pilot program so successful it's taken off in prisons and other facilities around the country—inmates training would-be service dogs of various sorts, a process that is as productive for society as it is healing for the women. Our very own Gould Farm has taken on this same program.

As it happens, people in prisons are people.

It's funny that so many of us miss that.

Whenever I don't, I figure I have the church to thank.

It's funny that people would prefer the strained calculus of social striving (Will this person be an asset or a liability? Will that person increase or decrease my social value?)—prefer this to entertaining the possibility that people, all people, are sackfuls of surprise and perhaps even delight, every single one an asset.

Whenever I prefer the second, I figure I've got the gospel to thank.

It's funny that people would hope for the kingdom out of fear of what might happen to them if they don't hope for the kingdom, rather than for the obvious much better reason—and, incidentally, much simpler reason. I mean I get *why* people do anticipate it in fear. Matthew's view of Christ's judgment is pretty intimidating, after all. But more compelling than some future threat is this present reality, that the kingdom, as promised to come and as already among us, is simply a more fun place to live.

You know, the prisoner you decide to visit might be clever, funny. That infirmed person you realize you should go see might be great at chess, and you love chess! That lunch lady you fall into conversation with might be as sweet as the dessert she so delightfully doles out.

You just never know.

Simple, right?

Too simple, simplistic even? Maybe.

But try it out, anyway. It might work. Really, it might be true—that there's a party going on, and everyone's invited, and none of us is going to want to miss it.

Thanks be to God.

Room for One More

Then I saw a new heaven and a new earth; for the first heaven and the first earth had passed away, and the sea was no more. And I saw the holy city, the new Jerusalem, coming down out of heaven from God, prepared as a bride adorned for her husband. And I heard a loud voice from the throne saying, "See, the home of God is among mortals. He will dwell with them; they will be his peoples, and God himself will be with them; he will wipe every tear from their eyes. Death will be no more; mourning and crying and pain will be no more, for the first things have passed away."

And the one who was seated on the throne said, "See, I am making all things new." Also he said, "Write this, for these words are trustworthy and true." Then he said to me, "It is done! I am the Alpha and the Omega, the beginning and the end. To the thirsty I will give water as a gift from the spring of the water of life . . . " (Revelation 21:1–6)

When he had gone out, Jesus said, "Now the Son of Man has been glorified, and God has been glorified in him. If God has been glorified in him, God will also glorify him in himself and will glorify him at once. Little children, I am with you only a little longer. You will look for me; and as I said to the Jews so now I say to you, 'Where I am going, you cannot come.' I give you a new commandment, that you love one another. Just as I have loved you, you also should love one another. By this everyone will know that you are my disciples, if you have love for one another." (John 13:31–35)

IMAGINE THIS. CLOSE YOUR eyes if that will help. You're feasting at the Lord's table in glory. Death is no more. Mourning and crying and pain are no more. The first things have passed away and all is made new. God's good purpose for creation has been fulfilled. God's power to redeem has left nothing to waste.

So you're feasting—life sustaining life. And you're laughing—joy coming at the cost of no one, high spiritedness coming as all are filled with the Holy Spirit. And you're recognizing—what you've trusted now you know, what you've believed now you see, what you've hoped for now is established.

Look around the table. The people you love are there. The people you long for are there. The people you've never quite connected with are there. So many strangers are all there. The whole creation, the whole of history, every experience however grand or minute—it's all there. Somehow all that is and has ever been and ever will be, all that might have been and might yet be, *all* is realized around that table. You breathe in, understanding. You breathe out, delight and surprise.

So, here's a question: Is Judas there?

"When he had gone out," the gospel reading this morning begins. "He" is Judas. The place from which he'd gone out is the upper room where Jesus was gathered with his friends for one last supper. And "out" is into the night to summon a detachment of Roman soldiers and some police from the chief priests.

Jesus had just said, "Very truly I tell you, one of you will betray me— the one to whom I give this piece of bread when I have dipped it in the dish." And when he'd given the bread to Judas Iscariot, he said to him, "Do quickly what you are going to do."

And the story is eager to note that no one at the table knew why he had said this to him; no one knew Jesus had said this to Judas: "Do quickly what you are going to do." Some thought that, because Judas held the common purse, Jesus was telling him to go quickly to buy what they'd need for the festival or to give something to the poor. But that wasn't it, as we know and as I think they too must have at least suspected. After all, Jesus would go on, from this moment after Judas had gone out, to preach to the disciples and to pray on behalf of the disciples some of the most significant things he's remembered to have said in this whole gospel. Wouldn't the disciples have noticed this? Wouldn't they have wondered at this, that Jesus sent Judas on an errand and then, though one of them was absent, got to the heart of the matter? If Judas truly was going on some Jesus-sent errand, wouldn't Jesus then wait for his return before really getting into things? What's going on here, wouldn't they have wondered? *Something's* going on here, they would at least have suspected.

And so it was. Something was going on. Satan had entered Judas— that adversarial spirit whose will is to divide, cast aspersion, suspicion. And now Judas would go out into the night.

How I'd like to have followed him out.

Here's how I'd have done it. I'd have snuck out so no one else would even have noticed—certainly not Judas, so needful was he to be alone and so pressed was he to do what he was to do; but also not the other disciples, though close by at the table, yet focused as they'd have been on Jesus' strange behavior of washing their feet and serving them dinner and on

Jesus' strange talk of being betrayed and being denied and in this being somehow glorified, glorified.

I'd have caught the door before it sounded itself shut, and slipped into the darkness that Judas was relying on. I'd have watched for which direction he would take through the city, and then I'd have taken the next street over, running parallel to his path. But I'd have outpaced him, and gotten ahead of him, and then a few blocks later rejoined the street he was taking. Then I'd have sat myself down on a stoop and waited for his approach.

And when he was near, he'd have spotted me and then slowed in his tracks or come even to a wavering stop, swaying in pained ambivalence, feeling God knows what.

Was he aggrieved that Jesus fell so short of the sort of Messiah the nation really needed and Judas himself had especially hoped for—a mighty warrior, a powerful king, someone to deal to Rome what they really deserved?

Or was he enraged at the role he was coming to play. Zealous he was, yes. But he wasn't a *bad* guy, and he wasn't *the* bad guy. So why was he starting to suspect that this is how he'd be seen?

Or was he confused as to whether the compulsion to betray his friend came from within him or beyond him—or came perhaps from his friend himself? "Do quickly what you are going to do," hadn't his friend said? So, fine, he would.

Or was he proud of the fact that he alone had the courage to do what needed to be done? He'd get rid of Jesus. Jesus, provoking the empire, provoking the Sanhedrin, provoking the temple authorities—and for what? They'd all just come down harder on the people. No, it's better for one man to die than for a whole nation to be destroyed. The high priest Caiaphas would say so himself.

Or was he ashamed that his envy—common, everyday envy—was about to get the better of him? Judas was zealous for his people; Jesus was indulgent of himself. Judas was entrusted with treasure and concerned for the poor; Jesus was a spendthrift. Judas hated Rome; Jesus ate with Roman tax collectors. Judas was devout; Jesus was beloved. Argghhh! The pain is as if your body was to begin feeding on itself.

"Judas," I'd say, and maybe this would cause him to come to himself. His name, his own name: it might have recalled to him that first call—to discipleship.

"Judas."

Meanwhile, back in the upper room Jesus was beginning the murmurings of what would come to be called his Farewell Discourse and his High Priestly Prayer. These are unfortunate names, hardly compelling to a potential reader or listener. But the preaching and the prayer were most likely a wonder when first heard: wonderful for being both sweet and strange.

For four chapters Jesus explains, proclaims, prays of things lovely and puzzling and sad and good. And it all begins with this, a new commandment: "Love one another. As I have loved you, so you should love one another. By this everyone will know that you are my disciples, if you have love for one another."

And, of course, the fact that our reading ends here shouldn't indicate to us that Jesus stopped speaking here, for he didn't. No, of course, the fact that the reading ends here reflects the decision of the lectionary advisors who decide upon the readings for the church's liturgical year, reflects their likely deciding that, with this gospel in particular, you need to keep the passages short. The Gospel of John is thick with significance. Though not as much happens as in the albeit shorter Gospel of Mark, though not as many characters come to bear as in the gospels of Matthew and Luke, the Gospel of John reverberates with meaning such that the readings are best served up a few verses at a time.

As exemplified in this one—a mere five verses but weighty with Jesus' glory, weighty with God's glory, weighty with the idea that in the cross Jesus is glorified.

Glory!

Glory?

When Tobias was young and we'd pray the Lord's Prayer before sleep, he'd ask me about the terms in the prayer, usually questioning one per night. My least favorite nights were when he'd ask me about glory. "What's glory?" he'd ask. "What does glory mean?" And I'd think, "Not again. Can't we wonder about kingdom or power? Can't I explain to you trespasses again, or temptation?" Because, really, how do you explain glory?

Here's how: glory means weight or significance. (I guess I should have just looked it up.) The Lord's Prayer would have us confess that all weight and significance belong to God. And John's Jesus would have us know that God signifies himself in Christ, weighs in as it were most especially with the cross—the cross of self-giving love.

So, this is a reading that, though thin in verses, is thick with the significance of Jesus' significance as signifying of God whom we should take to be self-giving love and whom we should then imitate in self-giving love.

Consider that for a time.

Come to think of it, maybe Jesus meant for us to, or meant at least for the disciples to—those gathered with him in that upper room. Yes, come to think of it, maybe this is exactly what Jesus meant for us to do—to consider this for a time. So, yes, maybe Jesus did pause here, or stop here. Though I just said the opposite—that we shouldn't take the fact that the reading ends here to mean that Jesus' thinking and speaking ends here—let's act as if he did, pausing here, "Love one another"; stopping here, glancing around the room; "Love one another," giving the disciples a moment to take it in and then perhaps to act.

Thinking of Judas, now prowling the night; thinking of the one who would be Jesus' enemy if he were to have his way; thinking of the one who would condemn himself (if the story of his suicide is correct) or would be condemned by history (if the story of his gruesome accident is correct)— perhaps Jesus paused here when having said, "Love one another. As I have loved you, so you should love one another. By this, everyone will know that you are my disciples, if you have love for one another." For this would have been a good time for at least one of those disciples to say, having now heard him, really heard him, "Jesus, just wait a minute while I go get Judas. We actually need him here."

Yes, this would have been a good time for at least one of the disciples to remember the story that Jesus told of the good shepherd who so loves his sheep that he'll risk everything to find even one sheep that has gone missing; or the story that Jesus told of the widow who lit a lamp and swept her entire house looking for that one coin that was lost; or the story that Jesus told about a wayward son who left his father's house and wasted his entire inheritance on things that do not satisfy only to return home with nothing but his own destitution and so begging to become his father's slave. (Didn't that father rejoice at his son's return?)

Yes, this would have been a good time for someone around that table to do just this: to light a lamp and search the streets of the city for the one who was going lost, to love and forgive that one back into the fold.

One commentator wrote of the scene at the table once Judas had left: "It is as if, when Judas departs, a pall lifts. Judas' departure rids the group of his evil presence . . ."[1] I disagree with this interpretation. I see no evidence that the disciples regarded Judas as evil. I see no evidence that his departure lightened the mood on that strangely somber evening. What I imagine is that the remaining eleven liked Judas, and loved Judas, and longed for his company around the table. He wasn't evil to them, he was their friend; and so they might have feared what they might find in him had they followed out of that upper room; and so they might have preferred instead to believe that he had simply gone out to do some errands while Jesus preached and prayed. And in so doing (so *not* doing), those eleven disciples fell (though understandably) short of being the sort of community that Christ had hoped they would be and that Christ would now preach them to be—searching the hedgerows and ditches for Judas; searching the night-fallen streets for confused, aggrieved, raging, resentful, envious Judas.

If so, then on it goes. In the long history of the church and its traditions, few are the people who've gone out in search of Judas, whereas many are the times when instead we've reveled in his loss. In this epic story, in this the gospel story of love and forgiveness and amazing grace, Judas is the one person whose condemnation we really enjoy. There's just something so pleasing about a traitor who gets what's coming. There's something so satisfying about retribution, just desserts.

It's a pleasure that John of Patmos seems to have known well—John of Patmos, the man behind the revelation that continues yet to spook and inspire. I want to be clear that, when John of Patmos imagined a new heaven and a new earth, many are the people who weren't there at that table. John's revelation is not of universal salvation but one in which some, many, don't make the cut. They're the usual suspects—the fornicators, the faithless, the murderers, the liars, the idolaters, the polluted. And some surprising others—the cowardly and the sorcerers.

But if he was offended by many sorts of people, I imagine he became so honestly. He was living under the fearsome press of occupation and war—Rome's centuries-long occupation of Jerusalem and Israel, and Rome's decades-long horrific War against the Jews.

For what it's worth, I just read a book about North Korea called *Nothing to Envy*, which had me rapt in the mindset of people who were starving to death en masse due to oppression, corruption, systematic generations-long deception and doublespeak; and I'd say that it's impossible to over-imagine how dehumanizing such things can be—whether now or then.

1. Donovan, "Biblical Commentary."

So, John was on the prison island of Patmos—held captive for trusting in Christ. And while this wasn't perhaps as horrific as a North Korean labor camp apparently is (it having better geography going for it, if nothing else), it might well have been just such a mawing, stripping, even psychotic experience.

And it might be for this reason that the book of Revelation itself almost didn't make the cut—that the author wasn't a credible witness, that he was (perhaps understandably) driven by paranoia and revenge. As you may or may not know, when the biblical cannon was first established, around the year 400, the book of Revelation was the last let in, and over some notable voices of dissent. Gregory of Nazianus and other bishops argued against it, citing difficulties in interpretation and risk of abuse. A millennium later, Martin Luther nearly cut it from the Protestant canon, considering it neither prophetic nor apostolic, stating, "I can in no way detect that Holy Spirit produced it," and that, in it, "Christ is neither taught nor known."[2] John Calvin, for his part, regarded it as authoritative, but left it as the only book in the Bible about which he never wrote a commentary.

What it has going for it, though, are these: a deep longing for justice; an unshakeable faith that balance and order will come through Christ who, though a Lamb, might somehow defeat the fearsome beast that lurks and attacks like so many empires the world has known; and a bold hope that this Christ is coming, which is good news indeed. What it also has going for it is its look to the end, its holding the end in sight in so confident and daring a gaze—and so it makes a suitable end to a library of books that dares to begin in the beginning. From Genesis to Revelation, the whole of history spans. So Revelation stays, with its final words, a hopeful plea: "Come, Lord Jesus."

Imagine that! Close your eyes if it helps. Jesus has come. History is fulfilled. All is reconciled, some strange cosmic reunion. You're feasting at the table, and you look around. A question: Is Judas there?

Another question: Who is Judas? One man, yes. He's many, as well. Men and women who single themselves out as traitors among us, they are those who've taken a dream we've held in common and betrayed it, destroyed it. They are those who've used a trust we share to take advantage, sometimes great advantage.[3] They are those who've spoken words we hold

---

2. Martin Luther in several editions to his New Testament, these produced between 1522 and 1527.

3. As I compile this collection, the events of June 17, 2015, at the Mother Emanuel

in common understanding and turned them to mean something utterly different, foreign, disingenuous, false. Are these people at that table?

If our answer is no, then we see something of ourselves. If our answer is the much more troubling yes, then we've learned something of Christ—Christ, who is, after all, the host at this table.

The gospel calls and sometimes our answer is harder to come to than others.

Thanks be to God.

AME Church in Charleston are not even a week in the past. So this is no academic question. The murderer sat and prayed for about an hour with those he would murder, relied on their hospitality to do the hateful deed he intended. This question, then, is real and pressing.

Afterword—A Sense of the Ending

WHEN I WAS PREGNANT with Tobias, my first, I had a dream that I could take him out. Each day, for just a few minutes. Even though he wasn't finished in the womb, he could take leave of it, though only for fifteen, twenty minutes at the most. So I would—I'd take him out, though still attached, and play with him, but with one eye always on the clock.

A parishioner once asked me a question she's often asked by others: how could she have hope for the end and still live fully in the world?

Remembering my dream, I thought, this is how: Take out the finished product and play with it now. Even though it's not finished, even though all is yet imperfect and incomplete, even though mourning and crying and pain yet persist, even though death is still a thing and the fear of it yet holds sway, even though, even though: take out God's promised, perfect end and play in its midst.

Make believe.

Patience is a virtue. I think impatience is too.

Bibliography
Suggested Reading & Listening

Alter, Robert. *The Five Books of Moses: A Translation with Commentary.* New York: W. W. Norton & Co., 2008.

Bailie, Gil. *Violence Unveiled: Humanity at the Crossroads.* New York: Crossroads, 1995.

Bass, Thomas. "Forgiveness Math." *Discover,* May 01, 1993. http://discovermagazine. com/1993/may/forgivenessmath212.

BBC News. "'World Peace' Hitcher Is Murdered." April 12, 2008. http://news.bbc.co.uk/2/ hi/europe/7344381.stm.

Berryman, Jerome. *Godly Play.* Minneapolis: Augsburg, 1995.

Blow, Charles. "The Perfect-Victim Pitfall." *New York Times,* December 3, 2014. http:// www.nytimes.com/2014/12/04/opinion/charles-blow-first-michael-brown-now-eric-garner.html?_r=0.

Brueggemann, Walter. *An Introduction to the Old Testament.* Louisville: Westminster John Knox, 2003.

———. *Out of Babylon.* Nashville: Abingdon, 2010.

Campbell, Charles and Johan Cilliers. *Preaching Fools: The Gospel as a Rhetoric of Folly.* Waco: Baylor University Press, 2012.

Carroll, James. *Constantine's Sword: The Church and the Jews.* New York: Houghton Mifflin Harcourt, 2002.

Cavanaugh, William. "Does Religion Cause Violence?" In *Harvard Divinity Bulletin* 35 (2007). http://bulletin.hds.harvard.edu/articles/springsummer2007/does-religion-cause-violence.

Coates, Ta-Nehisi. *Between the World and Me.* New York: Spiegel & Grau, 2015.

Craddock, Fred. *As One Without Authority.* Atlanta: Chalice, 2001.

"Culture Gabfest." *Slate Magazine.* Slate.com.

de Botton, Alain. *Religion for Atheists.* New York: Vintage, 2013.

———. "Religion for Everyone." In *The Wall Street Journal,* February 19, 2012. http:// www.wsj.com/articles/SB10001424052970204883304577221603720817864.

Demick, Barbara. *Nothing to Envy: Ordinary Lives in North Korea.* New York: Random House, 2009.

Dodd, C. H. *The Parables of the Kingdom.* London: James Nisbet & Co., 1961.

Donovon, Richard Niell. *Sermon Writer.* http://www.lectionary.org/EXEG_Engl_WEB/ NT/04-John-WEB/John%2013.31-35.htm.

Dykstra, Robert C. *Discovering a Sermon: Personal Pastoral Preaching.* Atlanta: Chalice, 2002.

Edwards, Bob. *The Heart of the Matter: A Case for Meaning in a Material World.* iUniverse, 2002.

Eliot, T. S. "Four Quartets: Burnt Norton." *The Complete Poems and Plays 1909–1950.* New York: Harcourt Brace, date unlisted.

Forgiarini, Matteo, et al. "Racism and the Empathy for Pain on Our Skin." In *Frontiers in Psychology,* May 23, 2011: 2:108. http://www.ncbi.nlm.nih.gov/pmc/articles/ PMC3108582/.

Gaita, Raymond. *A Common Humanity: Thinking About Love and Truth and Justice.* Melbourne: Routledge, 2002.

Heen, Erik. "Commentary on Hebrews 13:1–8, 15–6." WorkingPreacher.org. St. Paul: Luther Seminary. https://www.workingpreacher.org/preaching.aspx?commentary_id=1751.

Lee, Chang Rae. "Immovable Feast." In *The New Yorker,* November 3, 2104. http://www.newyorker.com/magazine/2014/11/03/immovable-feast.

Lepore, Jill. "The Disruption Machine: What the Gospel of Innovation Gets Wrong." *The New Yorker,* June 23, 2014. http://www.newyorker.com/magazine/2014/06/23/the-disruption-machine.

Long, Thomas. *Preaching from Memory to Hope.* Louisville: Westminster John Knox, 2009.

Lowe, Keith. *Savage Continent: Europe in the Aftermath of World War II.* London: Picador, 2013.

Macur, Juliet. "Outspoken Weir Will Be Quiet on Russian Law." In *The New York Times,* October 23, 2013. http://www.nytimes.com/2013/10/24/sports/outspoken-weir-will-be-quiet-on-russian-law.html?_r=0.

McGlothlin, Heidi and Melanie Killen. "How Social Experience Is Related to Children's Intergroup Attitudes." In *European Journal of Social Psychology,* May 13, 2010.

McThenia, Andrew W. "A Missionary Vocation: In the Strange Land of the Modern University: An Interview with William Willimon." In *The Witness,* September 2000. http://www.thewitness.org/archive/sept2000/willimon.html.

Murphy, Shaunna. "Johnny Weir's Olympic Fashion Is The Perfect Pro-Gay Putin Rebellion." In *Hollywood Life,* February 12, 2014. http://hollywoodlife.com/2014/02/12/johnny-weir-gay-winter-olympics-fashion-vladimir-putin-anti-gay-laws/.

Painter, Nell Irvin. *The History of White People.* New York: W. W. Norton, 2011.

Parker, Pat. *Movement in Black.* Ann Arbor: Firebrand, 1999.

Peterson, Eugene. *The Message: The Bible in Contemporary Language, Numbered Edition.* Colorado Springs, CO: NavPress, 2005.

Savage, Kirk. "Henceforth Free: The Emancipation Proclamation." *Backstory with the American History Guys,* Virginia Foundation for the Humanities, January 16, 2015. Accessed at http://backstoryradio.org/shows/henceforth-free/.

"Sermon Brainwave." *Workingpreacher.org.* Luther Seminary, St. Paul, MN.

Shavit, Ari. *My Promised Land: The Triumph and Tragedy of Israel.* New York: Spiegel and Grau, 2015.

Skinner, Matt. "Commentary on Mark 1:21–28." Working Preacher, https://www.workingpreacher.org/preaching.aspx?commentary_id=2343.

Taylor, Barbara Brown. "Remaining Human." In *The Christian Century* vol. 113, no. 5 (February 7, 1996).

Tillich, Paul. *The Shaking of the Foundations.* Eugene, OR: Wipf and Stock, 2012.

Tucker, Gene. "Proper 19 [24]." In *Preaching Through the Christian Year: Year C: A Comprehensive Commentary on the Lectionary* edited by Fred B. Craddock et al. New York: Bloomsbury, 1994.

van Zuylen-Wood, Simon. "Johnny Weir on Fooling Around in the Olympic Village and Being Gay in Socchi." In *Philadelphia,* Feburary 7, 2014. http://www.phillymag.com/news/2014/02/07/johnny-weir-2014-olympics-nbc-commentator-sochi/.

Wagner, Jane. *The Search for Signs of Intelligent Life in the Universe.* New York: HarperPerennial, 1986.

BIBLIOGRAPHY

Wesson, Jan. *They Asked, "Who's My Neighbor"* © 1982 The Hymn Society (Admin. Hope Publishing Company, Carol Stream, IL 60188). All rights reserved. Used by permission.

Williams, Rowan. *Faith in the Public Square.* London: Bloomsbury, 2012.

Wink, Walter. "Beyond Just War and Pacifism: Jesus' Nonviolent Way." http://www.cres. org/star/_wink.htm.

———. *The Powers that Be.* New York: Doubleday, 1999.

Winston, Kimberly. "Welcome to 'Aweism,' the Nonreligious Impulse You Can't Explain." Religious News Service, January 2, 2015. http://www.religionnews.com/2015/01/02/welcome-aweism-nonreligious-impulse-cant-explain/.

Woods, Aengus. "'Religion for Atheists': God, What Is He Good For?" Review of *Religion for Atheists*, by Alain de Botton, March 13, 2012. http://www.npr. org/2012/03/13/148142473/religion-for-atheists-god-what-is-he-good-for.

Woods, Janee. "12 Ways to Be a White Ally to Black People." In *The Root,* August 19, 2014. http://www.theroot.com/articles/culture/2014/08/ferguson_how_white_people_can_be_allies.html.

Zuckerman, Phil. http://atheistnexus.org/profiles/blogs/aweism-1.

Zuckerman, Phil. *Living the Secular Life: New Answers to Old Questions.* New York: Penguin, 2014.